D0194860

WORD
CHECK

WORD CHECK

✔ ✔ ✔ ✔ ✔

A CONCISE THESAURUS

based on

The American Heritage® Dictionary

of the English Language,

Third Edition

Houghton Mifflin Company

Boston   New York

Library of Congress Cataloging-in-Publication Data

Word check : a concise thesaurus : based on The American Heritage
    dictionary of the English language, third edition.
        p.   cm.
    Includes index.
    ISBN 0-395-75693-6
    1. English language — Synonyms and antonyms.   I. Houghton Mifflin
Company.   II. American Heritage dictionary of the English language.
PE1591.W69   1996   96-54
423'.1 — dc20   CIP

For information about this and other Houghton Mifflin trade and reference
books and multimedia products, visit The Bookstore at Houghton Mifflin on
the World Wide Web at http://www.hmco.com/trade/.

Manufactured in the United States of America

BP   10   9   8   7   6   5   4

CONTENTS

EDITORIAL AND PRODUCTION STAFF

Editorial Staff

Managing Editor
Marion Severynse

Senior Lexicographer
Joseph P. Pickett

Assistant Editors
Beth Anderson
Susan S. Chicoski, *Project Director*

Production Staff

Production and Manufacturing Manager
Christopher Leonesio

Production Supervisor
Elizabeth Rubè

Senior Art & Production Coordinator
Margaret Anne Miles

Database Production Supervisor
Thomas Endyke

Text Design
Melodie Wertelet

HOW TO USE THIS BOOK

Word Check is the most authoritative and convenient thesaurus available for the office or the classroom. Unlike a traditional thesaurus that prints exhaustive synonym lists without explaining the meaning of the words, *Word Check* provides synonym studies with definitions and examples that focus on the most important meanings and ideas and discriminate among many of the most frequently used — and misused — words in the English language. Whether you are looking for a more precise word to express a specific thought or idea, or simply for a synonym to express a general concept, *Word Check* is the place to look.

What Is a Synonym?

A synonym is a word with a meaning identical or very close to that of another word. While all of the synonyms in a group share an important aspect of meaning, there are usually differences in the shades of meaning between them. For example, *clever* and its synonyms *ingenious* and *shrewd* have the same basic meaning: they describe mental adroitness or ingenuity. *Clever* is the most general of the three. *Ingenious* usually refers to what is inventive or creative. And *shrewd* means sharply intelligent and practical.

Synonym Studies

Word Check contains two kinds of synonym studies. The first and simpler kind consists of an alphabetical list of synonyms that share a single, general meaning.

humane *humane compassionate humanitarian merciful*
The central meaning shared by these adjectives is "marked or motivated by concern with the alleviation of suffering": *a humane physician; compassionate toward disadvantaged people; released the prisoner for humanitarian reasons; is merciful to the repentant.*
  ✔ *Antonym:* **inhumane**

The second kind of study is longer and consists of fully discriminated synonyms listed in an order that reflects their interrelationship. A brief, general definition for all of the synonyms is given, and then each synonym is more specifically defined to clarify its own particular shade of meaning and usage.

envy *envy begrudge covet*
These verbs mean to feel resentful or painful desire for another's advantages or possessions. *Envy* is wider in range than the others since it combines discontent, resentment, and desire: *"When I peruse the conquered fame of heroes and the victories of mighty generals, I do not envy the generals"* (Walt Whitman). *Begrudge* stresses ill will and reluctance to acknowledge another's right or claim: *Why begrudge him his success?* *Covet* stresses desire, especially a secret or culpable longing, for something to which one has no right: *"as thorough an Englishman as ever coveted his neighbor's goods"* (Charles Kingsley).

In both entries, the part of speech of the synonyms is indicated, and antonyms, if they exist, are given at the end. Another feature of both types of study is the use of the synonyms in examples to further clarify meaning. In the longer studies, many of these illustrative examples are quotations from well-known authors.

In a few instances it is necessary to distinguish words with superscript numbers. For example, *mean*[1] is a main entry with the general meaning "to convey a particular idea". *Mean*[2] is a main entry with the general meaning "lacking in the elevation or dignity or falling short of the standards befitting human beings". The superscript numbers help you to distinguish between the two.

What Is an Antonym?

Antonyms are words that are opposite in meaning. They appear at the end of many of the synonym studies, as *inhumane* in the example *humane* given above. Some of the antonyms can be found as synonyms at other entries in the book. For example, *simple* is an antonym at the entry for *elaborate* (as an adjective); it is also a synonym found at several other synonym studies. Some words have many shades of meaning and so appear in various places in this thesaurus, while others may have one, more general, meaning. It should also be emphasized that antonyms usually apply only to the main entry words.

Index of Synonyms

All the words that are discussed in the synonym studies are listed in an alphabetical index beginning on page 229. All main entries at which synonym studies appear are printed in small capitals. Any word that is entered only as a synonym is printed in italics, and then followed by a colon and the main entry word at which it appears. If a word appears at more than one synonym list, all the main entry words are given and separated by commas. If a word is both a main entry and a synonym at another main entry with a similar meaning, it is given in both styles:

BATTER
batter: beat
bawl: shout
BE
BEAR
bear: produce

Index of Antonyms

The antonyms that appear in *Word Check* are indexed alphabetically and each is followed by the main entry word for the synonym study at which it is given:

displease: please
encourage: discourage
end: beginning
esteem: despise

If an antonym appears at more than one synonym study, the main-entry word for each study is given.

With its two kinds of synonym studies, antonyms, and convenient format, *Word Check* is the perfect thesaurus for everyday use. It can help you use the English language with color, variety, and precision.

ability   *ability capacity faculty talent skill
competence aptitude*
These nouns denote the qualities in a person that permit or fa-
cilitate achievement or accomplishment. *Ability* is the power,
mental or physical, to do something: *"The next three days demonstrated to her own complete satisfaction Miss Bart's ability to
manage her affairs without extraneous aid"* (Edith Wharton). *Capacity* refers to an innate potential for growth, development,
or accomplishment: *"In the meantime, he desired I would go on
with my utmost diligence to learn their language, because he was
more astonished at my capacity for speech and reason, than at the
figure of my body"* (Jonathan Swift). *Faculty* denotes an inherent
power or ability: *An unerring faculty for detecting hypocrisy is one
of her most useful attributes.* *Talent* emphasizes inborn ability, especially in the arts: *"There is no substitute for talent. Industry and
all the virtues are of no avail"* (Aldous Huxley). *Skill* stresses ability that is acquired or developed through experience: *"The intellect, character and skill possessed by any man are the product of
certain original tendencies and the training which they have received"* (Edward L. Thorndike). *Competence* suggests the ability
to do something satisfactorily but not necessarily outstand-
ingly well: *The concerto was performed by a violinist of unquestioned competence but limited imagination.* *Aptitude* implies inherent capacity for learning, understanding, or performing: *Even
as a child he showed an unusual aptitude for mathematics.*

abuse   *abuse misuse mistreat ill-treat maltreat*
These verbs mean to treat a person or thing wrongfully, incor-

rectly, or harmfully. **Abuse** applies to injurious, improper, or unreasonable treatment: *"We abuse land because we regard it as a commodity belonging to us"* (Aldo Leopold). **Misuse** stresses incorrect or unknowledgeable handling: *"How often misused words generate misleading thoughts"* (Herbert Spencer). **Mistreat, ill-treat,** and **maltreat** all share the sense of inflicting injury, often intentionally, as through malice: *"I had seen many more patients die from being mistreated for consumption than from consumption itself"* (Earl of Lytton). *The army of occupation had orders not to ill-treat the local citizenry.* *"When we misuse [a language other than our native language], we are in fact trying to reduce its element of foreignness. We let ourselves maltreat it as though it naturally belonged to us"* (Manchester Guardian Weekly).

accompany   *accompany conduct escort chaperon*

These verbs are compared when they mean to be with or to go with another or others. **Accompany** suggests going with another on an equal basis: *She went to Europe accompanied by her colleague.* **Conduct** implies guidance of others: *The usher conducted us to our seats.* **Escort** stresses protective guidance: *The picture shows the party chairperson escorting the candidate through the crowd.* **Chaperon** specifies adult supervision of young persons: *Teachers often chaperon their classes on field trips.*

acknowledge   *acknowledge admit own avow confess concede*

These verbs mean to make a disclosure, usually with reluctance or under pressure. To **acknowledge** is to accept responsibility for something one makes known: *He acknowledged that the purchase had been a mistake.* **Admit** usually implies marked reluctance in acknowledging one's acts or accepting a different point of view: *"The truly proud man knows neither superiors nor inferiors. The first he does not admit of: the last he does not concern* *himself about"* (William Hazlitt). **Own** stresses personal acceptance of and responsibility for one's thoughts or deeds: *She owned that she had fears for the child's safety.* **Avow,** a strong term, means to assert openly and boldly: *"Many a man thinks, what he is ashamed to avow"* (Samuel Johnson). **Confess** usually emphasizes disclosure of something damaging or inconvenient to oneself: *I have to confess that I lied to you.* To **concede** is to admit something, such as the validity of an argument, often against one's will: *The lawyer refused to concede that the two cases were at all similar.*

active   *active energetic dynamic vigorous lively*
These adjectives are compared as they mean engaged in activity. **Active,** the most neutral, merely means being in a state of action as opposed to being passive or quiescent: *an active toddler; an active imagination; saw active service in the army.* **Energetic** suggests sustained enthusiastic action with unflagging vitality: *an energetic fundraiser for the college.* **Dynamic** connotes energy and forcefulness that is often inspiring to others: *A dynamic speaker, the senator often persuades her colleagues to change their votes.* **Vigorous** implies healthy strength and robustness: *"a vigorous crusader against apartheid and government press restrictions"* (Christian Science Monitor). **Lively** suggests brisk alertness, animation, and energy: *I take a lively interest in politics.*

adapt   *adapt accommodate adjust conform fit reconcile*
The central meaning shared by these verbs is "to make suitable to or consistent with a particular situation or use": *adapted themselves to city life; can't accommodate myself to the new requirements; adjusting their behavior to the rules; conforming her life to accord with her moral principles; made the punishment fit the crime; couldn't reconcile his reassuring words with his hostile actions.*
  ✔ *Antonym:* **unfit**

adulterate   *adulterate debase doctor load sophisticate*

The central meaning shared by these verbs is "to make impure or inferior by adding foreign substances, especially by way of fraudulently increasing weight or quantity": *adulterate coffee with ground acorns; silver debased with copper; doctored the wine with water; rag paper loaded with wood fiber; alcohol sophisticated with ether.*

advance   *advance forward foster further promote*

The central meaning shared by these verbs is "to cause to move ahead, as toward a goal": *advance a worthy cause; forwarding their own interests; fostered friendly relations; furthering your career; efforts to promote sales.*

✔ Antonym: **retard**

advantage   *advantage edge handicap odds*

The central meaning shared by these nouns is "a factor or combination of factors conducive to superiority and success": *has the advantage of a superior education; a manufacturing edge given by sophisticated technology; a golfing champion with a handicap of 2; odds overwhelmingly in our favor.*

✔ Antonym: **disadvantage**

adventurous   *adventurous adventuresome audacious daredevil daring venturesome*

The central meaning shared by these adjectives is "taking, willing to take, or seeking out risks": *adventurous pioneers; an adventuresome prospector; an audacious explorer; a daredevil test pilot; daring acrobats; a venturesome investor.*

advice   *advice counsel recommendation*

The central meaning shared by these nouns is "an opinion as

to a decision or course of action": *sound advice for those looking for work; accepted the counsel of her attorney; refused to follow his recommendation.*

advise   *advise   counsel   recommend*
The central meaning shared by these verbs is "to give recommendations to someone about a decision or course of action": *advised him to take advantage of the opportunity; will counsel her to be prudent; recommended that we wait.*

affair   *affair   business   concern   lookout*
The central meaning shared by these nouns is "something that involves one personally": *I won't comment on that; it's not my affair. That's none of your business. Mind your own concerns. It's your lookout to see that your application is filed on time.*

affect   *affect   influence   impress   touch   move   strike*
These verbs are compared as they mean to produce a mental or emotional effect. To **affect** is to act upon a person's emotions: *The adverse criticism the book received didn't affect the author one way or another.* **Influence** implies a degree of control or sway over the thinking and actions, as well as the emotions, of another: *"Humanity is profoundly influenced by what you do"* (John Paul II). To **impress** is to produce a marked, deep, often enduring effect: *"The Tibetan landscape particularly impressed him"* (Doris Kerns Quinn). **Touch** usually means to arouse a tender response, such as love, gratitude, or compassion: *"The tributes [to the two deceased musicians] were fitting and touching"* (Daniel Cariaga). **Move** suggests profound emotional effect that sometimes leads to action or has a further consequence: *The account of her experiences as a refugee moved us to tears.* **Strike** implies keenness or force of mental response to a stimulus: *I was struck by the sudden change in his behavior.*

affectation   *affectation pose air mannerism*

These nouns refer to personal behavior assumed for effect. An **affectation** is an artificial habit, as of speech or dress, that is often adopted in imitation of an admired person and that can be identified by others as being unnatural: *"His [Arthur Rubinstein's] playing stripped away . . . the affectations and exaggerations that characterized Chopin interpretation before his arrival"* (Michael Kimmelman). **Pose** denotes an attitude adopted with the aim of calling favorable attention to oneself or making an impression on other people: *His humility is only a pose.* **Air,** meaning a distinctive but intangible quality, does not always imply sham: *an air of authority.* In the plural, however, it suggests affectation and especially a wish to seem more important than is actually the case: *Don't put on airs.* **Mannerism** denotes an idiosyncratic trait, manner, or quirk, often one that others find obtrusive and distracting: *He had a mannerism of closing his eyes as he talked, as if he were deep in thought.*

afflict   *afflict agonize excruciate rack torment torture*

The central meaning shared by these verbs is "to bring great harm or suffering to someone": *afflicted with arthritis; agonizing pain; excruciating spasms of neuralgia; racked with cancer; tormented by migraine headaches; tortured by painful emotions.*

afraid   *afraid apprehensive fearful*

The central meaning shared by these adjectives is "filled with fear": *afraid of snakes; feeling apprehensive before surgery; fearful of criticism.*
   ✔ *Antonym:* **unafraid**

ageless   *ageless eternal timeless*

The central meaning shared by these adjectives is "existing

unchanged forever": *the ageless themes of love and revenge; eternal truths; timeless beauty.*

agitate   *agitate churn convulse rock shake*

The central meaning shared by these verbs is "to cause to move to and fro violently": *land agitated by tremors; a storm churning the waves; buildings and streets convulsed by the detonation of a bomb; a tornado rocking trees and houses; an explosion that shook the ground.*

agree   *agree conform harmonize accord correspond coincide*

These verbs all indicate a compatible relationship between people or things. *Agree* may indicate mere lack of incongruity or discord: *The testimony of all the witnesses agrees on that point.* Often, however, it suggests acceptance of ideas or actions and thus accommodation: *We finally agreed on a price for the house.* *Conform* stresses correspondence in essence or basic characteristics, sometimes as a result of accommodation to established standards: *The kinds of books in her library conform to her level of education. Students are required to conform to the rules.* **Harmonize** implies a relationship of unlike elements combined or arranged to make a pleasing whole: *Beige harmonizes with black.* **Accord** implies harmonious relationship, unity, or consistency, as in feeling or essential nature: *"The creed [upon which America was founded] was widely seen as both progressive and universalistic: It accorded with the future, and it was open to all"* (Everett Carll Ladd). **Correspond** refers either to actual similarity in form or nature (*The dots on the pattern correspond with the seam allowance on the cut fabric*) or to similarity in function, character, or structure: *The Diet in Japan corresponds to the American Congress.* **Coincide** stresses exact agreement in space, time, or thought: *"His interest happily coincided with his duty"* (Edward A. Freeman).

✔ *Antonym:* **disagree**

aim aim direct level point train

The central meaning shared by these verbs is "to turn something in the direction of an intended goal or target": *aimed the camera at the guests; directing her eyes on the book; leveled criticism at the administration; pointing a finger at the suspect; trained the gun on the intruder.*

airy airy diaphanous ethereal filmy gauzy gossamer sheer transparent vaporous

The central meaning shared by these adjectives is "so light and insubstantial as to resemble air or a thin film": *an airy organdy blouse; a hat with a diaphanous veil; ethereal mist; the filmy wings of a moth; gauzy clouds of dandelion down; gossamer cobwebs; sheer silk stockings; transparent chiffon; vaporous muslin.*

alarm alarm alert tocsin warning

The central meaning shared by these nouns is "a signal that warns of imminent danger": *a burglar alarm; sirens signaling a bomb alert; a tocsin ringing from church steeples; factory whistles sounding a forest-fire warning.*

allocate allocate appropriate designate earmark

The central meaning shared by these verbs is "to set aside for a specified purpose": *allocated time for recreation; appropriated funds for public education; designated a location for the new hospital; money earmarked for a vacation.*

alone alone lonely lonesome solitary

These adjectives are compared as they describe lack of companionship. **Alone** emphasizes being apart from others but does not necessarily imply unhappiness: *"I am never less alone, than when I am alone"* (James Howell). **Lonely** often connotes painful awareness of being alone: *"We are for the most part more lonely when we go abroad among men than when we stay in our chambers"* (Henry David Thoreau). **Lonesome** emphasizes a plaintive desire for companionship: *"You must keep up your spirits, mother, and not be lonesome because I'm not at home"* (Charles Dickens). **Solitary** often shares the connotations of *lonely* and *lonesome*: *"Only solitary men know the full joys of friendship"* (Willa Cather). Frequently, however, it stresses physical isolation that is self-imposed: *She thoroughly enjoyed her solitary dinner.*

amateur   *amateur dabbler dilettante tyro*

The central meaning shared by these nouns is "one engaging in a pursuit but lacking professional skill": *a musician who is a gifted amateur, not a professional; a dabbler in the graphic arts; a sculptor but a mere dilettante; a tyro in the art of writing poetry.*
   ✔ *Antonym:* **professional**

ambiguous   *ambiguous equivocal obscure recondite abstruse vague cryptic enigmatic*

These adjectives mean lacking clarity of meaning. **Ambiguous** indicates the presence of two or more possible meanings: *Frustrated by ambiguous instructions, the parents were never able to assemble the new toy.* Something **equivocal** is unclear or misleading, sometimes as a result of a deliberate effort to avoid exposure of one's position: *"The polling had a complex and equivocal message for potential female candidates at all levels"* (David S. Broder). **Obscure** implies that meaning is hidden, either from lack of clarity of expression or from inherent difficulty of comprehension: *Those who do not appreciate Kafka's work say his style is obscure and too complex.* **Recondite** and **ab-**

struse connote the erudite obscurity of the scholar: *"some re-condite problem in historiography"* (Walter Laqueur). *The professor's lectures were so abstruse that students tended to avoid them.* What is **vague** is unclear because it is expressed in indefinite form or because it reflects imprecision of thought: *"Vague . . . forms of speech . . . have so long passed for mysteries of science"* (John Locke). **Cryptic** suggests a puzzling terseness that is often intended to discourage understanding: *The new insurance policy is written without cryptic or mysterious terms.* Something **enigmatic** is mysterious, puzzling, and often challenging: *I didn't grasp the meaning of that enigmatic comment until much later.*

ambush   *ambush ambuscade bushwhack waylay*

The central meaning shared by these verbs is "to attack suddenly and without warning from a place of concealment": *guerrillas ambushing a platoon of regulars; highwaymen ambuscading a stagecoach; tax collectors bushwhacked by moonshiners; a truck waylaid and its driver robbed.*

amenity   *amenity comfort convenience facility*

The central meaning shared by these nouns is "something that increases physical ease or facilitates work": *a sunny apartment with amenities including air conditioning; a suite with comforts such as a whirlpool bath; a kitchen with every convenience; a school with excellent facilities for students.*

amiss   *amiss afield astray awry wrong*

The central meaning shared by these adverbs is "not in the right way or on the proper course": *spoke amiss; straying far afield; afraid the letter would go astray; thinking awry; plans that went wrong.*
    ✔ *Antonym:* **aright**

amuse   *amuse   entertain   divert   regale*
These verbs refer to actions that provide pleasure, especially as a means of passing time. *Amuse,* the least specific, implies directing the attention away from serious matters: *I amused myself with a game of solitaire.* **Entertain** suggests acts undertaken to furnish amusement: *"They* [timetables and catalogs] *are much more entertaining than half the novels that are written"* (W. Somerset Maugham). **Divert** implies distraction from worrisome thought or care: *"I had neither Friends or Books to divert me"* (Richard Steele). To **regale** is to entertain with something enormously enjoyable: *"He loved to regale his friends with tales about the many memorable characters he had known as a newspaperman"* (David Rosenzweig).

analyze   *analyze   anatomize   dissect   resolve*
The central meaning shared by these verbs is "to separate into constituent parts for study": *analyze an ore to see if it contains iron; anatomizing the doctrine of free enterprise; medical students dissecting cadavers; vapor condensing and being resolved into water.*

ancestor   *ancestor   forebear   forefather   progenitor*
The central meaning shared by these nouns is "a person from whom one is descended": *ancestors who were farmers; an island once owned by his forebears; methods as old as our forefathers; the wisdom of our progenitors.*
   ✔ *Antonym:* **descendant**

anger   *anger   rage   fury   ire   wrath*
resentment   indignation
These nouns denote varying degrees of marked displeasure. *Anger,* the most general, is strong displeasure: *suppressed her anger; threw a book in a fit of anger.* **Rage** and **fury** are closely related in the sense of intense, explosive, often destructive emo-

tion: *"Heaven has no rage like love to hatred turned"* (William Congreve). *"Beware the fury of a patient man"* (John Dryden). **Ire** is a term for anger that is frequently encountered in literature: *"The best way to escape His ire / Is, not to seem too happy"* (Robert Browning). **Wrath** applies especially to fervid anger that seeks vengeance or punishment, often on an epic scale: *rebellious words sure to kindle a parent's wrath; the wrath of God.* **Resentment** refers to ill will and smoldering anger generated by a sense of grievance: *The strike can be traced to the personal resentment of the foreman against the factory owner.* **Indignation** is righteous anger at something regarded as being wrongful, unjust, or evil: *"public indignation about takeovers causing people to lose their jobs"* (Allan Sloan).

angry *angry furious indignant irate ireful mad wrathful*
The central meaning shared by these adjectives is "feeling or showing anger": *an angry retort; a furious scowl; an indignant denial; irate protesters; ireful words; mad at a friend; wrathful displeasure.*

announce *announce advertise broadcast declare proclaim promulgate publish*
The central meaning shared by these verbs is "to bring to public notice": *announced a cease-fire; advertise a forthcoming concert; broadcasting their beliefs; declared her intention to run for office; proclaiming his opinions; promulgated a policy of nonresistance; publishing the marriage banns.*

annoy *annoy irritate bother irk vex provoke aggravate peeve rile*
These verbs mean to disturb or disquiet a person so as to evoke moderate anger. **Annoy** refers to mild disturbance caused by an

act that tries one's patience: *The sound of footsteps on the bare floor annoyed the downstairs neighbors.* **Irritate** is closely related but somewhat stronger: *Your interruptions only serve to irritate the entire staff.* **Bother** implies troublesome imposition: *Hasn't he bothered them enough with his phone calls?* **Irk** connotes a wearisome quality: *The city council's failure to take action on the legislation irked the community.* **Vex** applies to an act capable of arousing anger or perplexity: *Hecklers in the crowd asked irrelevant questions for the sole purpose of vexing the speaker.* **Provoke** implies strong and often deliberate incitement to anger: *Her behavior was enough to provoke an angel.* **Aggravate** is an approximate equivalent: *"Threats only served to aggravate people in such cases"* (William M. Thackeray). **Peeve,** somewhat informal in tone, suggests rather minor disturbance that produces a querulous, resentful response: *The flippancy of your answer peeved me.* To **rile** is to upset one's equanimity and stir one up: *It riled me no end to listen to such lies.*

answer   *answer respond reply retort*

These verbs relate to action taken in return to a stimulus. **Answer, respond,** and **reply,** the most general, all mean to speak, write, or act in response: *"the attempt to answer questions, without first discovering precisely* what *question it is which you desire to answer"* (G.E. Moore). *You didn't really expect the President to respond personally to your letter, did you? The opposing team scored three runs; the home team replied with two of their own.* **Respond** also denotes a reaction to something that stimulates one to a course of action, often voluntary (*A bystander responded immediately to the victim's obvious need for help*), or to an involuntary emotional response (*She responded in spite of herself to the antics of the puppy*). To **retort** is to answer verbally in a quick, caustic, or witty manner: *"You don't need to worry about appearing too intelligent,"* retorted his opponent.

anxiety *anxiety worry care concern solicitude*
These nouns are compared as they refer to troubled states of mind. **Anxiety** suggests feelings of fear and apprehension, especially when these emotions seem unrelated to objective source: *"Feelings of resentment and rage over this devious form of manipulation cannot surface in the child . . . because he does not see through the subterfuge. At the most, he will experience feelings of anxiety, shame, insecurity, and helplessness"* (Alice Miller). **Worry** implies persistent doubt or fear that disturbs one's peace of mind: *"Rich people have about as many worries as poor ones, I think"* (Louisa May Alcott). **Care** denotes a burdened state of mind arising from heavy responsibilities: *"To be happy one must be . . . well fed, unhounded by sordid cares"* (H.L. Mencken). **Concern** stresses involvement in the source of mental unrest; it combines serious thought with emotion: *"Concern for man himself and his fate must always form the chief interest of all technical endeavors"* (Albert Einstein). **Solicitude** is active and sometimes excessive concern for the well-being of another or others: *"Animosity had given way first to grudging concessions of admiration and then to worried solicitude for Lindbergh's safety"* (Warren Trabant).

apology *apology apologetic apologia defense justification*
The central meaning shared by these nouns is "a statement that justifies or defends something, such as a past action or a policy": *a report that is an apology for capital punishment; an apologetic for fascism; a version of the story that is an apologia for malfeasance; offered a defense based on ignorance of the circumstances; an intellectually untenable justification for police brutality.*

apparent *apparent clear clear-cut distinct evident manifest obvious patent plain*
The central meaning shared by these adjectives is "readily

seen, perceived, or understood": *Angry for no apparent reason; a clear danger; clear-cut evidence of tampering; distinct fingerprints; evident hostility; manifest pleasure; obvious errors; patent advantages; making my meaning plain.*

appear   *appear   emerge   issue   loom   materialize   show*

The central meaning shared by these verbs is "to come into view": *a ship appearing on the horizon; a star that emerged from behind a cloud; a diver issuing from the water; a peak that loomed through the mist; a flash of lightning that seemed to materialize from nowhere; a ruffle showing at the edge of the sleeve.*

applaud   *applaud   cheer   root*

The central meaning shared by these verbs is "to express approval or encouragement in audible form, especially by clapping": *applauded at the end of the concert; cheered when the home team scored; rooting for the underdog in the tennis championship.*

appoint   *appoint   designate   name   nominate   tap*

The central meaning shared by these verbs is "to select for an office or position": *was appointed chairperson of the committee; expects to be designated leader of the opposition; a new commissioner of public safety named by the mayor; wants to be nominated as her party's candidate; was tapped for fraternity membership.*

appreciate   *appreciate   value   prize   esteem treasure   cherish*

These verbs mean to have a favorable opinion of someone or something. **Appreciate** applies especially when high regard is based on critical assessment, comparison, and judgment: *"As students so far from home, we have learned to appreciate those of life's pleasures that are not readily available in the People's Republic of China"* (Sports Illustrated). **Value** implies high regard for the importance or worth of the object: *"In principle, the modern university values nothing more than the free exchange of ideas necessary for the pursuit of knowledge"* (Eloise Salholz). **Prize** often suggests pride of possession: *"the nonchalance prized by teenagers"* (Elaine Louie). **Esteem** implies respect of a formal sort: *"If he had never esteemed my opinion before, he would have thought highly of me then"* (Jane Austen). **Treasure** and **cherish** stress solicitous care for what is considered precious and often suggest affectionate regard: *We treasure our freedom.* *"They seek out the Salish Indian woman for the wisdom of her 86 years, and to learn the traditions she cherishes"* (Tamara Jones).

apprehend   *apprehend comprehend understand grasp*
These verbs are compared as they denote perception of the nature and significance of something. **Apprehend** can imply awareness or consciousness that comes through the emotions or senses: *"We should not pretend to understand the world only by the intellect; we apprehend it just as much by feeling"* (Carl Jung). *Apprehend* also denotes taking in with the mind: *"Intelligence is quickness to apprehend"* (Alfred North Whitehead). Both **comprehend** and **understand** stress complete realization and knowledge: *"To comprehend is to know a thing as well as that thing can be known"* (John Donne). *"No one who has not had the responsibility can really understand what it is like to be President"* (Harry S. Truman). To **grasp** is to seize and hold an idea firmly: *"We have grasped the mystery of the atom and rejected the Sermon on the Mount"* (Omar N. Bradley).

appropriate   *appropriate arrogate commandeer confiscate preempt usurp*
The central meaning shared by these verbs is "to seize for oneself or as one's right": *appropriated the family car; arrogating to himself the most interesting tasks; commandeered a plane for the*

escape; confiscating alien property; preempted the glory for herself; usurped the throne.

approve   *approve endorse sanction certify accredit ratify*
These verbs mean to express a favorable opinion or to signify satisfaction or acceptance. Though **approve,** the most widely applicable, often means simply to consider right or good (*knew my parents wouldn't approve of what I had done*), it can also denote official consent: *"The colonel or commanding officer approves the sentence of a regimental court-martial"* (Charles James). **Endorse** implies the expression of support, often by public statement: *The senator will give a speech endorsing her party's gubernatorial candidate.* **Sanction** usually implies not only approval (*Public opinion ought not to sanction the use of force*) but also official authorization (*The privilege of voting is a right sanctioned by law*). **Certify** and **accredit** imply official approval based on compliance with requirements or standards: *"The proper officers, comparing every article with its voucher, certified them to be right"* (Benjamin Franklin). *The board of higher education will accredit only those institutions offering a sufficiently rigorous curriculum.* To **ratify** is to invest with legal authority by giving official sanction: *"Amendments . . . shall be valid . . . when ratified by the Legislatures of three fourths of the several States"* (U.S. Constitution, Article V).

arbitrary   *arbitrary capricious whimsical*
The central meaning shared by these adjectives is "determined by or arising from whim or caprice rather than judgment or reason": *an arbitrary decision; a capricious refusal; the butt of whimsical persecution.*

argue   *argue quarrel wrangle squabble bicker*
These verbs denote verbal exchange expressing conflict of po-

sitions or opinions. To **argue** is to present reasons or facts in an attempt to persuade an adversary in debate or to induce another to espouse a cause or point of view one advocates: *"I am not arguing with you — I am telling you"* (James McNeill Whistler). **Quarrel** stresses animosity and often a suspension of amicable relations: *There's no point in quarreling about the past.* **Wrangle** refers to loud, contentious argument: *"audiences . . . who can be overheard wrangling about film facts in restaurants and coffee houses"* (Sheila Benson). **Squabble** suggests disagreeable argument, usually over a petty or trivial matter: *"The one absolutely certain way of bringing this nation to ruin . . . would be to permit it to become a tangle of squabbling nationalities"* (Theodore Roosevelt). **Bicker** connotes sharp, persistent, bad-tempered exchange: *"(Our) whole political machinery presupposes a people so fundamentally at one that they can safely afford to bicker"* (Arthur James Balfour).

argumentative   *argumentative combative contentious disputatious quarrelsome scrappy*
The central meaning shared by these adjectives is "given to or fond of arguing": *an intelligent but argumentative child; combative impulses; a contentious mood; a disputatious lawyer; is quarrelsome when drinking; a scrappy litigator.*

arrange   *arrange marshal order organize sort systematize*
The central meaning shared by these verbs is "to distribute or dispose persons or things properly or methodically": *arranging figures in numerical sequence; marshal all the relevant facts for the presentation; tried to order my chaotic life; organizing and coordinating fund-raising efforts; sorted the sweaters according to color; systematizing a vast assortment of rules into a cohesive whole.*
   ✔ *Antonym:* **disarrange**

art   *art craft expertise knack know-how technique*
The central meaning shared by these nouns is "skill in doing or performing that is attained by study, practice, or observation": *the art of expressing oneself clearly; pottery that reveals craft and fine workmanship; political expertise; a knack for teaching; the know-how to sew one's own clothes; an outstanding keyboard technique.*

artificial   *artificial synthetic ersatz simulated*
These adjectives are compared as they refer to what is made by human beings rather than natural in origin. Of these terms **artificial** is broadest in meaning and connotation: *an artificial sweetener; artificial flowers.* **Synthetic** often implies the use of a chemical process to produce a substance that will look or function like the original, often with certain advantages, such as enhanced durability or convenience of use or care: *synthetic rubber; a synthetic fabric.* An **ersatz** product is a transparently inferior imitation: *ersatz coffee; ersatz mink.* **Simulated** refers to what is made to resemble or substitute for another often costlier substance: *a purse of simulated alligator hide; simulated mahogany paneling.*

ask   *ask question inquire query interrogate examine quiz*
These verbs mean to seek information from a person. **Ask** is the most neutral term: *asked her what was wrong; asked the way to the library; ask too many questions.* **Question** often implies the asking of a series of questions, as in determining the scope of a problem: *The prosecutor questioned the witness in great detail.* **Inquire,** which often implies a comprehensive search for knowledge or truth, in this sense refers to a simple request for information: *inquired where the books were kept; will inquire how we can be of help; inquired about her health.* **Query** usually suggests

questioning to settle a doubt: *The proofreader queried the spelling of the word.* **Interrogate,** a more formal word, applies especially to official questioning: *The suspects were called in and interrogated by detectives.* **Examine** refers particularly to close and detailed questioning to ascertain the extent of a person's knowledge or the adequacy of his or her qualifications: *At the end of the semester students are examined in every subject. Only lawyers who have been examined and certified by the bar association are admitted to practice.* **Quiz** is used most frequently to denote the informal examination of students to verify their comprehension of classwork or reading: *The teacher quizzed the pupils on the multiplication tables.*

assent   *assent agree accede acquiesce consent concur subscribe*

These verbs denote concurrence with another's views, proposals, or actions. **Assent** implies agreement, as with a statement or a proposal, especially when it results from deliberation: *They readily assented to our suggestion.* **Agree** and **accede** are related in the sense that assent has been reached after discussion or efforts at persuasion, but *accede* implies that one person or group has yielded, as to the insistence of the other: *"It was not possible to agree to a proposal so extraordinary and unexpected"* (William Robertson). *"In an evil hour this proposal was acceded to"* (Mary E. Herbert). **Acquiesce** suggests passive assent, often despite reservations, because of inability or unwillingness to oppose: *I had to acquiesce in her decision despite my private opinion.* **Consent** implies voluntary acquiescence to the desire or proposal of another: *Her parents refused to consent to her marriage.* **Concur** refers to agreement with another's position and may suggest that one has reached the same conclusion independently: *"I concurred with our incumbent in getting up a petition against the Reform Bill"* (George Eliot). **Subscribe** indicates hearty consent or approval: *"I am contented to subscribe to the opinion of the best-qualified judge of our time"* (Sir Walter Scott).

assistant   *assistant aide coadjutant coadjutor helper lieutenant second*
The central meaning shared by these nouns is "a person who holds a position auxiliary to another and assumes some of his or her responsibilities": *an editorial assistant; a senator's aide; the general's coadjutant; a bishop's coadjutor; a teacher's helper; a politician's lieutenant; a prizefighter's second.*

authentic   *authentic bonafide genuine real true undoubted unquestionable*
The central meaning shared by these adjectives is "not counterfeit or copied": *an authentic painting by Corot; a bona fide transfer of property; genuine crabmeat; a real diamond; true courage; undoubted evidence; an unquestionable antique.*
   ✔ *Antonym:* **counterfeit**

authorize   *authorize accredit commission empower license*
The central meaning shared by these verbs is "to give someone the authority to act": *authorized her partner to negotiate in her behalf; a representative who was accredited by his government; commissioned the real-estate agent to purchase the house for us; was empowered to make decisions during the president's absence; a pharmacist licensed to practice in two states.*

average   *average medium mediocre fair middling indifferent tolerable*
These adjectives indicate rank or position around the middle of a scale of evaluation. *Average* and *medium* apply to what is midway between extremes on such a scale; usually they imply both sufficiency and lack of distinction: *a novel of average merit; an or-*

ange of medium size. **Mediocre** stresses the undistinguished aspect of what is average: *"The caliber of the students . . . has gone from mediocre to above average"* (Judy Pasternak). What is **fair** is passable but substantially below excellent: *a fair student; in fair health; have a fair idea of what's going on.* **Middling** refers to middle position between best and worst: *gave a middling performance at best.* **Indifferent** applies to what is of less than striking character, being neither very good nor very bad: *"I've been fussing over the thing so long, I really don't know whether it's good, bad, or indifferent"* (Louisa May Alcott). Something that is **tolerable** is merely acceptable: *prepared a tolerable dinner.*

aware   **aware cognizant conscious sensible awake alert watchful vigilant**

These adjectives mean mindful or heedful of something. **Aware** implies knowledge gained through one's own perceptions, as of the attitudes of others, or by means of information: *Are you aware of your opponent's hostility? I am aware that Congress has passed the legislation.* **Cognizant** is a rather formal equivalent of aware: *"Our research indicates that the nation's youth are cognizant of the law"* (Jerry D. Jennings). **Conscious** emphasizes the recognition of something sensed or felt: *"an importance . . . of which even Americans are barely conscious"* (William Stanley Jevons). **Sensible** implies knowledge gained through intellectual perception or through intuition: *"I am sensible that the mention of such a circumstance may appear trifling"* (Henry Hallam). To be **awake** is to have full consciousness of something: *"as much awake to the novelty of attention in that quarter as Elizabeth herself"* (Jane Austen). **Alert** stresses quickness to recognize and respond: *alert enough to spot the opportunity when it came.* **Watchful** and **vigilant** imply being on the lookout for what is dangerous or potentially so: *a watchful parent with a toddler in tow; keeping a vigilant eye on every building where a fire might start.*

bad *bad evil wicked*

These adjectives are compared as they mean departing from moral or ethical standards. **Bad** is the most inclusive; it applies to what is regarded as being unpleasant, offensive, or blameworthy: *bad weather; a bad temper.* "*A bad book is as much of a labor to write as a good one*" (Aldous Huxley). **Evil,** a stronger term, adds to *bad* connotations of depravity and corruptive influence: "*The unconscious is not just evil by nature, it is also the source of the highest good*" (Carl Jung). **Wicked** suggests conscious or premeditated moral transgression: "*this wicked man Hitler, the repository and embodiment of many forms of soul-destroying hatred, this monstrous product of former wrongs and shame*" (Winston S. Churchill).

balance *balance equilibrium equipoise poise*

The central meaning shared by these nouns is "a state of stability resulting from the cancellation of all forces by equal opposing forces": *upsetting the balance of nature through the use of insecticides; equilibrium of power between Western and Eastern countries; the weights of a scale in equipoise; a poise between disparate and contradictory emotions.*

   ✔ Antonym: **imbalance**

band *band company corps party troop troupe*

The central meaning shared by these nouns is "a group of individuals acting together in a shared activity or enterprise": *a band of thieves; a company of scientists; a corps of drummers; a party of tourists; a troop of students on a field trip; a troupe of actors.*

banish *banish exile expatriate deport transport extradite*

These verbs mean to send away from a country or state. **Banish** applies to forced departure from a country by official decree:

was convicted of heresy and banished from the kingdom. **Exile** specifies departure from one's own country, either involuntarily because of legal expulsion or voluntarily because of adverse circumstances: *When the government was overthrown, the royal family was exiled.* **Expatriate** pertains to departure that is sometimes forced but often voluntary and may imply change of citizenship: *an immigrant whose citizenship was revoked and who was expatriated because he had concealed his criminal record.* **Deport** denotes the act of sending an alien abroad by governmental order: *was deported for entering the country illegally.* **Transport** pertains to the sending abroad, usually to a penal colony, of one convicted of a crime: *Offenders are no longer transported to Devil's Island.* **Extradite** applies to the delivery of an accused or convicted person to the state or country having jurisdiction over him or her: *The court refused to extradite political refugees.*

banter   *banter chaff josh kid rag razz rib*

The central meaning shared by these verbs is "to poke fun at good-humoredly": *bantered with her colleagues about their long coffee breaks; chaffed her for forgetting the appointment; joshed his brother about his strange new haircut; thought you were kidding me; ragged her about being so stubborn; razzed the teammate who missed the shot; ribbing a friend for being helplessly in love.*

bargain   *bargain compact contract covenant deal*

The central meaning shared by these nouns is "an agreement arrived at after discussion in which the parties involved promise to honor their respective obligations": *kept his end of the bargain and mowed the lawn; made a compact to correspond regularly; a legally binding contract to install new windows in the house; a covenant for mutual defense; annoyance that wasn't part of the deal.*

barrage   *barrage bombard pepper shower*
The central meaning shared by these verbs is "to direct a concentrated outpouring, as of missiles or words, at something or
someone": *barraging the speaker with questions; bombarded the
box office with ticket orders; peppered the senator with protests;
showered the child with gifts.*

baseless   *baseless groundless idle unfounded unwarranted*
The central meaning shared by these adjectives is "being without a basis or foundation in fact": *a baseless accusation; groundless rumors; idle gossip; unfounded suspicions; unwarranted jealousy.*

batter   *batter maim mangle maul mutilate*
The central meaning shared by these verbs is "to damage, injure, or disfigure by beating, abuse, or hard use": *a house battered by a hurricane; a wrist maimed in an accident; a mangled
corpse; a tent mauled by a hungry bear; mutilated the painting with
a razor blade.*

be   *be breathe exist live subsist*
The central meaning shared by these verbs is "to have life or
reality": *Her parents are no more. A nicer person has never
breathed. He is one of the worst actors who ever existed. Human beings cannot live without food and water. The benevolence subsisting
in her character draws her friends closer to her.*

bear   *bear endure stand abide suffer tolerate*
These verbs are compared in the sense of withstanding or sus-
taining what is difficult or painful to undergo. *Bear* pertains
broadly to capacity to withstand: *"Man performs, engenders, so
much more than he can or should have to bear. That's how he finds
that he can bear anything"* (William Faulkner). *Endure* specifies a
continuing capacity to face pain or hardship: *"Human life is ev-*

erywhere a state in which much is to be endured and little to be en-
joyed" (Samuel Johnson). **Stand** implies resoluteness of spirit:
The pain was too intense to stand. Actors who can't stand criticism
shouldn't perform in public. **Abide** and the more emphatic **suffer**
suggest resignation and forbearance: *She couldn't abide fools. He*
suffered their insults in silence. **Tolerate,** in its principal application to something other than pain, connotes reluctant acceptance despite reservations: *"A decent . . . examination of the*
acts of government should be not only tolerated, but encouraged"
(William Henry Harrison).

beat   *beat baste batter belabor buffet hammer*
lambaste pound pummel thrash
The central meaning shared by these verbs is "to hit heavily
and repeatedly with violent blows": *was mugged and beaten;*
basted him with a stick; was battered and bloodied in the prize ring;
rioting students belabored by squads of police officers; buffeted him
around the face with her open palm; hammered the opponent with
his fists; lambasting a horse thief with a riding crop; troops being
pounded with mortar fire; pummeled the bully soundly; an unruly
child who was thrashed with a birch cane.

beautiful   *beautiful lovely pretty handsome comely fair*
All these adjectives apply to what excites aesthetic admiration.
Beautiful, the most comprehensive, applies to what stirs a
heightened response both of the senses *(a beautiful child; beauti-*
ful country; a beautiful painting) and of the mind on its highest
level *(a persuasive and beautiful theory; a beautiful mathematical*
proof). **Lovely** applies to what inspires emotion rather than intellectual appreciation: *"They were lovely, your eyes, but you didn't*
know where to look" (George Seferis). *"Every man feels instinctively*
that all the beautiful sentiments in the world weigh less than a single
lovely action" (James Russell Lowell). What is **pretty** is beautiful

but in a delicate or graceful way; the word rarely applies to what is imposing: *a pretty face; a pretty song; a pretty room.* **Handsome** stresses visual appeal by reason of conformity to ideals of form and proportion: *a very large, handsome paneled library.* "*She is very pretty, but not so* extraordinarily *handsome*" (William M. Thackeray). **Comely** is usually restricted to wholesome physical attractiveness: "*Mrs. Hurd is a large woman with a big, comely, simple face*" (Ernest Hemingway). **Fair** in this context emphasizes visual appeal deriving from freshness or purity: "*In the highlands, in the country places, / Where the old plain men have rosy faces, / And the young fair maidens / Quiet eyes*" (Robert Louis Stevenson).

begin   *begin commence start initiate inaugurate*

These verbs are compared as they denote coming or putting into operation, being, or motion or setting about taking the first step, as in a procedure. **Begin** and **commence** are equivalent in meaning, though *commence* is more formal: *began the race; a play that begins at eight o'clock; commenced her career as a scientist; festivities that commenced with the national anthem.* **Start** is often interchangeable with *begin* and *commence* but can also imply setting out from a specific point, frequently following inaction: *Stand and visit with me for a few minutes until the train starts. The telephone started ringing.* **Initiate** applies to the act of taking the first steps in a process, without reference to what follows: *The public hoped the government would initiate restrictions on imported goods.* **Inaugurate** often connotes a formal beginning: "*The exhibition inaugurated a new era of cultural relations between the Soviet Union and United States*" (Serge Schmemann).

beginning   *beginning birth dawn genesis nascence rise*

The central meaning shared by these nouns is "the initial stage of a developmental process": *the beginning of a new era in computer technology; the birth of generative grammar; the dawn of*

civilization; the genesis of quantum mechanics; the nascence of classical sculpture; the rise and decline of an ancient city-state.
  ✔ Antonym: **end**

behavior *behavior conduct deportment*

These nouns all pertain to a person's actions as they constitute a means of evaluation by others. **Behavior** is the most general: *time off for good behavior; on their best behavior; guilty of contemptible behavior.* **Conduct** applies to actions considered from the standpoint of morality and ethics: *"The fate of unborn millions will now depend . . . on the courage and conduct of this army"* (George Washington). *"Life, not the parson, teaches conduct"* (Oliver Wendell Holmes, Jr.). **Deportment** more narrowly pertains to actions measured by a prevailing code of social behavior: *"[Old Mr. Turveydrop] was not like anything in the world but a model of Deportment"* (Charles Dickens).

belief *belief credence credit faith*

The central meaning shared by these nouns is "mental acceptance of the truth, actuality, or validity of something": *a statement unworthy of belief; an idea steadily gaining credence; testimony meriting credit; put no faith in a liar's assertions.*
  ✔ Antonym: **disbelief**

bend *bend crook curve round*

The central meaning shared by these verbs is "to swerve or cause to swerve from a straight line": *bent his knees and knelt; crooks her little finger when she holds a teacup; claws that curve under; rounding the lips to articulate an "o."*
  ✔ Antonym: **straighten**

beneficial *beneficial profitable advantageous*

These adjectives apply to what promotes benefit or gain. **Bene-**

ficial is said of what enhances well-being: *a temperate climate beneficial to the health; an arms limitation agreement beneficial to all countries.* **Profitable** refers to what yields material gain or useful compensation: *profitable speculation on the stock market; a profitable meeting to resolve difficulties.* Something **advantageous** affords improvement in relative position or in chances of success: *signed a contract that is advantageous to our company; found it socially advantageous to entertain often and well.*

benefit   *benefit capitalize profit*
The central meaning shared by these verbs is "to derive advantage from something": *benefited from the stock split; capitalized on her adversary's blunder; profiting from experience.*

benevolent   *benevolent charitable eleemosynary philanthropic*
The central meaning shared by these adjectives is "of, concerned with, providing, or provided by charity": *a benevolent fund; a charitable foundation; eleemosynary relief; philanthropic contributions.*

besiege   *besiege beleaguer blockade invest siege*
The central meaning shared by these verbs is "to surround with hostile forces": *besiege a walled city; a beleaguered settlement; blockaded the harbor; investing a fortress; a castle sieged by foot soldiers and cavalry.*

bet   *bet ante pot stake wager*
The central meaning shared by these nouns is "something valuable risked on an uncertain outcome": *placed a 50-dollar bet on a horse in the first race; raising the ante in a poker game; won the whole pot in bridge; defeated her opponent and took the stakes; laid a wager on who would get the role.*

bias *bias color jaundice prejudice warp*
The central meaning shared by these verbs is "to influence unfavorably or detrimentally": *past experiences that have biased his outlook; behavior that has colored my opinion of her; a view of campaign promises that has become jaundiced; lying that has prejudiced the public against the administration; bitterness that has warped your judgment.*

binge *binge fling jag orgy spree*
The central meaning shared by these nouns is "a period of uncontrolled self-indulgence": *a gambling binge; had a fling between commencement and graduate school; a crying jag; an eating orgy; a shopping spree.*

bite *bite champ gnaw*
The central meaning shared by these verbs is "to seize and tear or grind something with the teeth": *bite into a ripe tomato; horses champing grain; a dog gnawing a bone.*

bitter *bitter acerbic acrid*
The central meaning shared by these adjectives is "unpleasantly sharp or pungent in taste or smell": *a bitter cough syrup; acerbic barberries; acrid resin.*

blackball *blackball blacklist boycott ostracize*
The central meaning shared by these verbs is "to exclude from social, professional, or commercial activities": *blackballed from membership in the club; the movie industry blacklisting suspected Communists; winegrowers hiring union grape pickers for fear of being boycotted; ostracized by the community for immoral activities.*
   ✔ Antonym: **admit**

blackout   *blackout faint swoon syncope*
The central meaning shared by these nouns is "a temporary loss of consciousness": *suffers blackouts at high altitudes; fell in a dead faint at the sight of the cadaver; sank to the ground in a swoon; was taken to the emergency room in a state of syncope.*

blame   *blame fault guilt*
These nouns are compared in the sense of responsibility for an offense. **Blame** stresses censure or punishment for a lapse or misdeed for which one is held accountable: *The police laid the blame for the accident squarely on the driver's shoulders.* **Fault** is culpability for causing or failing to prevent the occurrence of something detrimental: *The student failed the examination, but not through any fault of his teacher.* **Guilt** applies to serious, willful breaches of conduct and stresses moral culpability: *The case was dismissed because the prosecution did not have sufficient evidence of the defendant's guilt.*

blameworthy   *blameworthy blamable blameful censurable culpable guilty reprehensible*
The central meaning shared by these adjectives is "meriting reproof or punishment": *blameworthy if not criminal behavior; blamable but understandable resentment; blameful capriciousness; censurable misconduct; culpable negligence; secret guilty deeds; reprehensible arrogance.*
    ✔ *Antonym:* **blameless**

blast   *blast blight dash nip wreck*
The central meaning shared by these verbs is "to have a pernicious, destructive, or ruinous effect on something": *prospects for peace blasted; blighted hopes; dashed ambitions; plans that were nipped in the bud; a wrecked life.*

blink   *blink nictitate twinkle wink*
The central meaning shared by these verbs is "to open and close the eyelids or an eyelid rapidly": *a dog blinking lazily at the fire; reptiles nictitating; twinkled, then laughed and responded; winking conspiratorially at his chum.*

block   *block hide obscure obstruct screen shroud*
The central meaning shared by these verbs is "to cut off from sight": *trees that block the view; a road hidden by brush; mist that obscures the mountain peak; skyscrapers obstructing the sky; a fence that screens the alley; a face shrouded by a heavy veil.*

bloody   *bloody gory sanguinary sanguineous*
The central meaning shared by these adjectives is "attended by or causing bloodshed": *a bloody battle; a gory murder; a sanguinary struggle; a sanguineous victory.*

bloom   *bloom blossom efflorescence florescence flower flush prime*
The central meaning shared by these nouns is "a condition or time of greatest vigor and freshness": *beauty in its full bloom; classical sculpture in its blossom; the efflorescence of humanitarianism; the florescence of baroque music; in the flower of her womanhood; in the flush of his popularity; the prime of life.*

blunder   *blunder bumble flounder lumber lurch stumble*
The central meaning shared by these verbs is "to move awkwardly or unsteadily": *blundered into the room and fell; flies bumbling against the open jam jar; floundered up the muddy mountain trail; a wagon lumbering along an unpaved road; twisted her ankle and lurched home; stumbled but regained his balance.*

boast   *boast brag crow vaunt*

These verbs all mean to speak with pride, often excessive pride, about oneself or something, such as one's possessions, related to oneself. ***Boast*** is the most general: *"We confide [i.e., have confidence] in our strength, without boasting of it; we respect that of others, without fearing it"* (Thomas Jefferson). ***Brag*** implies exaggerated claims and often an air of insolent superiority: *He bragged that his father was the most successful stockbroker on Wall Street.* ***Crow*** stresses exultation and loud rejoicing, as over a victory: *No candidate should crow until the votes have been counted.* ***Vaunt*** suggests ostentatiousness and lofty extravagance of expression: *"an elite that . . . vaunts diplomacy over national security concerns"* (Jim Hoagland).

bodily   *bodily corporal corporeal fleshly physical somatic*

The central meaning shared by these adjectives is "of or relating to the human body": *a bodily organ; a corporal defect; corporeal suffering; fleshly frailty; physical robustness; a somatic symptom.*

boil   *boil simmer seethe stew*

To ***boil*** is to cook in a liquid heated to a temperature at which it bubbles up and gives off vapor: *boil potatoes.* Figuratively *boil* pertains to intense agitation: *She boiled with resentment.* ***Simmer*** denotes gentle cooking just at or below the boiling point (*Let the stock simmer for several hours*); figuratively it refers to a state of gentle ferment (*Plans were simmering in his mind*). ***Seethe*** emphasizes in both senses the turbulence of steady boiling at high temperature: *Water seethed in the caldron.* *"The city had all through the interval been seething with discontent"* (John R. Green). ***Stew*** refers literally to slow boiling and figuratively to a persistent but not violent state of agitation: *I always add a little Madeira to the liquid when I stew prunes.* *"They don't want a man to fret and stew about his work"* (William H. Whyte, Jr.).

book   *book bespeak engage reserve*

The central meaning shared by these verbs is "to cause something to be set aside, as for one's use or possession, in advance": *will book a hotel room; bespoken merchandise; engaged a box for the opera season; reserving a table at a restaurant.*

boor   *boor barbarian churl lout vulgarian yahoo*

The central meaning shared by these nouns is "an uncouth and uncultivated person": *tourists acting like boors; a barbarian on the loose in a museum; consideration wasted on a churl; is both a lout and a bully; married a parvenu vulgarian; a yahoo and a blowhard.*

border   *border margin edge verge brink rim brim*

All these nouns refer to the line or narrow area that marks the outside limit of something such as a surface. *Border* refers either to the boundary line (*erected a fence along the border of the property*) or to the area that is immediately inside the boundary (*a picture frame with a wide border*). *Margin* is a border of more or less precisely definable width that is often distinguishable in other respects from the rest of the surface: *a boathouse near the margin of the pond; the margin of a little clearing in the forest. Edge* refers specifically to the precise bounding line formed by the continuous convergence of two surfaces: *sat on the edge of the chair. Verge* is an extreme terminating line or edge (*the sun's afterglow on the verge of the horizon*); figuratively it indicates a point at which something is likely to begin or to happen (*an explorer on the verge of a great discovery*). *Brink* denotes the edge of a steep place (*stood on the brink of the cliff*); in an extended sense it indicates the likelihood or imminence of a sudden change (*on the brink of falling in love*). *Rim* most often denotes the edge of something, such as a wheel, that is circular or curved: *a crack in the rim of the lens. Brim* applies to the upper edge or inner side of the rim of a container, such as a cup, or of something shaped like a basin: *lava issuing from the brim of the crater.*

boredom *boredom ennui tedium*
The central meaning shared by these nouns is "a condition of mental weariness, listlessness, and discontent": *a party so dull we thought we'd perish of boredom; took up a hobby to relieve the ennui of retirement; the oppressive tedium of routine tasks.*
   ✔ Antonym: **amusement**

boring *boring monotonous tedious irksome tiresome humdrum*
These adjectives refer to what is so lacking in interest as to cause mental weariness. *Boring* implies feelings of listlessness and discontent: *I had expected the book to be boring, but on the contrary it was fascinating.* What is *monotonous* bores because of lack of variety: *"There is nothing so desperately monotonous as the sea"* (James Russell Lowell). *Tedious* suggests dull slowness or long-windedness: *When we travel from coast to coast, we take a plane to avoid spending tedious days on the train.* *Irksome* describes what is demanding of time and effort and yet is dull and often unrewarding: *"I know and feel what an irksome task the writing of long letters is"* (Edmund Burke). Something *tiresome* fatigues because it seems to be interminable or to be marked by unremitting sameness: *"What a tiresome being is a man who is fond of talking"* (Benjamin Jowett). *Humdrum* refers to what is commonplace, trivial, or unexcitingly routine: *She led a humdrum existence — all work and no play.*

botch *botch blow bungle fumble muff*
The central meaning shared by these verbs is "to harm or spoil through inept or clumsy handling": *botch a repair; blow an op-*

portunity; a bungled performance; fumbled my chance for a promotion; an actor muffing his lines.

bouquet   bouquet nosegay posy

The central meaning shared by these nouns is "a bunch of cut flowers": *a bouquet of roses; a bride carrying a nosegay of lilies of the valley; gathered a posy of violets.*

branch   branch arm fork offshoot

The central meaning shared by these nouns is "something resembling or structurally analogous to a limb of a tree": *a branch of a railroad; an arm of the sea; the western fork of the river; an offshoot of a mountain range.*

brave   brave courageous fearless intrepid bold audacious valiant valorous doughty mettlesome plucky dauntless undaunted

These adjectives all mean having or showing courage under difficult or dangerous conditions. **Brave,** the least specific, is frequently associated with an innate quality: *"Familiarity with danger makes a brave man braver, but less daring"* (Herman Melville). **Courageous** implies an act of consciously rising to a specific test by drawing on a reserve of inner strength: *The young platoon leader set a courageous example for his soldiers by leading them safely into and out of jungle territory held by the enemy.* **Fearless** emphasizes absence of fear and resolute self-possession: *"world-class [boating] races for fearless loners willing to face the distinct possibility of being run down, dismasted, capsized, attacked by whales"* (Jo Ann Morse Ridley). **Intrepid** sometimes suggests invulnerability to fear: *Intrepid pioneers settled the American West.* **Bold** stresses not only readiness to meet danger or difficulty but often also a tendency to seek it out: *"If we shrink from the hard contests where men must win at the hazard of* *their lives . . . then bolder and stronger peoples will pass us by"* (Theodore Roosevelt). **Audacious** implies extreme confidence and boldness: *"To demand these God-given rights is to seek black power — what I call audacious power"* (Adam Clayton Powell, Jr.). **Valiant,** said principally of persons, suggests the bravery of a hero or a heroine: *"a sympathetic and detailed biography that sees Hemingway as a valiant and moral man"* (New York Times). **Valorous** applies to the deeds of heros and heroines: *"Her passengers, the other hostages, will never forget her calm, confident, valorous work"* (William W. Bradley). **Doughty,** a bit old-fashioned in flavor and often used humorously, suggests stalwartness: *The doughty old man battled his illness with fierce determination.* **Mettlesome** stresses spirit and love of challenge: *The mettlesome actress resumed her career after recovering from a stroke.* **Plucky** emphasizes spirit and heart in the face of unfavorable odds: *"Everybody was . . . anxious to show these Belgians what England thought of their plucky little country"* (H.G. Wells). **Dauntless** refers to courage that resists subjection or intimidation: *"So faithful in love, and so dauntless in war, / There never was knight like the young Lochinvar"* (Sir Walter Scott). **Undaunted** suggests courage and resolve that persist after being put to the test: *"Death and sorrow will be the companions of our journey; hardship our garment; constancy and valor our only shield. We must be united, we must be undaunted, we must be inflexible"* (Winston S. Churchill).

brawl   brawl broil donnybrook fracas fray free-for-all melee row ruction

The central meaning shared by these nouns is "a very noisy, disorderly, and often violent quarrel or fight": *a barroom brawl; a protest march that degenerated into a general broil between the demonstrators and the police; an incident that turned into a vicious legal donnybrook; putting down a violent fracas among prison in-*

mates; eager for the fray; a regular free-for-all in the schoolyard; po-
lice plunging into the melee; a terrific domestic row; a senseless ruc-
tion over trivia.

breach   *breach infraction violation transgression*
trespass infringement

These nouns denote an act or instance of breaking a law or reg-
ulation or failing to fulfill a duty, obligation, or promise. **Breach**
and **infraction** are the least specific: *Revealing the secret would be a*
breach of trust. Infractions of the rules will not be tolerated. A **viola-**
tion is an infraction committed willfully and with complete lack
of regard for legal, moral, or ethical considerations: *She failed to*
appear for the rehearsal, in flagrant violation of her contract. **Trans-**
gression refers most often to a violation of divine or moral law:
"The children shall not be punished for the father's transgression"
(Daniel Defoe). As it refers to the breaking of a statute, **trespass**
implies willful intrusion on another's rights, possessions, or
person: *"In the limited and confined sense [trespass] signifies no*
more than an entry on another man's ground without a lawful au-
thority" (William Blackstone). **Infringement** is most frequently
used specifically to denote encroachment on another's rights,
such as those granted by a copyright: *"Necessity is the plea for*
every infringement of human freedom" (William Pitt the Younger).

break   *break crack fracture burst split splinter shatter*
shiver smash

These verbs are compared as they mean to separate or cause to
separate into parts or pieces. **Break** is the most general and like
the other members of the set implies either the sudden application of force or the build-up of internal stress: *a window bro-*
ken by vandals; broke her leg; a delicate chair that will break under
a great weight. To **crack** is to break, often with a sharp snapping
sound, without dividing into parts: *I cracked the platter when I*

knocked it against the table. The foundation of the house cracked during the earthquake. The soil cracked from the drought. **Fracture** applies to a break or crack in a rigid body: *fractured her skull in the accident; a vertebra that fractured in the fall.* **Burst** implies a sudden coming apart, especially from internal pressure, and the dispersion of contents: *The child burst the balloon with a pin. Her appendix burst.* **Split** refers to a division into sections longitudinally or along the direction of the grain: *split the log with an ax; frost that caused the rock to split.* **Splinter** implies splitting into long, thin, sharp pieces: *The tree was struck by lightning and splintered. Repeated blows splintered the door.* To **shatter** is to break into many loose scattered pieces: *The bottle will shatter if you drop it. An exploding gas main shattered the tiles in the courtyard.* **Shiver** is a term rarely encountered outside literary contexts; like *shatter,* it indicates sudden force that causes fragmentation: *"Every statue was hurled from its niche . . . every painted window* [was] *shivered to atoms"* (John Lothrop Motley). *"The panels shivering in, like potsherds"* (Thomas Carlyle). **Smash** stresses force of blow or impact and suggests complete destruction: *My glasses slipped from my hand and smashed on the floor. The boat was smashed on the rocks.*

breeze *breeze cinch pushover snap walkaway walkover*
The central meaning shared by these nouns is "something that is easily accomplished": *The exam was a breeze. Chopping onions is a cinch with a food processor. Winning the playoffs was no pushover. The new computer program was a snap to learn. Getting elected to the council was a walkaway. It wasn't any walkover to alphabetize all those names.*

bright *bright brilliant radiant lustrous lambent luminous incandescent effulgent*
These adjectives refer to what emits or reflects light. **Bright** is

the most general: *bright sunshine; a bright blue; bright teeth.* **Brilliant** implies intense brightness and often suggests sparkling, glittering, or gleaming light: *a brilliant color; a brilliant gemstone.* Something that is **radiant** radiates or seems to radiate light: *a radiant sunrise; a radiant smile.* A **lustrous** object originates no light but reflects an agreeable sheen: *thick, lustrous auburn hair; a necklace of lustrous pearls.* **Lambent** applies to a soft, flickering light: *"its tranquil streets, bathed in the lambent green of budding trees"* (James C. McKinley). **Luminous** refers broadly to what shines with light but is said especially of something that glows in the dark: *The watch has a luminous dial.* **Incandescent** stresses burning brilliance, as of something white-hot: *Flames consist of incandescent gases.* **Effulgent** suggests splendid radiance: *"The crocus, the snowdrop, and the effulgent daffodil are considered bright harbingers of spring"* (John Gould).

broach *broach introduce moot raise*
The central meaning shared by these verbs is "to bring forward a point, topic, or question for consideration or discussion": *didn't know how to broach the subject tactfully; introduce a tax bill before the legislature; an idea that was approved when it was first mooted before the committee; raised the problem of dropouts with the faculty.*

broad-minded *broad-minded broad liberal*
open-minded tolerant
The central meaning shared by these adjectives is "having or showing an inclination to respect views and beliefs that differ from one's own" *a broad-minded but evenhanded judge; showed generous and broad sympathies; a liberal cleric; open-minded impartiality; a tolerant attitude.*

✔ *Antonym:* **narrow-minded**

brood *brood dwell fret mope stew worry*
The central meaning shared by these verbs is "to turn over in the mind moodily and at length": *brooding about his decline in popularity; dwelled on her defeat; fretting over the loss of their jobs; moping about his illness; stewing over her upcoming trial; worrying about the unpaid bills.*

brush *brush flick glance graze shave skim*
The central meaning shared by these verbs is "to make light and momentary contact with something in passing": *her arm brushing mine; flicked the paper with his finger; an arrow that glanced off the tree; a knife blade grazing the countertop; a taxi that shaved the curb; an oar skimming the surface of the pond.*

bulge *bulge balloon belly jut overhang project protrude*
The central meaning shared by these verbs is "to curve, spread, or extend outward past the normal or usual limit": *a wallet bulging with money; expenses ballooning; a sail bellying in the wind; a pipe jutting from his mouth; overhanging eaves; projecting teeth; a head protruding from the window.*

burden¹ *burden affliction cross trial tribulation*
The central meaning shared by these nouns is "something that is onerous or troublesome": *the burden of a guilty conscience; indebtedness that is an affliction; illness that is her cross; sitting still, a trial to the very young; domestic tribulations.*

burden² *burden substance core gist pith purport*
The central meaning shared by these nouns is "the essential import or significance of something spoken or written": *the burden of the President's speech; the substance of her complaint; the core of an article; the gist of the prosecutor's argument; the pith and marrow of an essay; the purport of a document.*

burn   *burn scorch singe sear char parch*

These verbs mean to injure or alter by means of intense heat or flames. **Burn,** the most general, applies to the effects of exposure to a source of heat or to something that can produce a similar effect: *burned the rug with a cigarette; left the onions on the stove and burned them; burned my fingers by handling dry ice.* **Scorch** usually refers to contact with flame or heated metal and involves superficial burning that discolors or damages the texture of something: *afraid that the iron might scorch the sheet; trees that were scorched in a forest fire.* **Singe** specifies superficial burning by brief exposure to flame and especially the deliberate removal of projections such as bristles or feathers from a carcass, such as a plucked fowl, before cooking: *a grease fire that singed my eyelashes; singed the Thanksgiving turkey, then roasted it.* **Sear** applies to surface burning of organic tissue, as by branding or cauterizing: *Sear the lamb over high heat before lowering the flame and adding liquid.* To **char** is most often to reduce a substance to carbon or charcoal by means of fire: *The timbers of the house were charred by the raging fire.* **Parch** in this sense emphasizes the drying and often fissuring of a surface from exposure to flame, the sun, or hot wind: *The torrid rays of the sun parched the soil.*

business   *business industry commerce trade traffic*

These nouns apply to forms of activity that have the objective of supplying commodities. **Business** pertains broadly to commercial, financial, and industrial activity: *decided to go into the oil business.* **Industry** is the production and manufacture of goods or commodities, especially on a large scale: *the computer industry; the arms industry.* **Commerce** and **trade** refer to the exchange and distribution of goods or commodities: *laws regulating interstate commerce; involved in the domestic fur trade; foreign commerce* (or *trade*). **Traffic** pertains broadly to commercial dealings but in particular to businesses engaged in the transportation of goods or passengers: *renovated the docks to attract shipping traffic.* The word may also suggest illegal trade, as in narcotics: *Traffic in stolen goods was brisk.*

cadge   cadge beg bum mooch panhandle

The central meaning shared by these verbs is "to ask, ask for, or get as charity": *cadged a cigarette; begging for forgiveness; bum a drink; mooching food; people forced to panhandle in subway stations.*

calculate   calculate compute reckon cipher figure

These verbs refer to the determination of a result, such as expense, through the use of mathematical methods. *Calculate,* the most comprehensive, often implies a relatively high level of abstraction or procedural complexity: *astronomers calculating the positions of the planets.* *Compute* applies in general to essentially straightforward though possibly lengthy arithmetic operations: *computing fees according to time spent.* *Reckon, cipher,* and *figure* suggest the use of simple arithmetic: *reckoned the number of hours before her departure; had to be taught to read and to cipher; trying to figure my share of the bill.*

call   call convene convoke muster summon

The central meaning shared by these verbs is "to demand or request to appear, come, or assemble": *called the doctor; convene a meeting; convoke the legislature; mustering the militia; summon a witness.*

calm   calm tranquil placid serene halcyon peaceful

These adjectives denote absence of excitement or disturbance. *Calm* implies freedom from emotional agitation: *calm acceptance of the inevitable.* *Tranquil* suggests a more enduring calm:

hoped for a more tranquil life in the country. **Placid** suggests a pleasant, often phlegmatic calm: *"Not everyone shared his placid temperament. Several cursed the delays"* (Samuel G. Freedman). **Serene** denotes a lofty, even spiritual repose: *remained serene in the midst of turbulence.* **Halcyon** suggests happy tranquillity: *halcyon days of youth.* **Peaceful** implies undisturbed serenity: *"I am . . . peaceful as old age tonight"* (Robert Browning).

campaign   campaign crusade drive push
The central meaning shared by these nouns is "a vigorous concerted effort to accomplish a purpose": *a fund-raising campaign; a crusade for improved social services; a drive to sell bonds; a push to get the bill through Congress.*

care   care charge custody keeping supervision trust
The central meaning shared by these nouns is "the function of watching, guarding, or overseeing": *left the house keys in my care; has charge of all rare books in the library; had custody of his friend's car during her absence; left the canary in the neighbors' keeping; assuming supervision of the first-grade pupils; documents that were committed to the bank's trust.*

careful   careful heedful mindful observant watchful
The central meaning shared by these adjectives is "cautiously attentive": *was careful not to get her shoes muddy; heedful of the danger; mindful of his health; observant to avoid giving offense; a watchful nurse tending a critically ill patient.*
　　✔ Antonym: **careless**

caress   caress cuddle fondle pet
The central meaning shared by these verbs is "to touch or handle affectionately": *caressed the little boy's forehead; cuddled the kitten in her arms; fondling my hand; petting his pony.*

catalyst   *catalyst ferment leaven leavening yeast*
The central meaning shared by these nouns is "an agent that stimulates or precipitates a reaction, development, or change": *a serious breach of trust that was the catalyst for the divorce; love, the most powerful ferment; the leaven of reform working in their minds; a leavening of humor; the yeast of revolution.*

catch   *catch enmesh ensnare entangle entrap snare tangle trap*
The central meaning shared by these verbs is "to take in and hold as if by using bait or a lure": *caught in her own lies; enmeshed in the neighbors' dispute; ensnaring an unsuspecting dupe with fast talk; became entangled in his own contradictions; entrapped by a skillful interviewer into making a damaging statement; snared by false hopes; tangled by his own duplicity; trapped into making an incriminating admission.*

celebrity   *celebrity hero luminary name notable personage*
The central meaning shared by these nouns is "a widely known person": *social celebrities; the heroes of science; a theatrical luminary; a big name in sports; a notable of the concert stage; a personage in the field of philosophy.*

center   *center focus headquarters heart hub seat*
The central meaning shared by these nouns is "a region, person, or thing around which something, such as an activity, is concentrated": *a great cultural center; the focus of research efforts; the headquarters of a multinational corporation; a town that is the heart of the colony; the hub of a steel empire; the seat of government.*

certain   *certain inescapable inevitable sure unavoidable*
The central meaning shared by these adjectives is "impossible

to avoid or evade": *certain death; an inescapable conclusion; an inevitable result; sudden but sure regret; an unavoidable accident.*

certainty   certainty certitude assurance conviction
These nouns mean freedom from doubt. **Certainty** implies an absence of doubt that is based on a thorough consideration of evidence: *"I give to Mr. Burke all his theatrical exaggerations for facts, and I then ask him, if they do not establish the certainty of what I here lay down?"* (Thomas Paine). **Certitude** is certainty that is based more on personal belief than on objective facts: *"Certitude is not the test of certainty"* (Oliver Wendell Holmes, Jr.). **Assurance** is a feeling of confidence resulting from subjective experience: *"There is no such thing as absolute certainty, but there is assurance sufficient for the purposes of human life"* (John Stuart Mill). **Conviction** is certainty arising from the vanquishment of doubt: *"The compensation of very early success is a conviction that life is a romantic matter"* (F. Scott Fitzgerald).

chafe   chafe abrade excoriate fret gall
The central meaning shared by these verbs is "to wear down or rub away a surface by or as if by scraping": *chafed my skin; a swift stream abrading boulders; an excoriated elbow; rope that fretted a groove in the post; his heel galled by an ill-fitting shoe.*

chance   chance random casual haphazard desultory
These adjectives apply to what is determined not by deliberation or method but by accident. **Chance** stresses lack of premeditation: *a chance meeting with a friend.* **Random** implies the absence of a specific pattern or objective and suggests a lack of direction that might or could profitably be imposed: *struck by a random shot; took a random guess.* **Casual** stresses lack of deliberation and often suggests an absence of due concern: *made a*

casual observation. **Haphazard** implies a carelessness or a willful leaving to chance: *offered a haphazard plan of action.* **Desultory** suggests a shifting about from one thing to another that reflects a lack of method: *engaged in a desultory conversation.*

charge   *charge freight imbue impregnate permeate pervade saturate suffuse*
The central meaning shared by these verbs is "to cause to be filled with a particular mood or tone": *an atmosphere charged with excitement; a pause freighted with meaning; poetry imbued with grace; a spirit impregnated with lofty ideals; optimism that permeates a group; letters pervaded with gloom; a novel saturated with imagination; a heart suffused with love.*

charm   *charm beguile bewitch captivate enchant entrance fascinate*
The central meaning shared by these verbs is "to attract strongly or irresistibly": *grace and manners that charmed the old curmudgeon; delicacies that beguile even the most discerning gourmet; a performance that bewitched the audience; a novel that captivates its readers; an evening that enchanted all the guests; music that entrances its listeners; a celebrity who fascinated his fellow guests.*
    ✔ *Antonym:* **repel**

chief   *chief principal main leading foremost primary prime*
These adjectives refer to what is first in rank or in importance. **Chief** applies to a person of the highest authority: *a chief magistrate.* Used figuratively, *chief* implies maximum importance or value: *Her children were her chief joy.* **Principal** applies to someone or something of the first order in rank, power, or significance: *the principal cellist in an orchestra; their*

principal source of entertainment. **Main** applies to what exceeds others in extent, size, or importance: *the main building on the campus; the main subject of conversation.* **Leading** suggests personal magnetism, a record of achievement, or suitability or capacity for influencing others: *She is one of the leading physicians of the city.* **Foremost** is closely related to *leading* but more strongly emphasizes first position and the sense of having forged ahead of others: *the foremost research scientist of the day.* **Primary** stresses first in the sense of origin, sequence, or development: *attending primary school.* It can also mean first in the sense of "basic" or "fundamental": *The primary function of a house is to provide warmth and shelter.* **Prime** applies to what is first in comparison with others and to what is of the best quality: *a theory of prime significance; prime veal; a prime Burgundy.*

choice   choice   alternative   option   preference   selection   election

Each of these nouns denotes the act, power, or right of choosing. **Choice** implies broadly the freedom to choose from a set, as of persons or things: *The store offers a wide choice of fruits and vegetables. I had no choice — their decision was final.* **Alternative** emphasizes a choosing between only two possibilities or courses of action: *"An unhappy alternative is before you, Elizabeth. . . . Your mother will never see you again if you do* not *marry Mr. Collins, and I will never see you again if you do"* (Jane Austen). **Option** often stresses a power or liberty to choose that has been granted, as by an authority: *The option lies between accepting the candidate the administration proposes and reconstituting the search committee.* **Preference** indicates choice based on one's values, bias, or predilections: *We were offered our preference of wines.* **Selection** suggests a variety of things or persons to choose from: *Parents should exercise care in their selection of the* *movies their young children see.* **Election** especially emphasizes the use of judgment in choosing: *The university recommends the election of courses in composition and literature.*

chronic   *chronic confirmed habitual inveterate*

The central meaning shared by these adjectives is "having long had a habit or a disease": *a chronic complainer; a confirmed bachelor; a habitual cheat; an inveterate smoker.*

circumference   *circumference circuit compass perimeter periphery*

The central meaning shared by these nouns is "a line around a closed figure or area": *the circumference of Earth; a park five acres in circuit; stayed within the compass of the yard; the perimeter of a rectangle; erected a fence around the periphery of the property.*

citizen   *citizen national subject*

The central meaning shared by these nouns is "a person owing allegiance to a nation or state and entitled to its protection": *an American citizen; a British national; a French subject.*

claim   *claim pretense pretension title*

The central meaning shared by these nouns is "a legitimate or asserted right to demand something as one's rightful due": *had a strong legal claim to the property; makes no pretense to scholarliness; pretensions to the chairmanship unjustified in every particular; has no title to our thanks.*

clean   *clean antiseptic cleanly immaculate spotless*

The central meaning shared by these adjectives is "free from dirt": *clean clothing; antiseptic surgical instruments; cats, cleanly animals; an immaculate tablecloth; spotless gloves.*

   ✔ *Antonym:* **dirty**

clear   *clear   limpid   lucid   pellucid   transparent*
The central meaning shared by these adjectives is "not opaque or clouded": *clear, sediment-free claret; limpid blue eyes; lucid air; a pellucid brook; transparent crystal.*

  ✔ Antonym: **opaque**

clever   *clever   ingenious   shrewd*
These adjectives are compared as they refer to mental adroitness or to practical ingenuity and skill. **Clever,** the most comprehensive, stresses mental quickness or adeptness: *"If I ever felt inclined to be timid as I was going into a room full of people, I would say to myself, 'You're the cleverest member of one of the cleverest families in the cleverest class of the cleverest nation in the world, why should you be frightened?'"* (Beatrice Webb). **Ingenious** implies originality and inventiveness: *"an ingenious solution to the storage problem"* (Linda Greider). **Shrewd** emphasizes mental astuteness and practical understanding: *"a woman of shrewd intellect and masculine character"* (Leslie Stephen).

cliché   *cliché   bromide   commonplace   platitude   truism*
The central meaning shared by these nouns is "an expression or idea that has lost its originality or force through overuse": *a short story weakened by clichés; the old bromide that we are what we eat; uttered the commonplace "welcome aboard"; taking comfort in the platitude that all will end well; a once-original thought that has become a truism.*

close   *close   immediate   near   nearby   nigh   proximate*
The central meaning shared by these adjectives is "not far from another in space, time, or relationship": *an airport close to town; her immediate family; his nearest relative; a nearby library; our nighest neighbor; a proximate neighborhood.*

  ✔ Antonym: **far**

clothe   *clothe cloak drape mantle robe*
The central meaning shared by these verbs is "to cover as if with clothes": *trees clothed in leafy splendor; mist that cloaks the mountains; a beam draped with cobwebs; a boulder mantled with moss; snow robing fields and gardens.*
   ✔ *Antonym:* **unclothe**

coagulate   *coagulate clot congeal curdle jell jelly set*
The central meaning shared by these verbs is "to change or be changed from a liquid into a thickened mass": *egg white coagulating when heated; gravy clotting as it cools; water congealing into ice; milk that had curdled; used pectin to jell the jam; jellied consommé; allowed the aspic to set.*

cold   *cold arctic chilly cool frigid frosty gelid glacial icy*
The central meaning shared by these adjectives is "marked by a low or an extremely low temperature": *cold air; an arctic climate; a chilly day; cool water; a frigid room; a frosty morning; gelid seas; glacial winds; icy hands.*
   ✔ *Antonym:* **hot**

collision   *collision concussion crash impact jar jolt shock*
The central meaning shared by these nouns is "violent forcible contact between two or more things": *the midair collision of two light planes; the concussion caused by an explosion; the crash of a car into a tree; the impact of a sledgehammer on pilings; felt repeated jars as the train ground to a halt; a series of jolts as the baby carriage rolled down the steps; experienced the physical shock of a sudden fall to hard pavement.*

comfort   *comfort console solace*
The central meaning shared by these verbs is "to give hope or

help to in time of grief or pain": *comforted the distressed child; consoling a woman on the death of her husband; solaced myself with a hot cup of coffee.*

comfortable   *comfortable cozy snug restful*

These words mean affording ease of mind or body. **Comfortable** implies the absence of sources of pain or distress: *sleeps in a comfortable bed; wears comfortable clothes.* The word may also suggest peace of mind: *felt comfortable with the decision; has a comfortable income.* **Cozy** evokes the image of a warm room in winter and suggests homey and reassuring ease: *sat in a cozy nook near the fire; had a cozy little chat.* **Snug** brings to mind the image of a warm, secure, compact shelter: *children snug in their beds.* **Restful** suggests a quiet conducive to tranquillity: *spent a restful hour reading; a room painted in restful colors.*

comment   *comment observation remark*

The central meaning shared by these nouns is "an expression of fact, opinion, or explanation": *made an unpleasant comment about my friend; a casual observation about the movie; an offensive personal remark.*

common   *common ordinary familiar vulgar*

These adjectives describe what is generally known or frequently encountered. **Common** applies to what is customary, takes place often, is widely used, or is well known: *a common problem; a common thief; the common dandelion.* The term also suggests lack of distinction and can imply coarseness or crudeness: *drank wine of the commonest sort; had a very common look about him.* **Ordinary** describes what is of the usual kind and is not distinguished in any way from others. In the latter sense it is sometimes derogatory: *A ballpoint pen is adequate for most ordinary purposes. The violinist gave a very ordinary performance* *marked by an occasional memory lapse.* **Familiar** applies to what is well known or quickly recognized through frequent occurrence or regular association: *a nursery rhyme familiar to most children; sang all the old familiar songs.* **Vulgar** describes what is associated with the great mass of people: *"He [Shakespeare] was not something sacred and aloof from the vulgar herd of men"* (William Hazlitt). The word usually connotes the lack of refinement of *common*: *Slurping soup directly from the bowl is vulgar.*

complex   *complex complicated intricate involved tangled knotty*

These adjectives mean having parts so interconnected as to make the whole perplexing. **Complex** implies a combination of many associated parts: *The composer transformed a simple folk tune into a complex set of variations.* **Complicated** stresses elaborate relationship of parts: *Middle Eastern politics is so complicated that even experts cannot agree on a cohesive policy.* **Intricate** refers to a pattern of intertwining parts that is difficult to follow or analyze: *"No one could soar into a more intricate labyrinth of refined phraseology"* (Anthony Trollope). **Involved** stresses confusion arising from the commingling of parts and the consequent difficulty of separating them: *The plot of the play has been criticized as being too involved.* **Tangled** strongly suggests the random twisting of many parts: *"Oh, what a tangled web we weave, / When first we practice to deceive!"* (Sir Walter Scott). **Knotty** stresses intellectual complexity leading to difficulty of solution or comprehension: *Even the professor couldn't clarify the knotty point.*

conceit   *conceit amour-propre egoism egotism narcissism vanity*

The central meaning shared by these nouns is "a regarding of oneself with often excessive favor": *constant boasting that re-*

veals conceit; insulted her amour-propre; imperturbable egoism; arrogance and egotism betrayed by a glance; lack of consideration arising from narcissism; immoderate and incurable vanity.

✔ *Antonym:* **humility**

condemn   *condemn damn doom sentence*
The central meaning shared by these verbs is "to fix the punishment or destiny of one found to be guilty or undeserving": *condemned the dissident to hard labor; damned to everlasting uncertainty; an attempt that was doomed to failure; sentenced the murderer to life in prison.*

confer   *confer consult parley treat*
The central meaning shared by these verbs is "to exchange views in order to reach a decision or resolve differences": *a doctor conferring with a patient; has to consult with an attorney; parleyed with enemy representatives during the cease-fire; delegates treating for the recognition of their union.*

conflict   *conflict contest combat fight affray*
These nouns denote struggle between opposing forces for victory or supremacy. **Conflict** applies both to open fighting between hostile groups and to a struggle, often an inner struggle, between antithetical forces: *"The kind of victory MacArthur had in mind — victory by the bombing of Chinese cities, victory by expanding the conflict to all of China — would have been the wrong kind of victory"* (Harry S. Truman). *"Fortunately analysis is not the only way to resolve inner conflicts. Life itself still remains a very effective therapist"* (Karen Horney). **Contest** can refer either to friendly competition or to a hostile struggle to achieve an objective: *an archery contest; a spelling contest; the gubernatorial contest.* **Combat** most commonly implies an encounter between two armed persons or groups: *"Alexander had appeared to*

him, armed for combat" (Connop Thirlwall). **Fight** usually refers to a clash, physical or figurative, involving individual adversaries: *A fight was scheduled between the world boxing champion and the challenger. "There is nothing I love as much as a good fight"* (Franklin D. Roosevelt). **Affray** suggests a public fight or brawl: *"Yet still the poachers came . . . for affrays in woods and on moors with liveried armies of keepers"* (Patricia Morison).

confuse   *confuse addle befuddle discombobulate fuddle muddle throw*
The central meaning shared by these verbs is "to cause to be unclear in mind or intent": *heavy traffic that confused the novice driver; problems that addle my brain; a question that befuddled even the professor; was discombobulated by the staggering number of possibilities; a plot so complex that it fuddles one's comprehension; a head that was muddled by endless facts and figures; behavior that really threw me.*

contain   *contain hold accommodate*
These verbs mean to have within or have the capacity for having within. **Contain** means to have within or have as a part or constituent: *This drawer contains all the cutlery we own. The book contains some amusing passages. Polluted water contains contaminants.* **Hold** can be used in that sense but primarily stresses capacity for containing: *The pitcher holds two pints but contains only one.* **Accommodate** refers to capacity for holding comfortably: *The restaurant accommodates 50 customers. Four hundred inmates were crowded into a prison intended to accommodate 200.*

contaminate   *contaminate befoul foul poison pollute taint*
The central meaning shared by these verbs is "to make dirty or impure": *a contaminated reservoir; shoes that were befouled with mud; noxious fumes that foul the air; chemicals poisoning*

the lake; polluted streams; food that had been tainted through improper storage.

continual *continual continuous constant ceaseless incessant perpetual eternal perennial interminable*

These adjectives are compared as they mean occurring over and over during a long period of time. **Continual** can connote absence of interruption (*lived in continual fear*) but is chiefly restricted to what is intermittent or repeated at intervals (*the continual banging of the shutter in the wind*). **Continuous** implies lack of interruption in time, substance, or extent: *She suffered a continuous bout of illness lasting six months. The horizon is a continuous line.* **Constant** stresses steadiness or persistence of occurrence and unvarying nature: *the constant chatter of the monkeys in the zoo; constant repetition of the exercise.* **Ceaseless** and **incessant** pertain to uninterrupted activity: *the ceaseless thunder of the surf against the rocks; incessant questions.* **Perpetual** emphasizes both steadiness and duration: *a perpetual struggle; a perpetual stream of visitors.* **Eternal** refers to what is everlasting, especially to what is seemingly without temporal beginning or end: *"That freedom can be retained only by the eternal vigilance which has always been its price"* (Elmer Davis). **Perennial** describes existence that goes on year after year, often with the suggestion of self-renewal: *wished for perennial youth; the perennial problem of urban poverty.* **Interminable** refers to what is or seems to be endless and is often applied to something prolonged and wearisome: *interminable talk; an interminable argument.*

convert *convert metamorphose transfigure transform transmogrify transmute*

The central meaning shared by these verbs is "to change into a different form, substance, or state": *convert stocks into cash; misery metamorphosing into happiness; a bare stage that was transfigured into an enchanted forest; a gangling adolescent transformed into a handsome adult; a sleepy town transmogrified by the boom into a bustling city; impossible to transmute lead into gold.*

correct   *correct rectify remedy redress reform revise amend*

These verbs mean to make right what is wrong. **Correct** refers to eliminating faults, errors, or defects: *correct spelling mistakes; correct a misapprehension.* **Rectify** stresses the idea of bringing something into conformity with a standard of what is right: *The omission of your name from the list will be rectified. I hope I can find a way to rectify your opinion of my behavior.* **Remedy** involves removing or counteracting something considered a cause of harm or damage: *Nothing has been done to remedy the lack. He took courses to remedy his abysmal ignorance.* **Redress** refers to setting right something considered immoral or unethical and usually involves making reparation: *The wrong is too great to be redressed.* **Reform** implies broad change that alters form or character for the better: *"Let us reform our schools, and we shall find little reform needed in our prisons"* (John Ruskin). *"Nothing so needs reforming as other people's habits"* (Mark Twain). **Revise** suggests change that results from reconsideration: *revise a manuscript; revising the tax laws; revise our judgment of the situation.* **Amend** implies improvement through alteration or correction: *"Whenever [the people] shall grow weary of the existing government, they can exercise their constitutional right of amending it, or their revolutionary right to dismember or overthrow it"* (Abraham Lincoln).

corrupt   *corrupt debase debauch deprave pervert vitiate*

The central meaning shared by these verbs is "to ruin utterly in character or quality": *was corrupted by limitless power; debased himself by pleading with the captors; a youth debauched by*

drugs and drink; indulgence that depraves the moral fiber; perverted her talent by putting it to evil purposes; a proof vitiated by a serious omission.

count *count import matter signify weigh*

The central meaning shared by these verbs is "to be of significance or importance": *an opinion that counts for a great deal; actions that import little; decisions that really matter; thoughts that signify much; considerations that do not weigh with her.*

crisis *crisis crossroad exigency head juncture pass*

The central meaning shared by these nouns is "a critical point or state of affairs": *a military crisis; government policy at the crossroad; had failed to predict the health-care exigency; a problem that is coming to a head; negotiations that had reached a crucial juncture; things rapidly coming to a desperate pass.*

critical *critical captious censorious faultfinding hypercritical*

The central meaning shared by these adjectives is "tending or marked by a tendency to find and call attention to errors and flaws": *a critical attitude; a captious pedant; censorious of petty failings; an excessively demanding and faultfinding tutor; hypercritical of colloquial speech.*

✔ Antonym: **uncritical**

criticize *criticize blame reprehend censure condemn denounce*

These verbs are compared as they mean to express an unfavorable judgment. **Criticize** can mean merely to evaluate good and bad points without necessarily finding fault: *"To criticize is to appreciate, to appropriate, to take intellectual possession"* (Henry James). Usually, however, the word implies the expression of disapproval: *The reviewer roundly criticized the novel.* **Blame** emphasizes the finding of fault and the fixing of responsibility: *"People are always blaming their circumstances for what they are"* (George Bernard Shaw). **Reprehend** implies sharp disapproval: *"reprehends students who have protested apartheid"* (New York Times). **Censure** refers to open and strong expression of criticism; often it implies a formal reprimand: *"No man can justly censure or condemn another, because indeed no man truly knows another"* (Thomas Browne). **Condemn** denotes the pronouncement of harshly adverse judgment: *"The wrongs which we seek to condemn and punish have been so calculated, so malignant and so devastating that civilization cannot tolerate their being ignored because it cannot survive their being repeated"* (Robert H. Jackson). **Denounce** implies public proclamation of condemnation or repudiation: *The press denounces clandestine support for the counterrevolution.*

crowd   *crowd crush flock horde mob press throng*
The central meaning shared by these nouns is "a large group of people gathered close to one another": *a crowd of onlookers; a crush of autograph seekers; a flock of schoolchildren; a horde of demonstrators; a mob of hard-rock enthusiasts; a press of shoppers; throngs of tourists.*

crude   *crude native raw*
The central meaning shared by these adjectives is "in a natural state and not yet processed for use": *crude rubber; native iron; raw cotton.*

crush   *crush mash pulp smash squash*
The central meaning shared by these verbs is "to press forcefully so as to reduce to a pulpy mass": *crush rose geranium leaves; mashed the sweet potatoes; pulped raspberries through a*

sieve; smashing bamboo stems with a hammer; squash an egg under one's foot.

cry   cry weep wail keen whimper sob blubber

These verbs mean to make inarticulate sounds of grief, unhappiness, or pain. **Cry** and **weep** both involve the shedding of tears; *cry* more strongly implies accompanying sound: *"And when he [William of Orange] died the little children cried in the streets"* (John Lothrop Motley). *"I weep for what I'm like when I'm alone"* (Theodore Roethke). **Wail** refers primarily to sustained, inarticulate mournful sound: *"The women . . . began to wail together; they mourned with shrill cries"* (Joseph Conrad). **Keen** suggests the wailing associated with lamentation for those who have died: *"It is the wild Irish women keening over their dead"* (George A. Lawrence). **Whimper** refers to low, plaintive broken or repressed cries, as those made by a child: *The condemned prisoner cowered and began to whimper for clemency.* **Sob** describes weeping or a mixture of broken speech and weeping marked by convulsive breathing or gasping: *"sobbing and crying, and wringing her hands as if her heart would break"* (Laurence Sterne). **Blubber** refers to noisy, unrestrained shedding of tears accompanied by broken or inarticulate speech: *He blubbered like a child who had been spanked.*

cure   cure heal remedy

The central meaning shared by these verbs is "to set right an undesirable or unhealthy condition": *cure an ailing economy; heal a wounded spirit; remedy a structural defect.*

curious   curious inquisitive snoopy nosy

These adjectives apply to persons who show a marked desire for information or knowledge. **Curious** most often implies an avid desire to know or learn, though it can suggest an undue interest in the affairs of others: *A curious child is a teacher's delight.* **Inquisitive** frequently suggests excessive curiosity and the asking of many questions: *"Remember, no revolvers. The police are, I believe, proverbially inquisitive"* (Lord Dunsany). Both *snoopy* and *nosy* imply an unworthy motive. **Snoopy** suggests underhanded prying: *The snoopy neighbor watched our activities all day.* **Nosy** implies impertinent curiosity likened to that of an animal using its nose to examine or probe: *I watched him flip through the letters on my desk in his nosy way.*

dark   dark dim murky dusky obscure opaque shady shadowy

These adjectives indicate the absence of light or clarity. **Dark,** the most widely applicable, can refer to insufficiency of illumination for seeing: *"Under the earth, in the flat, dark air, the wet, gloomy rock gave quarter grudgingly"* (Jimmy Breslin). The word can also denote deepness of shade or color (*dark brown*), absence of cheer (*a dark, somber mood*), or lack of rectitude: *"It* [gold] *serves what life requires, / But dreadful too, the dark Assassin hires"* (Alexander Pope). **Dim** suggests lack of clarity of outline, as of physical entities or mental processes such as recollection: *"life and the memory of it cramped, / dim, on a piece of Bristol board"* (Elizabeth Bishop); it can also apply to a source of light to indicate insufficiency: *"storied Windows richly dight, / Casting a dim religious light"* (John Milton). **Murky** implies darkness, often extreme, such as that produced by smoke or fog: *"an atmosphere murky with sand"* (Willa Cather). *"The path was altogether indiscernible in the murky darkness which surrounded them"* (Sir Walter Scott). Figuratively it can imply dark vagueness: *"the narrow crevice of one good deed in a murky life of guilt"* (Charles Dickens). **Dusky** applies principally to the dimness that is characteristic of diminishing light, as at twilight: *"The dusky night rides down the sky, / And ushers in the morn"*

(Henry Fielding); it often refers to deepness of shade of a color: *"A dusky blush rose to her cheek"* (Edith Wharton). **Obscure** usually means unclear to the mind or senses (*an obscure communiqué requiring clarification*), but it can refer to physical darkness (*the obscure rooms of a shuttered mansion*). **Opaque** means not admitting penetration by light (*opaque rock crystals*); figuratively it applies to something that is unintelligible: *"Nixon confined himself to opaque philosophical statements that indicated he was not ready for a discussion of basic assumptions"* (Henry A. Kissinger). **Shady** refers literally to what is sheltered from light, especially sunlight (*a shady grove of catalpas*) or figuratively to what is of questionable honesty (*shady business deals*). **Shadowy** also implies obstructed light (*a shadowy avenue through thick foliage*) but may suggest shifting illumination and indistinctness: *"[He] retreated from the limelight to the shadowy fringe of music history"* (Charles Sherman). The word can refer to something that seems to lack substance and is mysterious and possibly sinister: *a shadowy figure in a black Homburg traversing the fogbound park.*

daze   *daze bemuse benumb stun stupefy*

The central meaning shared by these verbs is "to dull or paralyze the mental capacities with or as if with a shock": *dazed by the defeat; bemused by the senator's resignation; a boring performance that benumbed the audience; stunned by their sudden death; a display that stupefied all onlookers.*

deceive   *deceive betray mislead beguile delude dupe hoodwink bamboozle double-cross*

These verbs mean to lead another into error, danger, or a disadvantageous position, for the most part by underhand means. **Deceive** involves the deliberate concealment or the misrepresentation of the truth: *"I do not mean to say that I am* *particularly observant or quick-sighted in general, but in such a case I am sure I could not be deceived"* (Jane Austen). **Betray** implies faithlessness or treachery: *"When you betray somebody else, you also betray yourself"* (Isaac Bashevis Singer). **Mislead** means to lead in the wrong direction or into error of thought or action: *"My manhood, long misled by wandering fires, / Followed false lights"* (John Dryden). **Beguile** suggests deceiving or misleading by means of pleasant or alluring methods: *They beguiled unwary investors with tales of overnight fortunes.* To **delude** is to mislead to the point where a person is unable to tell truth from falsehood or to form sound judgments: *The government deluded the public about the dangers of low-level radiation.* **Dupe** means to delude by playing upon another's susceptibilities or naiveté: *Gullible shoppers are easily duped by unscrupulous advertisers.* **Hoodwink** refers to deluding by trickery: *It is difficult to hoodwink a smart lawyer.* **Bamboozle** less formally means to delude by the use of such tactics as hoaxing, befuddling, or artful persuasion: *"Perhaps if I wanted to be understood or to understand I would bamboozle myself into belief, but I am a reporter"* (Graham Greene). **Double-cross** implies the betrayal of a confidence or the willful breaking of a pledge: *New members of the party felt they had been double-crossed by the old guard.*

decide   *decide determine settle rule conclude resolve*
These verbs are compared as they mean to make or cause to make a decision. **Decide** is the least specific: *"If two laws conflict with each other, the courts must decide on the operation of each"* (John Marshall). *Her parents' pleas decided her against dropping out of college.* **Determine** often involves somewhat narrower issues: *A jury will determine whether the charges are true or false.* **Settle** stresses finality of decision: *"The lama waved a hand to show that the matter was finally settled in his mind"* (Rudyard Kipling). **Rule** implies that the decision is handed down by

someone in authority: *The faculty committee ruled that changes in the curriculum should be implemented.* **Conclude** suggests that a decision, opinion, or judgment has been arrived at after careful consideration: *She concluded that it would be better to ignore the criticism.* **Resolve** stresses the exercise of choice in making a firm decision: *I resolved to lose weight. We resolved that nothing they said could induce us to trust them.*

decision   *decision conclusion determination*
The central meaning shared by these nouns is "a position, an opinion, or a judgment reached after consideration": *a decision unfavorable to the opposition; came to the conclusion not to proceed; satisfied with the panel's determination.*

decisive   *decisive conclusive crucial*
definitive determinative
The central meaning shared by these adjectives is "determining or having the power to determine an outcome": *the decisive vote; a conclusive reason; crucial experiments; a definitive verdict; the determinative battle.*
  ✔ *Antonym:* **indecisive**

decrease   *decrease lessen reduce dwindle abate*
diminish subside
These verbs mean to become or cause to become smaller or less. **Decrease** and **lessen,** interchangeable in most contexts, refer to steady or gradual diminution: *Traffic decreases on holidays. Lack of success decreases confidence. Use your seat belt to lessen the danger of injury in an accident. His appetite lessens as his illness progresses.* **Reduce** emphasizes bringing down, as in size, degree, or intensity: *The workers reduced their wage demands.* **Dwindle** suggests decreasing bit by bit to a vanishing point: *Their savings dwindled away.* **Abate** stresses a decrease in

amount or intensity and suggests a reduction of excess: *Toward evening the fire began to abate. Nothing can abate the force of that argument.* **Diminish** implies taking away or removal: *An occasional outburst didn't diminish my respect for her. The warden's authority diminished after the revolt.* **Subside** implies a falling away to a more normal level: *The wild enthusiasm the team's victory aroused did not subside.*

deep   *deep abysmal profound*

The central meaning shared by these adjectives is "extending far downward or inward from a surface": *a deep lake; falling from a cliff through abysmal space; a profound glacial chasm.*

✓ Antonym: **shallow**

defeat   *defeat conquer vanquish beat rout subdue subjugate overcome*

These verbs mean to get the better of an adversary. **Defeat** is the most general: *"Whether we defeat the enemy in one battle, or by degrees, the consequences will be the same"* (Thomas Paine). **Conquer** suggests decisive and often wide-scale victory: *"Our cruel and unrelenting enemy leaves us only the choice of brave resistance, or the most abject submission. We have, therefore, to resolve to conquer or die"* (George Washington). **Vanquish** emphasizes total mastery: *The forces of Napoleon were vanquished at Waterloo.* **Beat,** less formal, is often the equivalent of *defeat,* though *beat* may convey greater emphasis: *"To win battles . . . you beat the soul . . . of the enemy man"* (George S. Patton). **Rout** implies complete victory followed by the disorderly flight of the defeated force: *An entire division was routed during the first hours of the war.* **Subdue** suggests mastery and control achieved by overpowering: *"It cost [the Romans] two great wars, and three great battles, to subdue that little kingdom [Macedonia]"* (Adam Smith). **Subjugate** more strongly implies reducing an opponent to submission: *"The last foreigner to subjugate England was a Norman duke in the Middle Ages named William"* (Stanley Meisler). To **overcome** is to prevail over, often by persevering: *overcome an enemy; overcome temptation; overcome a physical handicap.*

defend   *defend protect guard preserve shield safeguard*

These verbs mean to make or keep safe from danger, attack, or harm. **Defend** implies the taking of measures to repel an attack: *defending the island against invasion; tried to defend his reputation.* **Protect** often suggests providing a cover to repel discomfort, injury, or attack: *bought a dog to protect the children from unfriendly strangers; wore sunglasses to protect my eyes; has to learn to protect herself.* **Guard** suggests keeping watch: *police guarding the entrance to the embassy; guarded the house against intruders.* To **preserve** is to take measures to maintain something in safety: *fighting to preserve freedom; ecologists working to preserve our natural resources.* **Shield** suggests protection likened to a piece of defensive armor interposed between the threat and the threatened: *His lawyers tried to shield him from the angry reporters.* **Safeguard** stresses protection against potential or less imminent danger and often implies preventive action: *The Bill of Rights safeguards our individual liberties.*

defy   *defy beard brave challenge dare face front*

The central meaning shared by these verbs is "to confront boldly and courageously": *an innovator defying tradition; bearded the power of the king; braving all criticism; challenged the opposition to produce proof; daring him to deny the statement; faced her accusers; front death with dignity.*

degrade   *degrade abase debase demean humble humiliate*

These verbs mean to deprive of self-esteem or self-worth. **De-**

grade implies reduction to a state of shame or disgrace: *"Charity degrades those who receive it and hardens those who dispense it"* (George Sand). **Abase** refers principally to loss of rank or prestige: *refused to abase herself by asking for an invitation.* **Debase** implies reduction in quality or value: *"debasing the moral currency"* (George Eliot). **Demean** suggests lowering in social position: *"It puts him where he can make the advances without demeaning himself"* (William Dean Howells). **Humble** can refer to lowering in rank or, more often, to driving out undue pride: *He dreamed of humbling his opponent.* To **humiliate** is to subject to loss of self-respect or dignity: *a defeat that humiliated both army and nation.*

delicate   *delicate   choice   dainty   elegant   exquisite   fine*
The central meaning shared by these adjectives is "appealing to refined taste": *a delicate flavor; choice exotic flowers; a dainty dish; elegant handwriting; an exquisite wine; the finest embroidery.*

delicious   *delicious   ambrosial   delectable   luscious   scrumptious   toothsome   yummy*
The central meaning shared by these adjectives is "extremely pleasing to the sense of taste": *a delicious pâté; ambrosial smoked salmon; delectable raspberries; luscious chocolate bonbons; a scrumptious peach; a toothsome apple; yummy fudge.*

demand   *demand   claim   exact   require*
The central meaning shared by these verbs is "to ask for urgently or insistently": *demanding better working conditions; claiming repayment of a debt; exacted obedience from the child; tax payments required by law.*

demote   *demote   break   bust   degrade   downgrade   reduce*
The central meaning shared by these verbs is "to lower in

grade, rank, or status": *was demoted from captain to lieutenant; a noncommissioned officer broken to the ranks; a detective who was busted to uniformed traffic patrol for insubordination; a supervisor degraded to an assistant; a popular author downgraded by critical opinion to a genre writer; a captain who was reduced from command of a battleship to administrative duty ashore.*

   ✔ Antonym: **promote**

deny   deny contradict contravene disaffirm gainsay negate negative traverse

The central meaning shared by these verbs is "to refuse to admit the existence, truth, or value of": *denied the rumor; contradicted the statement; contravene a conclusion; disaffirm a suggestion; trying to gainsay the evidence; negate reality; negatived the allegations; traverse an indictment.*

   ✔ Antonym: **affirm**

dependent   dependent conditional contingent relative subject

The central meaning shared by these adjectives is "determined or to be determined by something else": *a water supply dependent on adequate rainfall; conditional acceptance of the apology; assistance contingent on continuing need; the importance of a discovery as relative to its usefulness; promotion subject to merit.*

   ✔ Antonym: **independent**

deplete   deplete drain exhaust impoverish enervate

These verbs all mean to weaken severely by removing something essential. **Deplete** refers to using up gradually and only hints at harmful consequences: *I always replenish my food supply before it is depleted.* **Drain** suggests reduction by gradual drawing off and is stronger in implying harm: *War often drains a nation's economy.* **Exhaust** stresses reduction to a point of no further usefulness: *"The resources of civilization are not yet exhausted"* (William Ewart Gladstone). **Impoverish** refers to severe reduction of resources or qualities essential to adequate functioning: *"His death has eclipsed the gaiety of nations, and impoverished the public stock of harmless pleasure"* (Samuel Johnson). **Enervate** refers to weakening or destruction of vitality or strength: *Idleness enervates the will to succeed.*

depressed   depressed blue dejected dispirited downcast downhearted

The central meaning shared by these adjectives is "affected or marked by low spirits": *depressed by the loss of his job; lonely and blue in a strange city; is dejected but trying to look cheerful; a dispirited and resigned expression on her face; looked downcast after his defeat; a card welcomed by the downhearted patient.*

describe   describe narrate recite recount rehearse relate report

The central meaning shared by these verbs is "to tell the facts, details, or particulars of something verbally or in writing": *described the accident; narrated their experiences in the Far East; an explorer reciting her adventures; a mercenary recounting his exploits; parents rehearsing the dangers the children faced; related the day's events; came back and reported what she had seen.*

desire   desire covet crave want wish

The central meaning shared by these verbs is "to have a strong longing for": *desire peace; coveted the new convertible; craving fame and fortune; wanted a drink of water; got all she wished.*

despise   despise contemn disdain scorn scout

The central meaning shared by these verbs is "to regard with utter contempt": *despises incompetence; contemned the actions of the dictator; disdained my suggestion; scorns sentimentality; scouted simplistic explanations.*

  ✔ Antonym: **esteem**

despondent   *despondent   despairing   forlorn   hopeless*
The central meaning shared by these adjectives is "being without or almost without hope": *despondent about the failure of the enterprise; took a despairing view of world politics; a forlorn cause; a hopeless case.*

  ✔ Antonym: **hopeful**

detailed   *detailed   circumstantial   minute   particular*
The central meaning shared by these adjectives is "marked by attention to detail": *a detailed account of the trip; a circumstantial narrative; an exact and minute report; a faithful and particular description.*

development   *development   evolution   progress*
The central meaning shared by these nouns is "a progression from a simpler or lower to a more advanced, mature, or complex form or stage": *the development of an aptitude into an accomplishment; the evolution of a plant from a seed; attempts made to foster social progress.*

deviation   *deviation   aberration   divergence*
The central meaning shared by these nouns is "a departure from what is prescribed or expected": *tolerates no deviation from the rules; regretted the aberrations of her early life; the divergence of two cultures.*

dexterous   *dexterous   deft   adroit   handy   nimble*
These adjectives refer to skill and ease in performance. **Dexterous** implies physical or mental agility: *dexterous fingers.* "This

study [of law] *renders men acute, inquisitive, dexterous, prompt in attack, ready in defense, full of resources"* (Edmund Burke). **Deft** suggests quickness, sureness, neatness, and lightness of touch: *decorated the cake with a few deft strokes; defused the hostility with a deft turn of phrase.* **Adroit** implies ease and natural skill, especially in dealing with challenging situations: *an adroit skier; an adroit negotiator.* **Handy** suggests a more modest aptitude, principally in manual work: *handy with a saw and hammer.* **Nimble** stresses quickness and lightness in physical or mental performance: *nimble feet; nimble wits.*

dictate *dictate decree impose ordain prescribe*
The central meaning shared by these verbs is "to set forth expressly and authoritatively": *victors dictating the terms of surrender; confiscation of alien property decreed by the legislature; impose obedience; a separation seemingly ordained by fate; taxes prescribed by law.*

differ *differ disagree vary*
The central meaning shared by these verbs is "to be unlike or dissimilar": *Birds differ from mammals. The testimony of the two witnesses disagreed on significant points. People vary in intelligence.*

✔ *Antonym:* **agree**

difference *difference dissimilarity unlikeness divergence variation distinction discrepancy*
These nouns refer to a lack of correspondence or agreement. **Difference** is the most general: *differences in color and size; a difference of opinion.* **Dissimilarity** is difference between things otherwise alike or capable of close comparison: *a striking dissimilarity between the personalities of the sisters.* **Unlikeness** usually implies greater and more obvious difference: *more likeness than*

unlikeness among children of that age. **Divergence** suggests an often gradually increasing difference between things originally similar: *points of divergence between British and American English.* **Variation** is difference between things of the same class or species; often it refers to modification of something original, prescribed, or typical: *variations in temperature; a variation in shape.* **Distinction** often means a difference in detail between like or related things, determinable only by close inspection: *the distinction in meaning between "good" and "excellent."* A **discrepancy** is a difference between things that should correspond or match, as a conflict in two accounts of an incident: *a discrepancy between what was promised and what was done.*

difficulty   difficulty hardship rigor vicissitude

The central meaning shared by these nouns is "something that requires great effort to overcome": *grappling with financial difficulties; a life of hardship; undergoing the rigors of prison; withstood the vicissitudes of an army career.*

dip   dip douse duck dunk immerse souse submerge

The central meaning shared by these verbs is "to plunge briefly into a liquid": *dipped a doughnut into his coffee; doused her head in the shower; playmates ducking each other in the pool; dunked the dirty shirt into soapsuds; immersed the tomatoes in boiling water; managed to avoid falling and being soused in the puddle; tents and trailers submerged by the deluge.*

dirty   dirty filthy foul nasty squalid grimy

These adjectives apply to what is unclean, impure, or unkempt. **Dirty,** the most general, describes what is covered or stained with dirt: *dirty clothes; dirty feet; dirty sidewalks.* Something that is **filthy** is disgustingly dirty: *filthy rags; a room as filthy as a pigsty.* **Foul** suggests gross offensiveness, particularly to the sense of smell: *a foul exudation; a foul pond.* **Nasty** can refer to what is unpleasant because of the presence of dirt (*Scrubbing bathrooms is a nasty job*) but is often applied to what is merely annoying or unpleasant (*nasty ideas; a nasty trick*). **Squalid** suggests dirtiness, wretchedness, and sordidness: *lived in a squalid apartment.* **Grimy** describes something whose surface is smudged with dirt such as grime or soot: *grimy hands.*

disadvantage   *disadvantage detriment drawback handicap*
The central meaning shared by these nouns is "a condition, circumstance, or characteristic unfavorable to success": *poor health, a disadvantage to an athlete; is free to do as she wishes without detriment; responsibilities that are a drawback to our pleasure; illiteracy, a serious handicap in life.*
   ✔ Antonym: **advantage**

disappear   *disappear evanesce evaporate fade vanish*
The central meaning shared by these verbs is "to pass out of sight or existence": *a skyscraper disappearing in the fog; time seeming to evanesce; courage evaporating; hopes fading away; memories vanishing slowly but surely.*
   ✔ Antonym: **appear**

discourage   *discourage dishearten dispirit*
The central meaning shared by these verbs is "to make less hopeful or enthusiastic": *discouraged by the magnitude of the problem; lack of interest that disheartened the instructor; a failure that dispirited the team.*
   ✔ Antonym: **encourage**

discover   *discover ascertain determine learn*
The central meaning shared by these verbs is "to gain knowl-

edge or awareness of something not known before": *discovered that the world is round; ascertaining the facts; tried to determine the date of delivery; learned that her friend had married.*

discuss   *discuss argue debate dispute contend*

These verbs mean to talk with others in an effort to reach agreement, to ascertain truth, or to convince. *Discuss* involves close examination of a subject with interchange of opinions: *"Men are never so likely to settle a question rightly as when they discuss it freely"* (Thomas Macaulay). *Argue* emphasizes the presentation of facts and reasons in support of a position opposed by others: *"There is no good in arguing with the inevitable"* (James Russell Lowell). *Debate* involves formal, often public argument: *The candidates agreed to debate the campaign issues face to face. Dispute* implies differences of opinion and usually sharp argument: *members of the legislature disputing over increases in the military budget.* To **contend** is to strive in debate or controversy: *"I do really delight in your society and I only want to show you that I contended for a principle"* (Henry James).

disguise   *disguise camouflage cloak dissemble dissimulate mask*

The central meaning shared by these verbs is "to change or modify so as to conceal the true identity or character of": *disguised her interest with nonchalance; trying to camouflage their impatience; cloaked his anxiety with a smile; dissembling ill will with false solicitude; couldn't dissimulate her vanity; ambition that is masked as altruism.*

disgust   *disgust nauseate repel revolt sicken*

The central meaning shared by these verbs is "to offend the senses or feelings of": *a stench that disgusted us; hypocrisy that nauseated me; was repelled by such ruthlessness; brutality that revolts the sensibilities of civilized people; a fetid odor that sickened the hospital workers.*

dismay   *dismay appall daunt horrify shake*

These verbs mean to deprive a person of courage or the power to act as a result of fear or anxiety. **Dismay** is the least specific: *The news of plummeting stock prices dismayed speculators.* **Appall** implies a sense of helplessness caused by an awareness of the enormity of something: *"for as this appalling ocean surrounds the verdant land"* (Herman Melville). **Daunt** suggests an abatement of courage: *"captains courageous, whom death could not daunt"* (Anonymous ballad). **Horrify** implies dread, shock, or revulsion: *horrified by the possibility of nuclear war.* To **shake** is to dismay profoundly: *"A little swift brutality shook him to the very soul"* (John Galsworthy).

dismiss   *dismiss boot bounce can cashier discharge drop fire sack*

The central meaning shared by these verbs is "to terminate the employment of": *was dismissed for insubordination; was booted for being habitually tardy; afraid of being bounced for union activities; wasn't canned because his father-in-law owns the business; will be cashiered from the army; resort workers discharged at the end of the season; was dropped for incompetence; was fired on the spot for insolence; a reporter sacked for revealing a confidential source.*

display   *display array panoply parade pomp*

The central meaning shared by these nouns is "an impressive or ostentatious exhibition": *a tasteless display of wealth; an array of diamond rings in a showcase; a panoply of alpine peaks; a parade of knowledge and virtue; the pomp of a coronation ceremony.*

dissuade *dissuade deter discourage*

The central meaning shared by these verbs is "to persuade someone not to do something": *tried to dissuade the general from taking disciplinary action; couldn't be deterred from smoking; discouraged her from accepting the offer.*

   ✓ *Antonym:* **persuade**

distinct *distinct discrete separate several*

The central meaning shared by these adjectives is "distinguished from others in nature or qualities": *six distinct colors; a government with three discrete divisions; a problem consisting of two separate issues; performed the several steps of the process.*

distribute *distribute divide dispense dole deal ration*

These verbs mean to give out in portions or shares. **Distribute** is the least specific: *In the 19th century the government distributed land to settlers willing to cultivate it.* **Divide** implies giving out portions, often equal, on the basis of a plan or purpose: *The estate will be divided among the heirs.* **Dispense** stresses the careful determination of portions, often according to measurement or weight: *dispensing medication; dispensed tax dollars judiciously; dispense advice and sympathy.* **Dole,** often followed by **out,** implies careful, usually sparing measurement of portions; it can refer to the distribution of charity (*surplus milk and cheese doled out to the needy*) but more often suggests lack of generosity: *The professor seldom doled out praise, and even when he did it was with reluctance.* **Deal** implies orderly, equitable distribution, often piece by piece: *dealt out one hamburger each to the children.* **Ration** refers to equitable division of scarce items, often necessities, in accordance with a system that limits individual portions: *ration fuel in wartime; rationing water during the drought.*

doctrine   *doctrine dogma tenet*
The central meaning shared by these nouns is "a principle taught, advanced, or accepted, as by a group of philosophers": *the legal doctrine of due process; church dogma; experimentation, one of the tenets of the physical sciences.*

dramatic   *dramatic histrionic melodramatic stagy theatrical*
The central meaning shared by these adjectives is "suggestive of acting or of an emotional and often affected stage performance": *made a dramatic entrance in a swirling cape; a histrionic gesture; struck an attitude of melodramatic despair; stagy heroics; assumed a theatrical pose.*

dry   *dry dehydrate desiccate parch*
The central meaning shared by these verbs is "to remove the moisture from": *drying the dishes; add water to dehydrated eggs; a factory where coconut meat is shredded and desiccated; land parched by the sun.*
   ✓ *Antonym:* **moisten**

dull   *dull colorless drab humdrum lackluster pedestrian stodgy uninspired*
The central meaning shared by these adjectives is "lacking in liveliness, charm, or surprise": *a competent but dull performance of the role; a colorless and unimaginative person; a drab and boring job; a humdrum conversation; a lackluster life; a pedestrian movie plot; a stodgy dinner party; an uninspired lecture.*
   ✓ *Antonym:* **lively**

dumb   *dumb inarticulate mute speechless*
The central meaning shared by these adjectives is "lacking the faculty of speech or the power to speak": *dumb with fear; inarticulate with rage; mute with astonishment; speechless with horror.*

earn   *earn deserve merit rate win*
The central meaning shared by these verbs is "to gain as a result of one's behavior or effort": *earns a large salary; deserves our congratulations; a suggestion that merits consideration; an event that didn't even rate a mention in the news; a candidate who won wide support.*

easy   *easy simple facile effortless smooth light*
These adjectives mean requiring little effort or posing little if any difficulty. **Easy** applies both to tasks that require little effort and to persons who are not demanding: *"The diagnosis of disease is often easy, often difficult, and often impossible"* (Peter M. Latham). *Not wanting to be called an easy marker, the teacher graded the essays severely.* **Simple** implies lack of complexity that facilitates understanding or performance: *a simple game; a simple problem; "the faculty . . . of reducing his thought on any subject to the simplest and plainest terms possible"* (Baron Charnwood). **Facile** stresses readiness and fluency (*a facile speaker*); often, though, the word has unfavorable connotations, as of lack of care, glibness or insincerity, or superficiality: *The explanation is too facile for such a complex phenomenon.* **Effortless** refers to performance in which the application of great strength or skill makes the execution seem easy: *a skater performing an effortless double axel; wrote effortless prose.* **Smooth** suggests freedom from hindrances or difficulties that impede progress: *The path of the bill through the legislature was smooth and orderly.* **Light** refers to tasks or impositions that involve no taxing burdens or responsibilities: *light duties; light taxes.*

eat   *eat consume devour ingest*
The central meaning shared by these verbs is "to take food into the body by the mouth": *ate a hearty dinner; greedily consumed the sandwich; hyenas devouring their prey; whales ingesting krill.*

eccentricity   *eccentricity idiosyncrasy quirk*

These nouns refer to peculiarity of behavior. *Eccentricity* implies divergence from the usual or customary: *"England is the paradise of individuality, eccentricity, heresy, anomalies, hobbies, and humors"* (George Santayana). *Idiosyncrasy* more often refers to such divergency viewed as being peculiar to the temperament of an individualist and serving as an identifying trait: *The use of lowercase letters for capital letters was one of the idiosyncrasies of the poet e.e. cummings.* *Quirk,* a milder term, merely suggests an odd trait or mannerism: *"Every man had his own quirks and twists"* (Harriet Beecher Stowe).

echo   *echo reecho reflect resound reverberate*

The central meaning shared by these verbs is "to send back the sound of": *a cry echoed by the canyon; a cathedral roof reechoing joyous hymns; caves that reflect the noise of footsteps; cliffs resounding the thunder of the ocean; blasting reverberated by quarry walls.*

effect   *effect consequence result outcome upshot sequel*

These nouns denote something, such as an occurrence, a situation, or a condition, that is brought about by a cause. An *effect* is produced by the action of an agent or a cause and follows it in time: *"Every cause produces more than one effect"* (Herbert Spencer). A *consequence* also follows a cause and is traceable to it, but the relationship between them is less sharply definable: *"Servitude is at once the consequence of his crime and the punishment of his guilt"* (John P. Curran). A *result* is an effect, or the last in a series of effects, that is viewed as the end product of the operation of the cause: *"Judging from the results I have seen . . . I cannot say . . . that I agree with you"* (William H. Mallock). An *outcome* is a result but more strongly than *result* implies finality and may suggest the operation of a cause over a relatively long period: *If you had refused, the outcome would probably not have been very different.* An **upshot** is a decisive result, often of the nature of a climax: *"The upshot of the matter . . . was that she showed both of them the door"* (Robert Louis Stevenson). A **sequel** is a consequence that ensues after a lapse of time: *"Our dreams are the sequel of our waking knowledge"* (Ralph Waldo Emerson).

effective *effective effectual efficacious efficient*
The central meaning shared by these adjectives is "producing or capable of producing a desired effect": *an effective reprimand; an effectual complaint; an efficacious remedy; the efficient cause of the revolution.*
  ✔ *Antonym:* **ineffective**

elaborate *elaborate complicated intricate*
The central meaning shared by these adjectives is "marked by complexity of detail": *an elaborate lace pattern; the eye, a complicated organ; an intricate problem.*
  ✔ *Antonym:* **simple**

elegance *elegance grace polish urbanity*
The central meaning shared by these nouns is "refined and tasteful beauty of manner, form, or style": *a woman of unstudied elegance; walks with unconscious grace; comported herself with dignity and polish; tact and urbanity, the marks of a true diplomat.*
  ✔ *Antonym:* **inelegance**

element *element component constituent factor ingredient*
The central meaning shared by these nouns is "one of the individual parts of which a composite entity is made up": *the grammatical elements of a sentence; jealousy, a component of his*

character; melody and harmony, two of the constituents of a musical composition; ambition as a key factor in her success; humor, an effective ingredient of a speech.

elevation   *elevation altitude height*
The central meaning shared by these nouns is "the distance of something above a point of reference such as the horizon": *a city at an elevation of 3,000 feet above sea level; a blimp flying at an altitude of one mile; a boy who grew to a height of six feet.*

eliminate   *eliminate eradicate liquidate purge*
The central meaning shared by these verbs is "to wipe out someone or something undesirable, especially by using drastic methods such as banishment or execution": *eliminated all political opposition; eradicate guerrilla activity; liquidating traitors; purged all the imprisoned dissidents.*

embarrass   *embarrass abash chagrin discomfit disconcert faze rattle*
The central meaning shared by these verbs is "to cause someone to feel self-conscious and uneasy": *was embarrassed by her child's tantrum; felt abashed at the extravagant praise; will be chagrined if his confident prediction fails; was discomfited by the sudden personal question; is disconcerted by sarcastic remarks; refuses to be fazed by your objections; isn't easily rattled before an audience.*

emphasis   *emphasis accent stress*
The central meaning shared by these nouns is "special weight placed on something considered important": *laid a strong emphasis on the study of foreign languages; opposition to nuclear power plants, with the accent on total elimination; lay heavy stress on law and order.*

empty *empty vacant blank void vacuous bare barren*
These adjectives describe what contains nothing and inferentially lacks what it could or should have. **Empty** applies to what is without contents or substance: *an empty box; an empty room; empty promises*. **Vacant** refers to what is without an occupant or incumbent: *The auditorium is full of vacant seats. The presidency is vacant.* Figuratively the word refers to the absence of intelligent meaning or thought: *a vacant stare; a vacant mind*. **Blank** stresses the absence of something, especially on a surface, that would convey meaning or content: *blank pages; a blank expression*. **Void** applies to what is free from or completely destitute of discernible content: *space void of matter; gibberish void of all meaning*. **Vacuous** describes what is as devoid of substance as a vacuum is: *a vacuous smile; led a vacuous life*. Something that is **bare** lacks surface covering (*trees standing bare in November; a bare head*) or detail (*just the bare facts*); the word also denotes the condition of being stripped of contents or furnishings: *The closet is bare.* **Barren** stresses lack of productivity in both literal and figurative applications: *barren land; writing barren of insight.*

enclose *enclose cage coop fence hem pen wall*
The central meaning shared by these verbs is "to surround and confine within a limited area": *cattle enclosed in feedlots; was caged in the office all afternoon; was cooped up in a studio apartment; a garden fenced in by shrubbery; a battalion hemmed in by enemy troops; ships penned up in the harbor during a blockade; prisoners who were walled in.*

encourage *encourage animate cheer embolden hearten inspirit*
The central meaning shared by these verbs is "to impart courage, inspiration, and resolution to": *encouraged the student*

to enter the competition; played patriotic music to animate the troops; a visitor cheering the patient with his presence; was emboldened to sing for the guests; praise that heartened us; a half-time pep talk that inspirited the weary team.

✔ Antonym: **discourage**

endanger *endanger hazard imperil jeopardize risk*
The central meaning shared by these verbs is "to subject to danger, loss, or destruction": *driving that endangers passengers' lives; hazarded his well-being by constant smoking; a forest imperiled by acid rain; strikes that jeopardized the future of the business; risking her financial security by buying speculative stocks.*

enemy *enemy foe opponent*
The central meaning shared by these nouns is "one who is hostile to or opposes the purposes or interests of another": *was betrayed by his enemies; a foe of fascism; a political opponent.*

enforce *enforce implement invoke*
The central meaning shared by these verbs is "to cause to be applied or carried out": *enforced the rules; implementing the terms of the agreement; invoke emergency powers.*

engagement *engagement appointment assignation date rendezvous tryst*
The central meaning shared by these nouns is "a commitment to appear at a certain time and place": *a business engagement; a dental appointment; a secret assignation; a date to play tennis; a rendezvous of allied troops at the border; a lovers' tryst.*

enormous *enormous immense huge gigantic colossal mammoth tremendous stupendous gargantuan vast*
These adjectives describe what is extraordinarily large. *Enor-*

mous suggests a marked excess beyond the norm in size, amount, or degree: *an enormous boulder; enormous expenses.* **Immense** refers to boundless or immeasurable size or extent: *an immense crowd of people; immense pleasure.* **Huge** especially implies greatness of size or capacity: *a huge wave; a huge success.* **Gigantic** refers to size likened to that of a giant: *a gigantic redwood tree; a gigantic disappointment.* **Colossal** suggests a hugeness that elicits awe or taxes belief: *colossal crumbling ruins of an ancient temple; has a colossal nerve.* **Mammoth** is applied to something of clumsy or unwieldy hugeness: *a mammoth ship; a mammoth multinational corporation.* **Tremendous** suggests aweinspiring or fearsome size: *a tremendous monument 100 feet high; ate a tremendous meal.* **Stupendous** implies size that astounds or defies description: *an undertaking of stupendous difficulty.* "*The whole thing was a stupendous, incomprehensible farce*" (W. Somerset Maugham). **Gargantuan** especially stresses greatness of capacity, as for food or pleasure: *a gargantuan appetite.* **Vast** refers to greatness of extent, size, area, or scope: "*All the land was shrouded in one vast forest*" (Theodore Roosevelt). "*Of creatures, how few vast as the whale*" (Herman Melville).

enrapture   *enrapture entrance ravish thrill transport*
The central meaning shared by these verbs is "to have a powerful, agreeable, and often overwhelming emotional effect on someone": *enraptured by the music; a view of the Alps that entranced us; a painting that ravished the eye; thrilled by their success; transported with joy.*

envy   *envy begrudge covet*
These verbs mean to feel resentful or painful desire for another's advantages or possessions. **Envy** is wider in range than the others since it combines discontent, resentment, and desire: "*When I peruse the conquered fame of heroes and the victories*

of mighty generals, I do not envy the generals" (Walt Whitman).
Begrudge stresses ill will and reluctance to acknowledge another's right or claim: *Why begrudge him his success?* **Covet**
stresses desire, especially a secret or culpable longing, for
something to which one has no right: *"as thorough an Englishman as ever coveted his neighbor's goods"* (Charles Kingsley).

equipment   *equipment apparatus gear materiel outfit paraphernalia rig tackle*

The central meaning shared by these nouns is "the materials
needed for a purpose such as a task or a journey": *hiking equipment; laboratory apparatus; skiing gear; naval materiel; an explorer's outfit; sports paraphernalia; a climber's rig; fishing tackle.*

erase   *erase expunge efface delete cancel*

These verbs mean to remove or invalidate something, especially something recorded as by having been written down. To
erase is to wipe or rub out, literally or figuratively: *erased the
equation from the blackboard. Unconsciousness erased the details
of the accident from her memory.* **Expunge** implies thoroughgoing
removal that leaves no trace: *expunged their names from the list.*
Efface also refers to the removal of every trace: *effacing graffiti
from subway cars; tried to efface prejudice from his mind.* **Delete**
is used principally in the sense of removing matter from a
manuscript: *The expletives were deleted from the transcript.* **Cancel**
refers to invalidating by or as if by drawing lines through
something written or by indicating that the force or effect of
something has been terminated: *a postage stamp that had been
canceled; cancel vows; cancel a debt.*

estimate   *estimate appraise assess assay evaluate rate*

These verbs mean to form a judgment of worth or significance. **Estimate** usually implies a subjective and somewhat inexact judgment: *difficult to estimate the possible results in advance; could only estimate the size of the crowd.* **Appraise** stresses expert judgment: *appraised the furniture and works of art before distributing them to the heirs.* **Assess** implies authoritative judgment in setting a monetary value on something as a basis for taxation: *assessing an apartment on the amount for which it is likely to be rented.* **Assay** refers to careful examination, especially to chemical analysis of an ore to determine its quality, fineness, or purity: *cut a minute piece off the ingot to assay it.* In extended senses *appraise, assess,* and *assay* can refer to any critical analysis or appraisal: *appraised his character and found him wanting; assessing the impact of higher taxes on lower-income households; has no method for assaying merit.* **Evaluate** implies considered judgment in ascertaining value: *evaluating a student's thesis for content and organization; used projective tests to evaluate her aptitudes.* **Rate** involves determining the rank or grade of someone or something in relation to others: *Will history rate Picasso above Renoir?*

estrange   estrange alienate disaffect
These verbs refer to disruption of a bond of love, friendship, or loyalty. **Estrange** and **alienate** are often used with reference to two persons, such as a husband and wife, whose harmonious relationship has been replaced by hostility or indifference: *Political disagreements led to quarrels that finally estranged the two friends. His persistent antagonism caused his wife to be alienated from him.* **Disaffect** usually implies discontent, ill will, and disloyalty within the membership of a group: *Colonists were disaffected by the autocratic actions of the royal governor.*

evoke   evoke educe elicit
The central meaning shared by these verbs is "to draw forth or bring out something latent, hidden, or unexpressed": *evoke*

laughter; couldn't educe significance from the event; trying to elicit the truth.

exaggerate   *exaggerate inflate magnify overstate*

The central meaning shared by these verbs is "to represent something as being larger or greater than it actually is": *exaggerated the size of the fish he had caught; inflated her own importance; magnifying his part in their success; overstated their income on the mortgage application.*

✓ *Antonym:* **minimize**

example   *example instance case illustration sample specimen*

Each of these nouns refers to what is representative of or serves to explain a larger group or class. An **example** represents, usually typically, something of which it is a part and thereby demonstrates the character of the whole: *"Of the despotism to which unrestrained military power leads we have plenty of examples from Alexander to Mao"* (Samuel Eliot Morison). An **instance** is an example that is cited to prove or invalidate a contention or to illustrate a point: *an instance of flagrant corruption.* A **case** is an action, an occurrence, or a condition that constitutes a specific instance of something being discussed, decided, or treated: *a typical case of child neglect; very few cases of diphtheria.* An **illustration** is an example that clarifies or explains: *provided an illustration of the word in context; gave an illustration of her courage.* A **sample** is an actual part of something larger, presented as evidence of the quality or nature of the whole: *distributing samples of a new detergent; gave us a sample of her temper.* **Specimen** is sometimes synonymous with *sample,* but it often denotes an individual, representative member of a group or class: *This poem is a fair specimen of his work.*

excessive *excessive exorbitant extravagant immoderate inordinate extreme unreasonable*

These adjectives mean exceeding a normal, usual, reasonable, or proper limit. **Excessive** describes a quantity, an amount, or a degree that is more than what is justifiable, tolerable, or desirable: *excessive speed; excessive drinking.* **Exorbitant** usually refers to a quantity or degree that far exceeds what is customary or fair: *exorbitant interest rates; an exorbitant price.* **Extravagant** sometimes specifies excessive or unwise expenditure of money (*extravagant gifts*); often it implies unbridled divergence from the bounds of reason or sound judgment (*extravagant claims; extravagant praise*). **Immoderate** denotes lack of due moderation: *immoderate expenses; immoderate enthusiasm.* **Inordinate** implies an overstepping of bounds imposed by authority or dictated by good sense: *inordinate vanity; inordinate demands.* **Extreme** suggests the utmost degree of excessiveness: *extreme joy; extreme danger; extreme opinions.* **Unreasonable** applies to what exceeds reasonable limits: *charged an unreasonable rent; made an unreasonable request.*

existence *existence actuality being*

The central meaning shared by these nouns is "the fact or state of existing": *laws in existence for centuries; a fantasy that progressed from possibility to actuality; a point of view gradually coming into being.*

✔ *Antonym:* **nonexistence**

expect *expect anticipate hope await*

These verbs are related in various ways to the idea of looking ahead to something in the future. To **expect** is to look forward to the likely occurrence or appearance of someone or something: *You can expect us for lunch. "We should not expect something for nothing — but we all do and call it Hope" (Edgar W.*

Howe). **Anticipate** is sometimes used as a synonym of *expect,* but usually it involves more than expectation. Sometimes it refers to taking advance action, as to forestall or prevent the occurrence of something expected or to meet a wish or request before it is articulated: *anticipated the attack and locked the gates; anticipating her desires.* The term can also refer to having a foretaste of something expected before its occurrence: *anticipate trouble.* To **hope** is to look forward with desire and usually with a measure of confidence in the likelihood of gaining what is desired: *I hope to see you soon. Hope for the best, but expect the worst.* To **await** is to wait in expectation of; it implies certainty: *eagerly awaiting your letter.*

experience   *experience suffer sustain taste undergo*
The central meaning shared by these verbs is "to encounter or partake of personally": *experience happiness; suffer a loss; sustained an injury; tasted freedom; has undergone a religious conversion.*

explain   *explain elucidate expound explicate interpret construe*
These verbs mean to make understandable the nature or meaning of something. **Explain** is the most widely applicable: *explained the difficult words and obscure symbols; tried to explain himself.* To **elucidate** is to throw light on something complex: *"Man's whole life and environment have been laid open and elucidated"* (Thomas Carlyle). **Expound** and **explicate** imply detailed and usually learned and lengthy exploration or analysis: *"We must never forget that it is a* constitution *we are expounding"* (John Marshall). *"Ordinary language philosophers tried to explicate the standards of usage underlying the linguistic behavior of those who do not abuse this freedom"* (Jerrold J. Katz). To **interpret** is to reveal the underlying meaning of something by the

application of special knowledge or insight: *"If a poet interprets a poem of his own he limits its suggestibility"* (William Butler Yeats). **Construe** involves putting a particular construction or interpretation on something: *"I take the official oath today . . . with no purpose to construe the Constitution or laws by any hypercritical rules"* (Abraham Lincoln). *Why do you construe my silence as a sign of disapproval?*

explicit   *explicit categorical definite express specific*
The central meaning shared by these adjectives is "entirely clear and unambiguous": *explicit statements; a categorical refusal; a definite answer; my express wishes; a specific purpose.*
  ✓ *Antonym:* **ambiguous**

expressive   *expressive eloquent meaningful significant*
The central meaning shared by these adjectives is "effectively conveying a feeling, an idea, or a mood": *an expressive gesture; an eloquent speech; a meaningful look; a significant smile.*

extricate   *extricate disengage disentangle untangle*
The central meaning shared by these verbs is "to free from something that entangles": *extricated himself from an embarrassing situation; trying to disengage her attention from the subject that obsesses her; disentangled the oar from the water lilies; the efforts of a trapped animal to untangle itself from a net.*

face   *face countenance kisser mug pan physiognomy puss visage*
The central meaning shared by these nouns is "the front surface of the head": *turned her face away; a happy countenance; punched him in the kisser; caught a glimpse of his ugly mug; tripped and fell on her pan; caught him staring at my physiognomy; a menacing look on his puss; a noble-looking visage.*

fair *fair just equitable impartial unprejudiced unbiased objective dispassionate*

These adjectives mean free from favoritism, self-interest, or bias in judgment. *Fair* is the most general: *a fair referee; a fair deal; a fair fight; on a fair footing. Just* stresses conformity with what is legally or ethically right or proper: *a kind and just man; "a just and lasting peace"* (Abraham Lincoln). *Equitable* also implies justice, but justice dictated by reason, conscience, and a natural sense of what is fair to all concerned: *an equitable distribution of gifts among the children. Impartial* emphasizes lack of favoritism: *"the cold neutrality of an impartial judge"* (Edmund Burke). *Unprejudiced* means without favorable or unfavorable preconceived opinions or judgments: *an unprejudiced evaluation of the arguments for and against the proposal. Unbiased* implies absence of the preference or inclination inhibiting impartiality: *gave an unbiased account of her family problems. Objective* implies detachment that permits observation and judgment without undue reference to one's personal feelings or thoughts: *Try to be objective as you listen to the testimony. Dispassionate* means free from or unaffected by strong personal emotions: *A journalist should be a dispassionate reporter of fact.*

faithful *faithful loyal true constant fast steadfast staunch*

These adjectives mean adhering firmly and devotedly to someone or something, such as a person, cause, or duty, that elicits or demands one's fidelity. *Faithful* and *loyal* both suggest undeviating attachment; the words are often interchangeable, though *loyal* is the term more often applied to political allegiance: *a faithful employee; gave faithful service; a loyal companion; a loyal citizen. True* implies steadiness, sincerity, and reliability: *"I would be true, for there are those who trust me"* (Howard Arnold Walter). *Constant* stresses uniformity and invariability:

"But I am constant as the northern star" (William Shakespeare). **Fast** suggests loyalty that is not easily deflected: *fast friends.* **Steadfast** strongly implies fixed, unswerving loyalty: *a steadfast ally.* **Staunch** even more strongly suggests unshakable attachment or allegiance: *"He lived and died a staunch loyalist"* (Harriet Beecher Stowe).

fantastic *fantastic bizarre grotesque fanciful exotic*
These adjectives apply to what is very strange or strikingly unusual. **Fantastic** in this comparison describes what seems to have slight relation to the real world because of its strangeness or extravagance: *fantastic imaginary beasts such as the unicorn.* **Bizarre** stresses oddness of character or appearance that is heightened by striking contrasts and incongruities and that shocks or fascinates: *a bizarre art nouveau façade.* **Grotesque** refers principally to appearance or aspect in which deformity and distortion approach the point of caricature or even absurdity: *rainspouts terminating in gargoyles and other grotesque creatures.* **Fanciful** applies to a character, nature, or design strongly influenced by imagination, caprice, or whimsy: *a fanciful pattern with intertwined vines and flowers.* Something **exotic** is unusual and intriguing in appearance or effect: *exotic birds.*

fashion *fashion style mode vogue*
These nouns refer to a prevailing or preferred manner of dress, adornment, behavior, or way of life at a given time. **Fashion,** the broadest term, usually refers to what accords with conventions adopted by polite society or set by those in the forefront of the artistic or intellectual sphere: *wears clothes in the height of fashion; a time when pop art was very much in fashion.* **Style** is sometimes used interchangeably with *fashion* (*a gown that is out of style*), but *style,* like **mode,** often stresses adherence to standards of elegance: *The couple travels in style. Miniskirts were*

the mode in the late sixties. **Vogue** is applied to fashion that prevails widely (*the voluptuous figure in vogue at the time of Rubens*); the term often suggests enthusiastic but short-lived acceptance (*a game that enjoyed a vogue in its day*).

fashionable   *fashionable chic dashing in modish posh sharp smart stylish swank trendy*

The central meaning shared by these adjectives is "being or in accordance with the current fashion": *a fashionable restaurant; a chic dress; a dashing hat; the in place to go; modish jewelry; a posh address; a sharp jacket; a smart hotel; stylish clothes; a swank apartment; a trendy neighborhood.*

✓ *Antonym:* **unfashionable**

fast   *fast rapid swift fleet speedy quick hasty expeditious*

These adjectives refer to something, such as activity or movement, marked by great speed. **Fast** and **rapid** are often used interchangeably, though *fast* is more often applied to the person or thing in motion, and *rapid,* to the activity or movement involved: *a fast car; a fast plane; a rapid mountain stream; rapid development; a fast runner; rapid strides.* **Swift** suggests smoothness and sureness of movement (*a swift current; swift but unclear handwriting*), and **fleet,** lightness of movement (*The cheetah is the fleetest of animals*). **Speedy** refers to velocity (*a speedy worker*) or to promptness or hurry (*hoped for a speedy resolution to the problem*). **Quick** most often applies to what takes little time or to promptness of response or action: *Let's eat a quick snack. Only her quick reaction prevented an accident.* **Hasty** implies hurried action (*a hasty visit*) and often a lack of care or thought (*regretted the hasty decision*). **Expeditious** suggests rapid efficiency: *sent the package by the most expeditious means.*

fasten *fasten anchor fix moor secure*

The central meaning shared by these verbs is "to cause to remain firmly or fast in position or place": *fastened our seat belts; anchored the television antenna to the roof; fixed the flagpole in concrete; mooring the rowboat at the dock; secures her chignon with hairpins.*

✓ *Antonym:* **unfasten**

fate *fate destiny kismet lot portion*

The central meaning shared by these nouns is "something that is inevitably destined to happen to a person": *deserved a worse fate; complained about their miserable destiny; a meeting foreordained by kismet; has a happy lot; success that was her portion.*

favorable *favorable propitious auspicious benign conducive*

These adjectives describe what is indicative of a successful outcome. **Favorable** can refer to people, conditions, or circumstances that contribute in a positive way to the attainment of a goal: *I hope you will give favorable consideration to my suggestion. The performance received a favorable review.* **Propitious** implies a favorable tendency or inclination: *"Miracles are propitious accidents, the natural causes of which are too complicated to be readily understood"* (George Santayana). **Auspicious** refers to what by its favorable nature presages good fortune: *The project had an auspicious beginning.* **Benign** applies to people or things that exert a beneficial influence: *"I lingered round them, under that benign sky . . . and wondered how anyone could ever imagine unquiet slumbers, for the sleepers in that quiet earth"* (Emily Brontë). Something **conducive** leads or contributes to a result, often a desirable one: *"Nothing is more conducive to happiness than the free exercise of the mind in pursuits congenial to it"* (Thomas Macaulay).

fawn *fawn apple-polish bootlick kowtow slaver toady truckle*

The central meaning shared by these verbs is "to curry favor by behaving obsequiously and submissively": *fawned on her superior; students apple-polishing the teacher; bootlicked to get a promotion; lawyers kowtowing to a judge; slavered over his rich uncle; toadying to members of the occupation force; nobles truckling to the king.*

fear *fear fright dread terror horror panic alarm dismay consternation trepidation*

These nouns all denote the agitation and anxiety caused by the presence or imminence of danger. *Fear* is the most general term: *fear of change; fear of flying; fear of death. "Fear is the parent of cruelty"* (J.A. Froude). *Fright* is sudden, usually momentary fear characterized by great agitation: *In her fright she forgot to lock the door. Dread* is strong fear of something impending, especially of what one is powerless to avoid: *He looked forward with dread to the scheduled surgery. Terror* is intense, overpowering fear: *"the weapon which most readily conquers reason: terror and violence"* (Adolf Hitler). *Horror* is a combination of fear and aversion or repugnance: *Murder arouses widespread horror. Panic* is sudden frantic fear, often groundless: *The fire caused a panic among the horses. Rumors of the President's illness resulted in panic on the world stock markets. Alarm* is fright aroused by the first realization of danger: *I watched with alarm as the current carried the raft and its passengers toward the dam. Dismay* is apprehension that robs one of courage or the power to act effectively: *The appearance of a comet caused universal dismay in the ancient world. Consternation* is a state of often paralyzing dismay characterized by confusion and helplessness: *Consternation spread throughout the city as the invading army approached. Trepidation* is dread characteristically marked by trembling or hesitancy: *"They were . . . full of trepidation about things that were never likely to happen"* (John Morley).

feat   *feat achievement exploit masterstroke*
The central meaning shared by these nouns is "an extraordinary deed or action": *feats of bravery; achievements of diplomacy; military exploits; a masterstroke of entrepreneurship.*

fertile   *fertile fecund fruitful productive prolific*
The central meaning shared by these adjectives is "marked by great productivity": *fertile farmland; a fecund imagination; fruitful efforts; a productive meeting; a prolific writer.*
   ✔ *Antonym:* **infertile**

field   *field bailiwick domain province realm sphere territory*
The central meaning shared by these nouns is "an area of activity, thought, study, or interest": *the field of comparative literature; considers psychology her bailiwick; the domain of physics; the province of politics; the realm of constitutional law; the nation's sphere of influence; the territory of historical research.*

figure   *figure design device motif pattern*
The central meaning shared by these nouns is "an element or a component in a decorative composition": *a tapestry with a floral figure; a rug with a geometric design; a brooch with a fanciful and intricate device; a scarf with a heart motif; fabric with a plaid pattern.*

financial   *financial pecuniary fiscal monetary*
These adjectives mean of or relating to money (*a financial adviser; pecuniary motives; a fiscal year; monetary considerations*), but they often differ in application. **Financial** frequently refers

to transactions involving money on a large scale: *Many software corporations are experiencing financial reverses.* **Pecuniary** is more appropriate to the private, small-scale dealings of individuals: *He received thanks but no pecuniary compensation for his services.* **Fiscal** applies especially to a nation's financial practices and policies: *The Secretary of the Treasury is the chief fiscal officer of our government.* **Monetary** has special reference to the coinage, printing, or circulation of currency: *The basic monetary unit of the United States is the dollar.*

firm   *firm hard solid*
The central meaning shared by these adjectives is "tending not to yield to external pressure, touch, or force": *a firm mattress; hard as granite; solid ice.*
   ✔ Antonym: **soft**

flirt   *flirt dally play toy trifle*
The central meaning shared by these verbs is "to deal lightly, casually, or flippantly with someone or something": *flirted with the idea of getting a job; dallying with music; can't play with life; toyed with the problem; a person not to be trifled with.*

flourish   *flourish brandish wave*
The central meaning shared by these verbs is "to swing back and forth boldly and dramatically": *flourished her newly signed contract; brandish a sword; waving a baton.*

flow   *flow current flood flux rush stream tide*
The central meaning shared by these nouns is "something suggestive of running water": *a flow of thought; the current of history; a flood of ideas; a flux of words; a rush of sympathy; a stream of complaints; a tide of immigration.*

flutter   *flutter flicker flit flitter hover*

The central meaning shared by these verbs is "to move quickly, lightly, and irregularly like a bird in flight": *children fluttering around a birthday cake; flames that flickered in the night; guests flitting from table to table; sunlight flittering over the ocean; admirers hovering around a celebrity.*

follow   *follow succeed ensue result supervene*

These verbs mean to come after something or someone. **Follow,** which has the widest application, can refer to coming after in time or order, as a consequence or result, or by the operation of logic: *Night follows day. If you disregard the doctor's orders, a relapse will follow. Though he disapproves of violence, it doesn't follow that he won't defend himself.* To **succeed** is to come next after another in time or order, especially in planned order determined by considerations such as rank, inheritance, or election: *"The son of a mandarin has no prescriptive right to succeed his father"* (H.G. Wells). *The heir apparent succeeded to the throne.* **Ensue** applies to what follows something, usually as a consequence or by way of logical development: *If a forest fire cannot be extinguished, devastation is sure to ensue.* **Result** implies that what follows is caused by what has preceded: *Failure to file an income tax return can result in a fine.* **Supervene,** in contrast, refers to the coming after of a thing that has little relation to what has preceded and that is often unexpected: *"A bad harvest supervened. Distress reached its climax"* (Charlotte Brontë).

foolish   *foolish silly fatuous absurd preposterous ridiculous ludicrous*

These adjectives are applied to what is so devoid of wisdom or good sense as to be laughable. **Foolish,** the least emphatic and derogatory, usually implies poor judgment or lack of wisdom or soundness: *a foolish young fellow; a foolish expenditure of time* *and energy.* **Silly** suggests lack of point or purpose: *a silly argument; silly mistakes; suggestions that aren't brilliant but aren't silly either.* **Fatuous** applies especially to what is foolish in a vacuous, smug, and unconscious way: *seems to take pride in making fatuous remarks.* **Absurd,** preposterous, ridiculous, and ludicrous apply to what is risible because of a departure from reason, logic, or common sense: *It would be absurd for us both to drive, since we're headed for the same destination.* **Preposterous** describes what is contrary to reason or sense: *"It would be preposterous to take so grave a step on the advice of an enemy"* (J.A. Froude). **Ridiculous** refers to what inspires ridicule: *"Clara's conceited assumption of a universal interest in her dull children was ridiculous"* (Arnold Bennett). **Ludicrous** applies to what causes scornful laughter: *It is ludicrous to call a simple split-level house a mansion.*

forbid   forbid ban enjoin interdict prohibit proscribe

The central meaning shared by these verbs is "to refuse to allow": *laws that forbid speeding; banned smoking; was enjoined from broadcasting the news item; interdict trafficking in drugs; rules that prohibit swimming in the reservoir; proscribed the importation of raw fruits and vegetables.*

✔ *Antonym:* **permit**

force   force compel coerce constrain oblige obligate

These verbs mean to cause a person or thing to follow a prescribed or dictated course. **Force,** the most general, usually implies the exertion of strength, especially physical power, or the operation of circumstances that permit no alternative to compliance: *Tear gas forced the fugitives out of their hiding place. Lack of funds will eventually force him to look for work.* **Compel** is often interchangeable with *force,* but it applies especially to an act dictated by one in authority: *Say nothing unless you're compelled* *to. His playing compels respect, if not enthusiasm.* **Coerce** invariably implies the use of strength or harsh measures in securing compliance: *"The way in which the man of genius rules is by persuading an efficient minority to coerce an indifferent and self-indulgent majority"* (James Fitzjames Stephen). **Constrain** suggests that one is bound to a course of action by physical or moral means or by the operation of compelling circumstances: *"I am your anointed Queen. I will never be by violence constrained to do anything"* (Elizabeth I). **Oblige** is applicable when compliance is brought about by the operation of authority, necessity, or moral or ethical considerations: *"Work consists of whatever a body is obliged to do"* (Mark Twain). **Obligate** applies when force is exerted by the terms of a legal contract or promise or by the dictates of one's conscience or sense of propriety: *I am obligated to repay the loan.*

foreign   *foreign alien exotic strange*
The central meaning shared by these adjectives is "of, from, or characteristic of another place or part of the world": *a foreign accent; alien customs; exotic birds; moved to a strange city.*

foretell   *foretell augur divine prophesy vaticinate*
The central meaning shared by these verbs is "to tell about something beforehand by or as if by supernatural means": *foretelling the future; augured scandal from a distance; divined the enemy's victory; prophesying a stock-market boom; atrocities vaticinated by the antifascists.*

forgive   *forgive pardon excuse condone*
These verbs mean to refrain from imposing punishment on an offender or demanding satisfaction for an offense. The first three can be used as conventional ways of offering apology, as for minor infractions of social proprieties: *Please forgive me for*

being late. I hope you'll pardon the length of this letter. Excuse me,
but I disagree with you. More strictly, to **forgive** is to grant pardon
without harboring resentment: *"Children begin by loving their*
parents; as they grow older they judge them; sometimes they forgive
them" (Oscar Wilde). **Pardon** more strongly implies release from
the liability for or penalty entailed by an offense: *After the revo-*
lution all political prisoners were pardoned. *"God may pardon you,*
but I never can" (Elizabeth I). To **excuse** is to pass over a mistake
or fault without demanding punishment or redress: *"There are*
some acts of injustice which no national interest can excuse" (J.A.
Froude). To **condone** is to overlook an offense, usually a serious
one; the word often suggests tacit forgiveness: *Failure to protest*
police brutality may indicate a willingness to condone it.

forte *forte métier specialty thing*
The central meaning shared by these nouns is "something at
which a person is particularly skilled": *Writing fiction is her*
forte. The theater is his métier. The professor made the description
of the Semitic languages her specialty. Mountain climbing is really
her thing.

found *found create establish institute organize*
The central meaning shared by these verbs is "to bring something into existence and set it in operation": *founded a colony;*
created a trust fund; establishing an advertising agency; instituted
an annual ball to benefit the homeless; organizing the mortgage-
lending division of a bank.

fragile *fragile breakable frangible delicate brittle*
These adjectives mean easily broken or damaged. **Fragile** applies to objects whose lightness or delicacy of material requires
that they be handled with great care: *a collection of fragile porce-*
lain plates. **Breakable** and **frangible,** which are identical in

meaning, mean capable of being broken but do not necessarily imply inherent weakness: *Even earthenware pottery is breakable. The museum stored all frangible articles in a locked showcase.* **Delicate** refers to what is so soft, tender, or fine as to be susceptible to injury: *The peach is a delicate fruit.* **Brittle** refers to hardness and inelasticity of material that makes something especially likely to fracture or snap when it is subjected to pressure: *brittle bones.*

fragrance   fragrance aroma bouquet perfume redolence scent

The central meaning shared by these nouns is "a pleasant or sweet odor": *the fragrance of lilacs; the aroma of sizzling bacon; the bouquet of a fine Burgundy wine; the perfume of roses; the redolence of freshly brewed coffee; the scent of newly mown hay.*

frank   frank candid outspoken straightforward open

These adjectives mean revealing or disposed to reveal one's thoughts freely and honestly. **Frank** implies forthrightness of expression, sometimes to the point of bluntness: *You can tell me what you think, and you may just as well be frank.* **Candid** stresses openness and sincerity and often suggests refusal to evade difficult or unpleasant issues: *"Save, save, oh save me from the candid friend!"* (George Canning). **Outspoken** usually implies bold lack of reserve: *It is possible to be outspoken without being rude.* **Straightforward** denotes directness of manner and expression: *"George was a straightforward soul . . . 'See here!' he said. 'Are you engaged to anybody?'"* (Booth Tarkington). **Open** suggests freedom from all trace of reserve or secretiveness: *"I will be open and sincere with you"* (Joseph Addison).

freedom   freedom liberty license

These nouns refer to the power to act, speak, or think without externally imposed restraints. **Freedom** is the most general term: *"In giving freedom to the slave, we assure freedom to the free"* (Abraham Lincoln). *"The freedom of the press is one of the great bulwarks of liberty"* (George Mason). **Liberty** is often used interchangeably with *freedom;* often, however, it especially stresses the power of free choice: *liberty of opinion; liberty of worship; at liberty to choose whatever occupation she wishes; "liberty, perfect liberty, to think, feel, do just as one pleases"* (William Hazlitt). **License** sometimes denotes deliberate deviation from normally applicable rules or practices to achieve a desired effect, as in literature or art: *poetic license.* Frequently, though, it denotes undue freedom: *"the intolerable license with which the newspapers break . . . the rules of decorum"* (Edmund Burke).

frighten   *frighten scare alarm terrify terrorize startle panic*

These verbs mean to cause a person to experience fear. **Frighten** and the less formal **scare** are the most widely applicable terms: *"Better be killed than frightened to death"* (Robert Smith Surtees). *Don't let the size of the task scare you.* **Alarm** implies the often sudden onset of fear or apprehension: *Her sudden and inexplicable loss of weight alarmed her doctor.* **Terrify** implies overwhelming, often paralyzing fear: *"The regulars, terrified by the yells of the Indians . . . gathered themselves into a body"* (George Bancroft). **Terrorize** implies fear that intimidates; the word sometimes suggests deliberate coercion: *"premeditated and systematized terrorizing of the civil populations"* (Edith Wharton). **Startle** suggests fear that shocks momentarily and may cause a sudden, involuntary movement of the body: *The clap of thunder startled us.* **Panic** implies sudden frantic fear that often impairs self-control and rationality: *The radio drama was so realistic that it panicked listeners who tuned in after it had begun.*

frown   frown glower lower scowl

The central meaning shared by these verbs is "to contract the brows in displeasure": *frowns when he is annoyed; glowered sullenly at being interrupted; lowering at the rambunctious child; scowled at me when I came home late.*

function   function duty office role

The central meaning shared by these nouns is "the actions and activities assigned to, required of, or expected of a person": *the function of a teacher; a bank clerk's duty; assumed the office of financial adviser; the role of a parent.*

futile   futile barren bootless fruitless unavailing useless vain

The central meaning shared by these adjectives is "producing no result or effect": *a futile effort; a barren search; bootless entreaties; fruitless labors; an unavailing attempt; a useless discussion; vain regrets.*
    ✔ Antonym: **useful**

gather   gather collect assemble congregate accumulate amass

These verbs mean to bring or come together in a group or mass. **Gather** is the most general term and therefore the most widely applicable: *The tour guide gathered the visitors in the hotel lobby. A group of students gathered in front of the administration building to demand divestiture. I gathered sticks as kindling for the fire. Clouds gather before a thunderstorm.* **Collect** is often interchangeable with *gather: A proctor will collect (or gather) the examination papers at the end of the hour. Tears collected (or gathered) in her eyes.* Frequently, however, *collect* refers to the careful selection of like or related things that become part of an organized whole: *collects antiques; collected stamps.* **Assemble** in all of its senses implies that the persons or things involved have a definite and usually close relationship. With respect to persons the term suggests convening out of common interest or purpose: *Assembling an able staff was more difficult than raising the funds to finance the venture. The new legislature will assemble in January.* With respect to things *assemble* implies gathering and fitting together components, as of a structure or machine: *The curator is devoting time and energy to assembling an interesting exhibit of Stone Age artifacts.* **Congregate** refers chiefly to the coming together of a large number of persons or animals: *After the lecture the physicians congregated in the library to compare notes.* **Accumulate** applies to the increase of like or related things over an extended period: *They gradually accumulated enough capital to be financially secure after retirement. Old newspapers and magazines are accumulating in the basement.* **Amass** refers to the collection or accumulation of things, especially valuable things, to form an imposing quantity: *families who amassed great fortunes in the days before income tax.*

gaudy   *gaudy flashy garish loud meretricious tawdry*

The central meaning shared by these adjectives is "tastelessly showy": *a gaudy costume; a flashy ring; garish colors; a loud sport shirt; a meretricious yet stylish book; tawdry ornaments.*

gaze   *gaze stare gape glare peer ogle*

These verbs mean to look long and intently. **Gaze** refers to prolonged looking that is often indicative of wonder, fascination, awe, or admiration: *gazing at the stars; gazed into her eyes.* To **stare** is to gaze fixedly; the word can indicate curiosity, boldness, insolence, or stupidity: *stared at them in disbelief; staring into the distance.* **Gape** suggests a prolonged open-mouthed look reflecting amazement, awe, or lack of intelligence: *tourists gaping at the sights.* To **glare** is to fix another with a hard, piercing stare: *He glared furiously at me when I contradicted him.* To **peer** is to look narrowly, searchingly, and seemingly with difficulty: *peered through her spectacles at the contract.* To **ogle** is to stare in an amorous, usually impertinent manner: *construction workers on their lunch hour ogling passing women.*

general   *general common generic universal*
The central meaning shared by these adjectives is "belonging to, relating to, or affecting the whole": *the general welfare; a common enemy; generic differences between birds and reptiles; universal military conscription.*
   ✔ Antonym: **particular**

gesture   *gesture gesticulation sign signal*
The central meaning shared by these nouns is "an expressive, meaningful bodily motion": *an emphatic gesture of disapproval; frantic gesticulations in an attempt to get help; made a sign for silence; giving the signal to advance.*

giddy   *giddy dizzy vertiginous*
The central meaning shared by these adjectives is "producing a sensation of whirling and a tendency to fall": *a giddy precipice; a dizzy pinnacle; a vertiginous height.*

glad   *glad happy cheerful lighthearted joyful joyous*
These adjectives mean being in or showing good spirits. *Glad* often refers to the feeling that results from the gratification of a wish or from satisfaction with immediate circumstances: *is glad of her success; was glad he had seen her.* "*Some folks rail against other folks, because other folks have what some folks would be glad of*" (Henry Fielding). **Happy** applies to a pleasurable feeling of contentment, as from a sense of fulfillment: "*Ask*

yourself whether you are happy, and you cease to be so" (John Stuart Mill). **Cheerful** suggests the good spirits characteristic of a person who is pleased with something or who has a naturally outgoing nature: *She was as cheerful as anyone confined to a hospital bed could be.* **Lighthearted** stresses the absence of care: *"He whistles as he goes, lighthearted wretch, / Cold and yet cheerful"* (William Cowper). **Joyful** and **joyous** suggest lively, often exultant happiness: *a joyful heart; a joyful state of affairs; joyous laughter; joyous news.*

glib   *glib slick smooth-tongued*
The central meaning shared by these adjectives is "being, marked by, or engaging in ready but often insincere or superficial discourse": *a glib denial; a slick commercial; a smooth-tongued hypocrite.*

gossip   *gossip blab tattle*
The central meaning shared by these verbs is "to engage in or communicate idle, indiscreet talk": *gossiping about the neighbors' domestic problems; can't be trusted with a secret — he always blabs; is disliked by her classmates for tattling on mischief makers.*

gracious   *gracious cordial genial sociable*
The central meaning shared by these adjectives is "marked by kindness, sympathy, and unaffected politeness": *gracious even to unexpected visitors; a cordial welcome; a genial guest; enjoyed a sociable chat.*
   ✔ Antonym: **ungracious**

grand   *grand magnificent imposing stately majestic august grandiose*
These adjectives mean strikingly large in size, scope, or extent. Both *grand* and *magnificent* apply to what is physically or aes-

thetically impressive. **Grand** implies dignity, sweep, or eminence: *buildings on a grand scale; a grand coronation ceremony; a performance in the grand manner.* **Magnificent** suggests splendor, sumptuousness, and grandeur: *a magnificent cathedral; magnificent jewels; a magnificent poem.* **Imposing** describes what impresses by virtue of its size, bearing, or power: *an imposing residence; mountain peaks of imposing height.* **Stately** refers principally to what is dignified and handsome, as in size or proportions: *stately homes; stately columns; a stately oak.* **Majestic** suggests lofty dignity or nobility: *the majestic Alps; a majestic wave of the hand.* **August** describes what inspires solemn reverence or awe, as because of exalted rank or character: *was ushered into the archbishop's august presence.* **Grandiose** refers to what is marked by imposing largeness (*simple but grandiose architecture*); it often suggests pretentiousness, affectation, or pompousness (*grandiose ideas; a grandiose writing style*).

graphic   *graphic lifelike realistic vivid*
The central meaning shared by these adjectives is "strikingly sharp and accurate": *a graphic account of the battle; a lifelike portrait; a realistic description; a vivid recollection of the accident.*

grieve   *grieve lament mourn sorrow*
The central meaning shared by these verbs is "to feel, show, or express grief, sadness, or regret": *grieved over her father's sudden death; lamenting over the decline in academic standards; mourning for lost hopes; sorrowed over the innocent victims of the dictatorship.*
   ✓ *Antonym:* **rejoice**

guide   *guide lead pilot shepherd steer usher*
The central meaning shared by these verbs is "to conduct on or direct to the way": *guided me to my seat; led the troops into battle; a teacher piloting his pupils through the museum; shepherd-*

ing tourists to the chartered bus; steered the applicant to the proper department; ushering a visitor out.

habit   *habit practice custom usage use wont habitude*

These nouns denote patterns of behavior established by continual repetition. **Habit** applies to a way of acting so ingrained in an individual that it is done without conscious thought: *trying to break the smoking habit; has a habit of closing his eyes when he tells a story.* "Habit rules the unreflecting herd" (William Wordsworth). **Practice** denotes a customary, often chosen pattern of individual or group behavior: *It is our practice to eat an early dinner.* "You will find it a very good practice always to verify your references, sir" (Martin Joseph Routh). **Custom** is either individual or group behavior as established by long practice and especially by accepted conventions: *"No written law has ever been more binding than unwritten custom supported by popular opinion"* (Carrie Chapman Catt). **Usage** refers to customary practice that has become an accepted standard for a group and thus regulates individual behavior: *"laws . . . corrected, altered, and amended by acts of parliament and common usage"* (William Blackstone). **Use** and **wont** are terms for the customary and distinctive practice of an individual or a group: *"situations where the use and wont of their fathers no longer meet their necessities"* (J.A. Froude). **Habitude** refers to an individual's habitual disposition to behave in a certain way rather than to a specific act: *"His real habitude gave life and grace / To appertainings and to ornament"* (William Shakespeare).

hamper   *hamper fetter handcuff hobble hog-tie manacle shackle trammel*

The central meaning shared by these verbs is "to restrict the activity or free movement of": *a swimmer hampered by clothing; prisoners fettered by chains; handcuffed by rigid regulations; hob-*

bled by responsibilities; an aspiring leadership that refused to be hog-tied; imagination manacled by fear; shackled by custom; trammeled by debts.

happen *happen befall betide chance occur*

The central meaning shared by these verbs is "to come about": *What would happen if you said no? Who can predict the misery that may befall humankind? Woe betide the poor soldier. It chanced that we succeeded. The accident occurred recently.*

happy *happy fortunate lucky providential*

The central meaning shared by these adjectives is "attended by luck or good fortune": *a happy outcome; a fortunate omen; a lucky guess; a providential recovery.*

✔ Antonym: **unhappy**

harass *harass harry hound badger pester plague bait*

These verbs are compared as they mean to trouble persistently or incessantly. *Harass* and *harry* imply systematic persecution by besieging with repeated annoyances, threats, demands, or misfortunes: *The landlord harassed tenants who were behind in their rent. "Of all the griefs that harass the distress'd"* (Samuel Johnson). *A gang of delinquents harried the storekeeper.* **Hound** suggests unrelenting pursuit to gain a desired end: *Reporters hounded the celebrity for an interview.* To **badger** is to nag or tease persistently: *The child badgered his parents to buy him a new bicycle.* To **pester** is to inflict a succession of petty annoyances: *"How she would have pursued and pestered me with questions and surmises"* (Charlotte Brontë). **Plague** refers to the infliction of tribulations, such as worry or vexation, likened to an epidemic disease: *"As I have no estate, I am plagued with no tenants or stewards"* (Henry Fielding). To **bait** is to torment by or as if by taunting, insulting, or ridiculing: *Hecklers baited the speaker mercilessly.*

harden *harden acclimate acclimatize season toughen*
The central meaning shared by these verbs is "to make resistant to hardship, especially through continued exposure": *was hardened to life on the frontier; is becoming acclimated to the tropical heat; was acclimatized by long hours to overwork; became seasoned to life in prison; toughened by experience and criticism.*
   ✔ Antonym: **soften**

haste *haste celerity dispatch expedition hurry speed*
The central meaning shared by these nouns is "rapidity or promptness of movement or activity": *left the room in haste; a legal system not known for celerity; advanced with all possible dispatch; cleaned up the room with remarkable expedition; worked systematically but without hurry; driving with excessive speed.*
   ✔ Antonym: **deliberation**

healthy *healthy sound wholesome hale robust well hardy vigorous*
These adjectives are compared as they mean being in or indicative of good physical or mental health. **Healthy** stresses the absence of disease and often implies energy and strength: *a rosy, healthy infant. If you exercise regularly and eat properly, you'll stay fit and healthy.* **Sound** emphasizes freedom from injury, imperfection, or impairment: *"The man with the toothache thinks everyone happy whose teeth are sound"* (G.B. Shaw). **Wholesome** suggests appealing healthiness and well-being: *"a broad grin on his ugly wholesome face"* (Archibald Marshall). *"Exercise develops wholesome appetites"* (Louisa May Alcott). **Hale** stresses freedom from infirmity, especially in elderly persons, while **robust** emphasizes healthy strength and ruggedness: *"He is pretty well advanced in years, but hale, robust, and florid"* (Tobias Smollett). **Well** indicates absence of or recovery from sickness: *Her mother is not a well woman.* **Hardy** implies robust and sturdy good

health: *hardy mountaineers of Alpine regions*. **Vigorous** suggests healthy, active energy and strength: *"a vigorous old man, who spent half of his day on horseback"* (W.H. Hudson).

heap *heap bank mound pile stack*

The central meaning shared by these nouns is "a group or collection of things lying one on top of the other": *a heap of old newspapers; a bank of thunder clouds; a mound of boulders; a pile of boxes; a stack of firewood.*

heavy *heavy weighty hefty massive ponderous cumbersome*

These adjectives mean having a relatively great weight. **Heavy** refers to what has great weight (*a heavy boulder; a heavy load*); figuratively it applies to what is burdensome or oppressive to the spirit (*heavy responsibilities; heavy losses*). **Weighty** literally denotes having considerable weight (*a weighty package*); figuratively it describes what is onerous, serious, or important (*the weighty cares of a head of state; a weighty problem; a weighty decision*). **Hefty** refers principally to physical heaviness or brawniness: *a hefty dictionary; a tall, hefty wrestler*. **Massive** describes what is bulky, heavy, solid, and strong: *a massive head; massive marble columns; a massive gold chain*. **Ponderous** refers to what has great mass and weight and usually implies unwieldiness: *ponderous prehistoric beasts*. Figuratively it describes what is complicated, involved, or lacking in grace: *a book with a ponderous plot; a ponderous compliment*. Something **cumbersome** is difficult to move, handle, or deal with because it is heavy, bulky, or clumsy: *cumbersome luggage; a cumbersome writing style.*

help *help aid assist succor*

These verbs mean to contribute to the fulfillment of a need, the furtherance of an effort, or the achievement of a purpose

or end. **Help** and **aid,** the most general, are frequently interchangeable: *a medication that helps (or aids) the digestion; a fine
sense of rhythm that helped (or aided) the student in learning
music. Help,* however, sometimes conveys a stronger suggestion of effectual action: *Nothing will help. I'll help you move the
piano. He helped her out of the car.* **Assist** usually implies making
a secondary contribution or acting as a subordinate: *A team of
kitchen apprentices assisted the chef in preparing the banquet.* **Succor** refers to going to the relief of one in want, difficulty, or distress: *"Mr. Harding thought . . . of the worn-out, aged men he had
succored"* (Anthony Trollope).

heritage   *heritage inheritance legacy tradition*
The central meaning shared by these nouns is "something immaterial, such as a custom, that is passed from one generation
to another": *a heritage of moral uprightness; an inheritance of
knowledge from the past; a legacy of philosophical thought; the tradition of noblesse oblige.*

hide   *hide conceal secrete cache screen bury cloak*
These verbs mean to keep from the sight or knowledge of others. **Hide** and **conceal** are the most general and are often used interchangeably: *I used a throw rug to hide (or conceal) the stain on
the carpet. Don't hide (or conceal) your money in the cookie jar —
it's the first place a thief would look. Fog hid (or concealed) the
mountain. She smiled to hide (or conceal) her hurt feelings. "The
other America, the America of poverty, is hidden today"* (Michael
Harrington). *"The true use of speech is not so much to express our
wants as to conceal them"* (Oliver Goldsmith). **Secrete** and **cache**
involve concealment in a place unknown to others; *cache* often
implies storage for later use: *The lioness secreted her cubs in the
tall grass. The mountain climbers cached their provisions for the descent in a cave they could easily locate but that was inaccessible to*

animals. To **screen** is to shield or block from the view of others by interposing something such as a screen: *Tall shrubs screen the actor's home from the curious.* **Bury** implies covering over so as to conceal: *buried the treasure; buried his hands in his pockets; buried the point of the article in a mass of details.* To **cloak** is to conceal something, such as a thought, a plan, or an intention, by masking or disguising it: *"On previously cloaked issues, the Soviets have suddenly become forthcoming"* (John McLaughlin).

honesty *honesty honor integrity probity rectitude*
These nouns denote the quality of being upright in principle and action. **Honesty** implies truthfulness, fairness in dealing with others, and refusal to engage in fraud, deceit, or dissembling: *Honesty is the best policy.* **Honor** implies principled uprightness of character and a worthy adherence to a strict moral or ethical code: *"Never give in except to convictions of honor and good sense"* (Winston S. Churchill). **Integrity** is moral soundness, especially as it is revealed in dealings that test steadfastness of purpose, responsibility, or trust: *"Integrity without knowledge is weak and useless, and knowledge without integrity is dangerous and dreadful"* (Samuel Johnson). **Probity** is proven integrity: *A judge must be a person of unquestioned probity.* **Rectitude** is moral righteousness both in principle and in practice: *"The name of Brutus would be a guaranty to the people of rectitude of intention"* (J.A. Froude).

humane *humane compassionate humanitarian merciful*
The central meaning shared by these adjectives is "marked or motivated by concern with the alleviation of suffering": *a humane physician; compassionate toward disadvantaged people; released the prisoner for humanitarian reasons; is merciful to the repentant.*
   ✔ *Antonym:* **inhumane**

idea   *idea thought notion concept conception*
These nouns refer to what is formed or represented in the mind as the product of mental activity. **Idea** has the widest range: *Fruit is not her idea of a dessert. Don't get any ideas about revenge. "Human history is in essence a history of ideas"* (H.G. Wells). **Thought** is applied to what is distinctively intellectual and thus especially to what is produced by contemplation and reasoning as distinguished from mere perceiving, feeling, or willing: *Quiet — she's trying to collect her thoughts. I have no thought of going to Europe. "Language is the dress of thought"* (Samuel Johnson). **Notion** often refers to a vague, general, or even fanciful idea: *"She certainly has some notion of drawing"* (Rudyard Kipling). **Concept** and **conception** are applied to mental formulations on a broad scale: *He seems to have absolutely no concept of time. "Every succeeding scientific discovery makes greater nonsense of old-time conceptions of sovereignty"* (Anthony Eden).

imitate   *imitate copy mimic ape parody simulate*
These verbs mean to follow something or someone taken as a model. To **imitate** is to act like or follow a pattern or style set by another: *The adults drank their tea in a ceremonious manner, and the children imitated them. The decorator had the wood paneling painted to imitate marble. "Art imitates Nature"* (Richard Franck). To **copy** is to duplicate an original as precisely as possible: *tried to copy her cultivated accent; a building that evokes the neoclassic style of architecture without copying it.* To **mimic** is to make a close imitation, as of another's actions, speech, or mannerisms, often with an intent to ridicule: *"fresh carved cedar, mimicking a glade / Of palm and plaintain"* (John Keats). *In private the candidate mimicked his opponent's stammer.* To **ape** is to follow another's lead slavishly but often with an absurd result: *"Those* [superior] *states of mind do not come from aping an alien culture"* (John Russell). To **parody** is either to imitate

with comic effect or to attempt a serious imitation and fail: *"All these peculiarities [of Samuel Johnson's literary style] have been imitated by his admirers and parodied by his assailants"* (Thomas Macaulay). To **simulate** is to feign or falsely assume the appearance or character of something: *"I . . . lay there simulating death"* (W.H. Hudson).

immaterial   *immaterial incorporeal insubstantial*
metaphysical spiritual
The central meaning shared by these adjectives is "lacking material body, form, or substance": *immaterial apparitions; an incorporeal spirit; imaginary and insubstantial victories; metaphysical forces; spiritual beings.*
    ✔ Antonym: **material**

impact   *impact repercussion*
The central meaning shared by these nouns is "a strong effect exerted by one person or thing on another": *the far-reaching impact of an oil embargo; a strike that had dire repercussions.*

importance   *importance consequence moment*
significance import weight
These nouns refer to the state or quality of being significant, influential, or worthy of note or esteem. **Importance** is the most general term: *The importance of a proper diet in maintaining health should not be disregarded. In this profession, training and experience are of equal importance. Cartoonists are considered by some to be artists of secondary importance.* **Consequence** is especially applicable to persons or things of notable rank or position (*scholars of consequence*) and to what is important because of its possible outcome, result, or effect (*Changes in the tax law are of consequence to all investors*). **Moment** implies importance or consequence that is readily apparent: *Heads of*

state are confronted with making decisions of great moment. **Significance** *and* **import** refer to the quality of something, often not obvious, that gives it special meaning or value: *Your vote can be of real significance in the outcome of the election. The works of John Locke are of great social import.* **Weight** is frequently used when a personal evaluation or judgment of importance is suggested: *"The popular faction at Rome . . . was led by men of weight"* (J.A. Froude).

impression *impression impress imprint print stamp*

The central meaning shared by these nouns is "a visible mark made on a surface by pressure": *an impression of a notary's seal on wax; the impress of bare feet in the sand; a medal marked with the imprint of a bald eagle; a tar driveway with the print of automobile tires; a gold ingot with the refiner's stamp.*

improve *improve better help ameliorate*

These verbs mean to advance to a more desirable, valuable, or excellent state. **Improve** and **better**, the most general terms, are often interchangeable: *improve* (or *better*) *the mind through study; had a haircut to improve* (or *better*) *his appearance; practicing to improve* (or *better*) *her golf game. It is sometimes difficult for disadvantaged people to improve* (or *better*) *their situation in life.* **Help** in this sense usually implies limited relief or change for the better: *Gargling helps a sore throat.* To **ameliorate** is to improve or better circumstances that demand change: *Volunteers could do little to ameliorate conditions in the refugee camp.*

incisive *incisive trenchant biting cutting crisp clear-cut*

These adjectives are synonymous when they refer to keenness and forcefulness of thought, expression, or intellect. **Incisive** and **trenchant** suggest penetration to the heart of a subject and clear, sharp, and vigorous expression: *an incisive and piquant style of writing; trenchant wit*. **Biting** and **cutting** apply to penetration and discernment that often have a sarcastic or sardonic quality capable of wounding or stinging: *"Biting remarks revealed her attitude of contempt"* (D.H. Lawrence). *"He can say the driest, most cutting things in the quietest of tones"* (Charlotte Brontë). **Crisp** suggests clarity, conciseness, and briskness: *a crisp retort; crisp banter*. **Clear-cut** specifies distinctness and sharpness of definition: *The wording of the lease is so clear-cut that no one could possibly misinterpret its meaning*.

increase   *increase expand enlarge extend augment multiply*

These verbs mean to make or become greater or larger. **Increase** applies most widely; it sometimes suggests steady growth: *"Absence diminishes mediocre passions and increases great ones"* (La Rochefoucauld). *The mayor's political influence rapidly increased*. To **expand** is to increase in size, area, volume, bulk, or range: *He does exercises to expand his chest*. *"Work expands so as to fill the time available for its completion"* (C. Northcote Parkinson). **Enlarge** refers to expansion in size, extent, capacity, or scope: *The landowner enlarged her property by repeated purchases. Our group of friends is enlarging by leaps and bounds*. To **extend** is to lengthen in space or time or to broaden in range, as of application: *The transit authority extended the subway line to the next town. The baseball season may be extended. "His [Jefferson's] eye, like his mind, sought an extended view"* (Dumas Malone). **Augment** usually applies to what is already developed or well under way: *augmented her collection of books; depression that augments with each visit to the hospital*. To **multiply** is to increase in number, especially by propagation or procreation: *"As for my cats, they multiplied"* (Daniel Defoe). *"May thy days be multiplied!"* (Sir Walter Scott).

indicate   *indicate argue attest bespeak betoken testify witness*
The central meaning shared by these verbs is "to give grounds for supposing or inferring the existence or presence of something": *a fever indicating illness; a shabby house that argues poverty; paintings that attest the artist's genius; disorder that bespeaks negligence; melting snows that betoken spring floods; a comment testifying ignorance; a stunned silence that witnessed his astonishment.*

indispensable   *indispensable essential necessary needful requisite*
The central meaning shared by these adjectives is "pressingly needed": *foods indispensable to good nutrition; funds essential to the completion of the project; necessary tools and materials; provided them with all things needful; lacking the requisite qualifications for the position.*
   ✔ *Antonym:* **dispensable**

infinite   *infinite boundless eternal illimitable sempiternal*
The central meaning shared by these adjectives is "being without beginning or end": *infinite wisdom; boundless ambition; eternal beauty; illimitable space; sempiternal truth.*
   ✔ *Antonym:* **finite**

inquiry   *inquiry inquest inquisition investigation probe research*
The central meaning shared by these nouns is "a quest for knowledge, data, or truth": *filed an inquiry about the lost shipment; holding an inquest to determine whether the dead man had been murdered; refused to cooperate with the inquisition into her political activities; a criminal investigation; a probe into alleged police corruption; scientific research.*

intelligent *intelligent right brilliant knowing quick-witted smart intellectual*

These adjectives mean having or showing mental keenness. *Intelligent* usually implies the ability to cope with demands arising from novel situations and new problems and to use the power of reasoning and inference effectively: *The most intelligent students do additional reading to supplement the material in the textbook.* **Bright** implies quickness or ease in learning: *Some children are brighter in one subject than in another.* **Brilliant** suggests unusually impressive mental acuteness: *"The dullard's envy of brilliant men is always assuaged by the suspicion that they will come to a bad end"* (Max Beerbohm). **Knowing** implies the possession of knowledge, information, or understanding: *Knowing furniture collectors bought American antiques before the prices soared.* **Quick-witted** suggests mental alertness and prompt response: *We were successful not because we were quick-witted but because we persevered.* **Smart** refers to quick intelligence and often a ready capability for taking care of one's own interests: *The smartest lawyers avoid the appearance of manipulating juries.* **Intellectual** stresses the working of the intellect and especially implies the capacity to grasp difficult or abstract concepts: *The scholar's interest in the intellectual and analytical aspect of music didn't prevent her from enjoying concerts.*

intention *intention intent purpose goal end aim object objective*

These nouns refer to what one intends to do or achieve. *Intention* simply signifies a course of action that one proposes to follow: *It is not my intention to argue with you.* **Intent** more strongly implies deliberateness: *The executor tried to comply with the intent of the testator.* **Purpose** strengthens the idea of resolution or determination: *"His purpose was to discover how long these guests intended to stay"* (Joseph Conrad). **Goal** may suggest an idealistic or even a remote purpose: *"Black Power . . . is a call for black people to begin to define their own goals"* (Stokely Carmichael and Charles V. Hamilton). **End** suggests a long-range goal: *It has been said that the end justifies the means.* **Aim** stresses the direction one's efforts take in pursuit of an end: *The aim of every performing artist is to achieve perfection of execution.* An **object** is an end that one tries to carry out: *"The chief object of the English was to establish . . . a great empire on the Continent"* (Thomas Macaulay). **Objective** often implies that the end or goal can be reached: *"A major objective [of political liberalism] is the protection of the economic weak"* (Wayne Morse).

interfere   *interfere meddle tamper*

These verbs are compared as they mean to put oneself forward and intervene in the affairs of others when unasked to do so and often in an impudent or indiscreet manner. *Interfere* and *meddle* are sometimes interchangeable. **Meddle,** however, is the stronger in implying unwanted, unwarranted, or unnecessary intrusion: *"wholly unacquainted with the world in which they are so fond of meddling"* (Edmund Burke). It is somewhat weaker than **interfere** in implying action that seriously hampers, hinders, or frustrates: *"It was his peculiar doctrine that a man has a perfect right to interfere by force with the slaveholder, in order to rescue the slave"* (Henry David Thoreau). To **tamper** is to interfere by making unsought, unwelcome, often destructive changes or by trying to influence another in an improper way: *"a large number of persons accused of . . . tampering with ballot boxes"* (James Bryce). *"He began another practice, to tamper with the justices"* (John Strype).

irrelevant   *irrelevant extraneous immaterial impertinent*

The central meaning shared by these adjectives is "not pertinent to the subject under consideration": *an irrelevant com-*

ment; a question extraneous to the discussion; an objection that is immaterial after the fact; mentioned several impertinent facts before finally coming to the point.

✓ Antonym: **relevant**

isolate   *isolate insulate seclude segregate sequester*

The central meaning shared by these verbs is "to separate from others": *a mountain village that is isolated from all other communities; trying to insulate herself from the chaos surrounding her; a famous actor who was secluded from public scrutiny; characteristics that segregate leaders from followers; sequestering a jury during its deliberations.*

item   *item detail particular*

The central meaning shared by these nouns is "an individual, often specialized element of a whole": *a shopping list with numerous items; discussed all the details of their trip; furnished the particulars of the accident.*

jealous   *jealous covetous envious*

The central meaning shared by these adjectives is "resentfully or painfully desirous of another's advantages": *jealous of her friend's success; covetous of his neighbor's possessions; envious of their art collection.*

jerk   *jerk snap twitch wrench yank*

The central meaning shared by these verbs is "to move with a sudden short, quick motion": *jerked the rope and broke it; a lock snapping shut; her mouth twitching with suppressed amusement; wrenched the stick out of his hand; yanked the door open.*

join   *join combine unite link connect relate associate*

These verbs mean to fasten or affix or become fastened or affixed. *Join* applies to the physical contact, connection, or union of at least two separate things and to the coming together of persons, as into a group: *The children joined hands. Join the panels of fabric at the selvages.* "*Join the union, girls, and together say* Equal Pay for Equal Work" (Susan B. Anthony). *Combine* suggests the mixing or merging of components, often for a specific or shared purpose: *The cook combined whipped cream, sugar, and vanilla to make a topping for the compote.* "*When bad men combine, the good must associate*" (Edmund Burke). *Unite* stresses the coherence or oneness of the persons or things joined: *Can strips of plastic be united with epoxy? The attack on their country united squabbling political factions in a common purpose.* *Link* and *connect* imply a firm attachment in which individual components nevertheless retain their identities: *linked poverty and unemployment to the social unrest besetting the city. The chief of police is in no way connected with the scandal.* *Relate* refers to connection of persons through marriage or kinship (*Though they have the same surname, the two are not even distantly related*) or of things through logical association (*The two events seem to be related*). *Associate* usually implies a relationship of persons as partners or allies: *His daughter is associated with him in the family business.* It can also refer to a relationship of things that are similar or complementary or that have a connection in one's thoughts: *I can forgive his bluntness because it is associated with a basic kindliness of spirit.*

judge   *judge arbitrator arbiter referee umpire*

These nouns denote persons who make decisions that determine points at issue. A *judge* is one capable of making rational, dispassionate, and wise decisions: *The members of the jury are the sole judges of what the truth is in this case.* An *arbitrator* works to settle controversies and is either appointed or derives authority from the consent of the disputants, who choose him or her or approve the selection: *The mayor appointed an experienced arbitrator to mediate between the sides and resolve the transit strike.* An **arbiter** is one who may or may not have official status but whose opinion or judgment is recognized as being unassailable or binding: *a critic who considers himself the supreme arbiter of literary taste.* Less often *arbiter* is used interchangeably with *arbitrator.* A **referee** is an attorney appointed by a court to make a determination of a case or to investigate and report on it (*a bankruptcy case handled by a referee*), and an **umpire** is a person appointed to settle an issue that arbitrators are unable to resolve (*umpires studying complex tax cases*). In sports *referee* and *umpire* refer to officials who enforce the rules and settle points at issue.

justify   *justify warrant*

The central meaning shared by these verbs is "to be a proper or sufficient reason for": *an angry outburst justified by extreme provocation; drastic measures not warranted by the circumstances.*

keep   *keep retain withhold reserve*

These verbs mean to have and maintain in one's possession or control. **Keep** is the most general: *We received a tempting offer for the house but decided to keep it. I don't know which is more difficult — to earn money or to keep it.* **Retain** means to continue to hold, especially in the face of possible loss: *"The executor . . . is allowed to pay himself first, by retaining in his hands so much as his debt amounts to"* (William Blackstone). **Withhold** implies reluctance or refusal to give, grant, or allow: *The tenants withheld their rent until the landlord repaired the boiler.* To **reserve** is to hold back for the future or for a special purpose: *I will reserve my questions for the discussion period. The farmer reserved two acres for an orchard.*

knowledge *knowledge information learning erudition lore scholarship*

These nouns refer to what is known, as by having been acquired through study or experience. *Knowledge* is the broadest; it includes facts and ideas, understanding, and the totality of what is known: *"A knowledge of Greek thought and life, and of the arts in which the Greeks expressed their thought and sentiment, is essential to high culture"* (Charles Eliot Norton). *"Science is organized knowledge"* (Herbert Spencer). *Information* is usually construed as being narrower in scope than *knowledge*; it often implies a collection of facts and data: *"Obviously, a man's judgment cannot be better than the information on which he has based it"* (Arthur Hays Sulzberger). *Learning* usually refers to knowledge that is gained by schooling and study: *"Learning is not attained by chance, it must be sought for with ardor and attended to with diligence"* (Abigail Adams). *Erudition* implies profound knowledge, often in a specialized area: *"Some have criticized his poetry as elitist, unnecessarily impervious to readers who do not share his erudition"* (Elizabeth Kastor). *Lore* is usually applied to knowledge about a particular subject that is gained through tradition or anecdote: *Early peoples passed on plant and animal lore through legend.* *Scholarship* is the knowledge of a scholar whose mastery of a particular area of learning is reflected in the scope, thoroughness, and quality of his or her work: *a book that gives ample evidence of the author's scholarship.*

lack *lack want need*

These verbs mean to be without something, especially something that is necessary or desirable. *Lack* emphasizes the absence of the thing in question or the inadequacy of its supply: *She lacks the money to buy new shoes. The plant died because it lacked moisture. What he lacks in courage he compensates for in bravado.* *Want* and *need* stress the urgent necessity for filling a void or remedying an inadequacy: *"Her pens were uniformly bad and wanted fixing"* (Bret Harte). *I need help. The garden needs care.* *"All his faculties seemed to be needed to guide him over and past obstructions"* (Stephen Crane).

large   large big great

The central meaning shared by these adjectives is "being notably above the average in size or magnitude": *a large city; a large sum of money; a big brown barn; a big sweep of open lawn; a great old oak tree; a great ocean liner.*
  ✔ Antonym: **small**

last   last final terminal eventual ultimate

These adjectives mean coming after all others in chronology or sequence. *Last* applies to what comes at the end of a series, as of like things: *the last day of the month; the last piece of candy. The last time I saw them they were fine.* Something **final** comes at the end of a progression or process; the term stresses the definitiveness and decisiveness of the conclusion: *This is our final offer. The decision of the board of trustees will be final.* *"I believe that unarmed truth and unconditional love will have the final word in reality"* (Martin Luther King, Jr.). **Terminal** applies to what marks or forms a limit or boundary, as in space, time, or development: *In order to increase its freight revenues the railroad chose as its terminal city a town with a large harbor.* Something **eventual** will inevitably come about as a result of a particular circumstance or contingency: *If prices continue to spiral out of control, it is reasonable to expect the eventual collapse of the stock market.* **Ultimate** applies to what concludes a series, process or progression, to what constitutes a final result or objective, and to what is most distant or remote, as in time: *the ultimate sonata of that opus; our ultimate goal; the ultimate effect; an ultimate authority.* *"I know no safe depository of the ulti-*

mate powers of the society but the people themselves" (Thomas Jefferson).

lazy   *lazy fainéant idle indolent slothful*

The central meaning shared by these adjectives is "not disposed to exertion, work, or activity": *too lazy to wash the breakfast dishes; fainéant aristocrats; an idle drifter; a good-natured but indolent hanger-on; slothful employees.*

lean¹   *lean slant incline slope tilt tip*

The central meaning shared by these verbs is "to depart or cause to depart from true vertical or horizontal": *leaned against the railing; rays of the setting sun slanting through the window; inclined her head toward the speaker; a sloping driveway; tilted her hat at a rakish angle; tipped his chair against the wall.*

lean²   *lean spare skinny scrawny lank lanky rawboned gaunt*

These adjectives mean lacking excess flesh. **Lean** emphasizes absence of fat: *The farmer tried to fatten the lean cattle for market.* **Spare** sometimes suggests trimness and good muscle tone: *"an old man, very tall and spare, with an ascetic aspect"* (William H. Mallock). *She has the spare figure of a marathon runner.* **Skinny** and **scrawny** imply unattractive thinness, as that associated with undernourishment: *The child has skinny, freckled legs with prominent knees.* *"He* [had] *a long, scrawny neck that rose out of a very low collar"* (Winston Churchill). **Lank** describes one who is thin and tall, and **lanky** one who is thin, tall, and ungraceful: *"He was . . . exceedingly lank, with narrow shoulders"* (Washington Irving). *She was transformed from a lanky adolescent into a willowy young woman.* **Rawboned** suggests a thin, bony, gangling build: *a rawboned cowhand with a weather-beaten, tanned face.* **Gaunt** implies thinness and boniness and a haggard appearance; it may suggest illness or hardship: *a white-haired pioneer, her face gaunt from overwork and worry.*

learned   *learned erudite scholarly*
The central meaning shared by these adjectives is "having or showing profound knowledge": *a learned jurist; an erudite professor; a scholarly treatise.*

letter   *letter epistle missive note*
The central meaning shared by these nouns is "a written communication directed to another": *received a letter of complaint; the Epistles of the New Testament; a missive of condolence; a thank-you note.*

lie   *lie equivocate fib palter prevaricate*
The central meaning shared by these verbs is "to evade or depart from the truth": *a witness who lied under oath; didn't equivocate about her real purpose in coming; fibbed to escape being scolded; paltering with an irate customer; didn't prevaricate but answered forthrightly and honestly.*

lift   *lift raise rear elevate hoist heave boost*
These verbs mean to move something from a lower to a higher level or position. **Lift** sometimes stresses the expenditure of effort: *a trunk too heavy to lift; requires three men to lift the piano.* **Raise** often implies movement to an approximately vertical position: *raised the window slightly; raising a monument to the war dead.* **Rear** is frequently interchangeable with *raise*: *rear a ladder; rear a flagpole.* "Her family reared a sumptuous mausoleum over her remains" (Thomas Macaulay). **Elevate** is sometimes synonymous with the preceding terms (*used two pillows to keep his head elevated*), but it more often suggests exalting, ennobling, or raising morally or intellectually: "*A generous and elevated*

mind is distinguished by nothing more certainly than an eminent degree of curiosity" (Samuel Johnson). **Hoist** is applied principally to the lifting of heavy objects, often by mechanical means: *hoist a sunken ship; uses a crane to hoist the construction beams.* To **heave** is to lift or raise with great effort or force: *heaved the pack onto his back.* **Boost** suggests upward movement effected by or as if by pushing from below: *boosted the child into the saddle; boost sales; boost morale.*

likeness   likeness similarity similitude resemblance analogy affinity

These nouns denote agreement or conformity, as in character, nature, or appearance between persons or things. **Likeness** implies close agreement: *"There is a devil haunts thee in the likeness of a fat old man"* (William Shakespeare). *It was your uncanny likeness to my sister that made me stare at you.* **Similarity** and **similitude** suggest agreement only in some respects or to some degree: *They were drawn to each other by similarity of interests. "A striking similitude between the brother and sister now first arrested my attention"* (Edgar Allan Poe). **Resemblance** refers to similarity in appearance or in external or superficial details: *"The child . . . bore a remarkable resemblance to her grandfather"* (Lytton Strachey). **Analogy** is similarity, as of properties or functions, between unlike things that are otherwise not comparable: *The operation of a computer presents an interesting analogy to the working of the human brain.* **Affinity** is likeness deriving from kinship or from the possession of shared or compatible properties, characteristics, or sympathies: *There is a discernible stylistic affinity between the compositions of Brahms and those of Dvořák.*

limp   limp flabby flaccid floppy

The central meaning shared by these adjectives is "lacking in

stiffness or firmness": *a limp shirt collar; flabby, wrinkled flesh; flaccid cheeks; a floppy hat brim.*
  ✓ Antonym: **firm**

logical *logical analytic ratiocinative rational*
The central meaning shared by these adjectives is "capable of or reflecting the capability for correct and valid reasoning": *a logical mind; an analytic thinker; the ratiocinative process; a rational being.*
  ✓ Antonym: **illogical**

loud *loud earsplitting stentorian strident*
The central meaning shared by these adjectives is "marked by or producing great volume and often disagreeable intensity of sound": *loud trumpets; earsplitting shrieks; stentorian tones; strident, screeching brakes.*
  ✓ Antonym: **soft**

love *love affection devotion fondness infatuation*
These nouns denote feelings of warm personal attachment or strong attraction to another person. *Love* suggests a more intense feeling than that associated with the other words of this group: *married for love.* *Affection* is a less ardent and more unvarying feeling of tender regard: *parental affection.* *Devotion* is earnest, affectionate dedication; it implies a more selfless, often more abiding feeling than *love: The devotion of the aged couple is inspiring.* *Fondness* is strong liking or affection: *showed their fondness for their grandchildren by financing their education.* *Infatuation* is foolish or extravagant attraction, often of short duration: *Their infatuation blinded them to the fundamental differences in their points of view.*

luxury *luxury extravagance frill*
The central meaning shared by these nouns is "something de-

sirable that is not a necessity": *a fur coat that is a real luxury; antique porcelain, an extravagance we should have resisted; caviar, smoked salmon, and other culinary frills.*

✔ Antonym: **necessity**

makeshift   *makeshift expedient resort stopgap*
The central meaning shared by these nouns is "something used as a substitute when other means fail or are not available": *lacked a cane but used a stick as a makeshift; exhausted every expedient and finally filed suit; will use force only as a last resort; a crate serving as a stopgap for a chair.*

malleable   *malleable ductile plastic pliable pliant*
The central meaning shared by these adjectives is "capable of being shaped, bent, or drawn out": *malleable metals such as gold; ductile copper; plastic substances such as wax; soaked the leather to make it pliable; pliant molten glass.*

manipulate   *manipulate exploit maneuver*
The central meaning shared by these verbs is "to influence, manage, use, or control to one's advantage by artful or indirect means": *manipulates people into helping him; exploiting her friends; maneuvering to gain an edge over their corporate competitors.*

mark   *mark brand label tag ticket*
The central meaning shared by these verbs is "to place a mark of identification on": *marked the furs with their place of origin; brand cattle; labeled the boxes on the shelf; tagging suitcases; ticketed the new merchandise.*

mature   *mature age develop ripen*
The central meaning shared by these verbs is "to bring or come to full development or maximum excellence": *maturing*

the wines in vats; aged the brandy for 100 years; developed the fla-vor slowly; fruits that were ripened on the vine.

mean¹   mean denote import signify

The central meaning shared by these verbs is "to convey a par-ticular idea": *what does the word* serendipity *mean? The prefix* pro– *may denote "earlier" or "anterior." Philadelphia is the city of brotherly love; that is what its name imports. A crown signifies royal power.*

mean²   mean low base abject ignoble sordid

These adjectives mean lacking in the elevation or dignity or falling short of the standards befitting human beings. **Mean** suggests pettiness; it may also connote traits such as spite or niggardliness: *"chok'd with ambition of the meaner sort"* (Shake-speare). *"Never ascribe to an opponent motives meaner than your own"* (J.M. Barrie). Something **low** violates standards of morality, ethics, or propriety: *low cunning; a low trick.* **Base** suggests a contemptible, mean-spirited, or selfish lack of human decency: *"that liberal obedience, without which your army would be a base rabble"* (Edmund Burke). **Abject** means brought low in condition; it often indicates starkness or hopelessness: *abject submission; abject poverty.* **Ignoble** means lacking those qualities, such as elevated moral character, that give human beings distinc-tion of mind and soul: *"For my part I think it a less evil that some criminals should escape than that the government should play an ignoble part"* (Oliver Wendell Holmes, Jr.). **Sordid** suggests foul, repulsive degradation: *"It is through art . . . that we can shield ourselves from the sordid perils of actual existence"* (Oscar Wilde).

meaning   meaning acceptation import sense significance signification

The central meaning shared by these nouns is "the idea that is conveyed by something, such as a word, an action, a gesture, or a situation": *Synonyms are words that have the same or approximately the same meaning. In one of its acceptations* value *is a technical term in music. The import of his statement is ambiguous. The term* anthropomorphism *has only one sense. The significance of a green traffic light is generally understood. Scientists have been unable to determine the signification of most Etruscan inscriptions.*

memory   *memory remembrance recollection reminiscence*
These nouns denote the act or an instance of remembering, or something remembered. **Memory** is the faculty of retaining and reviving impressions or recalling past experiences: *He has a bad memory for facts and figures.* "*Even memory is not necessary for love*" (Thornton Wilder). The word also applies to something recalled to the mind, a sense in which it often suggests a personal, cherished quality: "*My earliest memories were connected with the South*" (Thomas B. Aldrich). **Remembrance** most often denotes the process or act of recalling: *The remembrance of his humiliation was almost too painful to bear.* **Recollection** is sometimes interchangeable with *memory*: *My recollection of the incident differs from yours.* Often, though, the term suggests a deliberate, concentrated effort to remember: *After a few minutes' recollection she produced the answer.* **Reminiscence** is the act or process of recollecting past experiences or events within one's personal knowledge: "*Her mind seemed wholly taken up with reminiscences of past gaiety*" (Charlotte Brontë). When the word refers to what is remembered, it may involve the sharing of the recollection with another or others: *They spent some time in reminiscence before turning to the business that had brought them together.*

mercy   *mercy leniency lenity clemency charity*
These nouns mean kind, forgiving, or sympathetic and hu-

mane treatment of or disposition toward others. **Mercy** is compassionate forbearance: *"We hand folks over to God's mercy, and show none ourselves"* (George Eliot). **Leniency** and **lenity** imply mildness, gentleness, and often a tendency to reduce the severity or harshness of punishment: *"When you have gone too far to recede, do not sue [appeal] to me for leniency"* (Charles Dickens). *"His Majesty gave many marks of his great lenity, often . . . endeavoring to extenuate your crimes"* (Jonathan Swift). **Clemency** is mercy shown by one in a position of authority or power and especially by one charged with administering justice: *The judge believed in clemency for youthful offenders.* **Charity** is goodwill and benevolence, especially as it manifests itself in kindly forbearance in judging others: *"But how shall we expect charity towards others, when we are uncharitable to ourselves?"* (Thomas Browne).

miscellaneous   miscellaneous heterogeneous motley mixed varied assorted

These adjectives mean consisting of a number of different kinds. **Miscellaneous** implies a varied, often haphazard combination: *The shop carries suits, coats, shirts, and miscellaneous accessories.* *"My reading . . . had been extremely miscellaneous"* (William Godwin). **Heterogeneous** emphasizes diversity and dissimilarity: *The population of the United States is vast and heterogeneous.* **Motley** emphasizes difference to the point of incongruity and discordance and is sometimes used derogatorily: *The audience consisted of a motley crowd of property owners, renters, and drifters.* **Mixed** suggests a combination of differing but not necessarily conflicting elements: *The orchestra offered a mixed program of baroque and contemporary fare.* **Varied** stresses absence of uniformity: *"The assembly was large and varied, containing clergy and laity, men and women"* (Nicholas P.S. Wiseman). **Assorted** often suggests the purposeful arrangement of different but complementary elements: *The centerpiece is a luxuriant arrangement of assorted garden flowers.*

mix   *mix blend mingle coalesce merge amalgamate fuse*
These verbs mean to put into or come together in one mass so that constituent parts or elements are diffused or commingled. **Mix** is the least specific, implying only components capable of being combined: *mix water and wine; motives that were mixed. Greed and charity don't mix.* To **blend** is to mix intimately and harmoniously so that the components shade into each other, losing some or all of their original definition: *blended mocha and java coffee beans; snow-covered mountains blending into the clouds.* **Mingle** implies combination without loss of individual characteristics: *"Respect was mingled with surprise"* (Sir Walter Scott). *"His companions mingled freely and joyously with the natives"* (Washington Irving). **Coalesce** involves a union, often slowly achieved, with a distinct new identity: *Indigenous peoples and conquerors gradually coalesced into the present-day population.* **Merge** implies the absorption of one entity into another with resultant homogeneity: *Tradition and innovation are merged in this new composition. Twilight merged into night.* **Amalgamate** implies the integration of elements: *"The four sentences of the original are amalgamated into two"* (William Minto). **Fuse** emphasizes an enduring union, as that formed by heating metals, strongly marked by the merging of parts: *"He diffuses a tone and spirit of unity, that blends, and (as it were) fuses, each into each"* (Samuel Taylor Coleridge).

mixture   *mixture blend admixture compound composite amalgam*
These nouns refer to a combination produced by mixing. **Mixture** has the widest application: *a mixture of tea and honey; yarn that is a mixture of nylon and cotton.* "He showed a curious mix-

ture of eagerness and terror" (Francis Parkman). **Blend** denotes an intimate, harmonious mixture in which the original components lose their distinctness: *The novel is a fascinating blend of illusion and reality.* **Admixture** suggests that one of the components of the mixture is dissimilar to the others: *The essential oil in the perfume contains a large admixture of alcohol.* A **compound** is a combination of elements or parts that together constitute a new and independent entity: *The word* houseboat *is a compound. Creative genius is a compound made up of exceptional intellect and superior imagination.* A **composite** usually lacks the unity of a compound since the components may not wholly lose their identities: *The suite is a composite of themes for various parts of the opera.* **Amalgam** implies an intimate union of diverse elements likened to an alloy of mercury and another metal: *an amalgam of charming agreeability and indefatigable humor.*

moderate   *moderate qualify temper*
The central meaning shared by these verbs is "to make less extreme or intense": *moderated the severity of the rebuke; qualified her criticism; admiration tempered with fear.*
    ✔ Antonym: **intensify**

moment   *moment instant minute second jiffy flash*
These nouns denote a brief interval of time. A **moment** is an indeterminately short but not insignificant period: *I'll be with you in a moment. It took him a moment to answer.* **Instant** is a period of time almost too brief to detect; it implies haste and often urgency: *She hesitated for just an instant. Stop it this instant.* **Minute** and **second,** used strictly, refer to measured intervals of time; often, though, *minute* is interchangeable with *moment* (*Wait a minute. The plane will be arriving in a minute*), and *second* with *instant* (*I slipped out of the room for a few seconds to*

turn the oven on). **Jiffy** and **flash** occur principally in combinations preceded by *in a*; *in a jiffy* means in a short space of time, while *in a flash* suggests the almost imperceptible duration of a flash of light: *"He was on his stool in a jiffy, driving away with his pen"* (Charles Dickens). *She was on her feet in a flash when the doorbell rang.*

monopolize   *monopolize absorb consume*
engross preoccupy
The central meaning shared by these verbs is "to have exclusive possession or control of": *desirable housing monopolized by the wealthy; study that absorbs all her time; was consumed by fear; engrossed herself in her reading; a mind that was preoccupied with financial worries.*

mood   *mood humor temper*
These nouns refer to a temporary state of mind or feeling. **Mood** is the most inclusive term: *a contentious mood; a cheerful mood.* *"I was in no mood to laugh and talk with strangers"* (Mary Wollstonecraft Shelley). **Humor** often implies a state of mind resulting from one's characteristic disposition or temperament; it sometimes suggests fitfulness or variability: *The humor of the Cabinet shifted after the scandal was exposed.* *"All which had been done . . . was the effect not of humor, but of system"* (Edmund Burke). **Temper** most often refers to a state of mind marked by irritability or anger: *"The nation was in such a temper that the smallest spark might raise a flame"* (Thomas Macaulay).

moral   *moral ethical virtuous righteous*
These adjectives mean in accord with principles or rules of right or good conduct. **Moral** applies to personal character and behavior, especially sexual conduct, measured against prevailing standards of rectitude: *"The fact that man knows right from*

wrong proves his intellectual *superiority to the other creatures; but the fact that he can do wrong proves his* moral *inferiority to any creature that* cannot" (Mark Twain). **Ethical** stresses conformity with idealistic standards of right and wrong, as those applicable to the practices of lawyers and doctors: *"The world has achieved brilliance without conscience. Ours is a world of nuclear giants and ethical infants"* (Omar N. Bradley). **Virtuous** implies moral excellence and loftiness of character; in a narrower sense it refers to sexual chastity: *"The life of the nation is secure only while the nation is honest, truthful, and virtuous"* (Frederick Douglass). **Righteous** emphasizes moral uprightness and especially the absence of guilt or sin; when it is applied to actions, reactions, or impulses, it often implies justifiable outrage: *"The effectual fervent prayer of a righteous man availeth much"* (James 5:16). *"He was . . . stirred by righteous wrath"* (John Galsworthy).

morale   *morale esprit esprit de corps*
The central meaning shared by these nouns is "a spirit, as of dedication to a common goal, that unites a group": *the high morale of the troops; the esprit of an orchestra; the esprit de corps of a football team.*

muscular   *muscular athletic brawny burly sinewy*
The central meaning shared by these adjectives is "strong and powerfully built": *a muscular boxer; a robust and athletic young woman; brawny arms; a burly stevedore; a lean and sinewy frame.*

mysterious   *mysterious esoteric arcane occult inscrutable*
These adjectives mean beyond human power to explain or understand. Something **mysterious** arouses wonder and inquisitiveness and at the same time eludes explanation or comprehension: *a mysterious noise; mysterious symbols. "The sea lies all about us. . . . In its mysterious past it encompasses all the dim ori-*

gins of life" (Rachel Carson). What is **esoteric** is mysterious because it is known and understood by only a small, select group, as by a circle of initiates or the members of a profession: *a compilation of esoteric philosophical theories*. **Arcane** applies to what is hidden from the knowledge of all but those having the key to a secret: *the arcane science of dowsing*. **Occult** suggests knowledge reputedly gained only by secret, magical, or supernatural means: *occult powers; the occult sciences*. Something that is **inscrutable** cannot be fathomed by means of investigation or scrutiny: *an inscrutable smile*. *"It is not for me to attempt to fathom the inscrutable workings of Providence"* (Earl of Birkenhead).

naive   *naive simple ingenuous unsophisticated natural unaffected guileless artless*
These adjectives mean free from guile, cunning, or sham. **Naive** suggests the simplicity of nature; it sometimes connotes a credulity that impedes effective functioning in a practical world: *"this naive simple creature, with his straightforward and friendly eyes so eager to believe appearances"* (Arnold Bennett). **Simple** stresses absence of complexity, artifice, pretentiousness, or dissimulation; it may imply a favorable quality, such as openness of character, or an unfavorable one, such as lack of good sense: *"Those of highest worth and breeding are most simple in manner and attire"* (Francis Parkman). *"He was one of those simple men that love and sympathize with children"* (W.H. Hudson). *"Among simple people she had the reputation of being a prodigy of information"* (Harriet Beecher Stowe). **Ingenuous** denotes childlike directness, simplicity, and innocence; it connotes an inability to mask one's feelings: *an ingenuous admission of responsibility*. **Unsophisticated** indicates absence of worldly wisdom: *The sights of Paris bowled over the unsophisticated tourists*. **Natural** stresses spontaneity that is the result of

freedom from self-consciousness or inhibitions: *"When Kavanagh was present, Alice was happy, but embarrassed; Cecelia, joyous and natural"* (Henry Wadsworth Longfellow). **Unaffected** implies sincerity and lack of affectation: *"With men he can be rational and unaffected, but when he has ladies to please, every feature works"* (Jane Austen). **Guileless** signifies absence of insidious or treacherous cunning: *a harmless, honest, guileless creature; a guileless, disarming look.* **Artless** stresses absence of plan or purpose, as to mislead, and suggests a lack of concern for or awareness of the reaction produced in others: *a woman of artless grace and simple goodness.*

native   *native   indigenous   endemic   autochthonous   aboriginal*

These adjectives mean of, belonging to, or connected with a specific place or country by virtue of birth or origin. **Native** implies birth or origin in the specified place: *a native Frenchman; the native North American sugar maple.* **Indigenous** specifies that something or someone is native rather than coming or being brought in from elsewhere: *The tomato is indigenous to South America. The Ainu are indigenous to the northernmost islands of Japan.* Something **endemic** is prevalent in or peculiar to a particular locality or people: *Food shortages and starvation are endemic in certain parts of the world.* **Autochthonous** applies to what arises in the locality where it is found and has not been exposed to or has resisted change from outside sources: *Bartók collected autochthonous folk melodies and used them in his compositions.* **Aboriginal** describes what has existed from the beginning; it is often applied to the earliest known inhabitants of a place: *aboriginal chiefs; the aboriginal population; aboriginal nature.*

nautical   *nautical   marine   maritime   naval*

The central meaning shared by these adjectives is "of or relating to the sea, ships, shipping, sailors, or navigation": *nautical charts; marine insurance; maritime law; a naval officer.*

neat   *neat tidy trim shipshape spick-and-span spruce trig*

These adjectives mean marked by good order and cleanliness. **Neat** implies a pleasingly clean and orderly condition: *a neat room; neat hair.* **Tidy** emphasizes precise arrangement and order: *"When she saw me come in tidy and well dressed, she even smiled"* (Charlotte Brontë). **Trim** stresses especially smart appearance resulting from neatness, tidiness, and pleasing proportions: *"A trim little sailboat was dancing out at her moorings"* (Herman Melville). **Shipshape** evokes the meticulous order and neatness that might be found aboard a ship: *"We'll try to make this barn a little more shipshape"* (Rudyard Kipling). **Spick-and-span** suggests the immaculate freshness and cleanliness of something new: *"young men in spick-and-span uniforms"* (Edith Wharton). **Spruce** implies neatness and smartness, as of dress or appearance: *"a good-looking man; spruce and dapper, and very tidy"* (Anthony Trollope). **Trig** suggests sprightly smartness: *"the trig corporal, with the little visorless cap worn so jauntily"* (William Dean Howells).

negligent   *negligent derelict lax neglectful remiss slack*

The central meaning shared by these adjectives is "guilty of a lack of due care or concern": *an accident caused by a negligent driver; was derelict in his civic responsibilities; lax in attending classes; neglectful of her own financial security; remiss of you not to pay your bill; slack in maintaining discipline.*

news   *news advice intelligence tidings word*

The central meaning shared by these nouns is "information about hitherto unknown events and happenings": *just heard the good news; sent advice that the mortgage would be foreclosed; a source of intelligence about the negotiations; tidings of victory; received word of the senator's death.*

noise   noise din racket uproar pandemonium hullabaloo hubbub clamor babel

These nouns refer to loud, confused, or disagreeable sound or sounds. **Noise** is the least specific: *deafened by the noise in the subway; the noise of cannon fire.* A **din** is a jumble of loud, usually discordant sounds: *The din in the factory ends abruptly when the noon whistle sounds.* **Racket** is loud, distressing noise: *Can you imagine the racket made by a line of empty trailer trucks rolling along cobblestone streets?* **Uproar, pandemonium,** and **hullabaloo** imply disorderly tumult together with loud, bewildering sound: *"The evening uproar of the howling monkeys burst out"* (W.H. Hudson). *"When night came, it brought with it a pandemonium of dancing and whooping, drumming and feasting"* (Francis Parkman). *The first performance of the iconoclastic composition caused a tremendous hullabaloo in the audience.* **Hubbub** emphasizes turbulent activity, as of those engaged in commerce, and concomitant din: *We couldn't hear the starting announcement above the hubbub of bettors, speculators, tipsters, and touts.* **Clamor** is loud, usually sustained noise, as of a public outcry of dissatisfaction: *"not in the clamor of the crowded street"* (Henry Wadsworth Longfellow). *The debate was interrupted by a clamor of opposition.* **Babel** stresses confusion of vocal sounds arising from simultaneous utterance and random mixture of languages: *My outstanding memory of the diplomatic reception is of elegantly dressed guests chattering in a babel of tongues.*

normal   normal regular natural typical

These adjectives mean not deviating from what is common, usual, or to be expected. **Normal** stresses adherence to an established standard, model, or pattern: *normal body temperature;*

normal curiosity. **Regular** indicates unvarying conformity with a fixed rule or principle or a uniform procedure: *her regular bedtime; regular attendance at school.* What is **natural** is proper to, consonant with, or in accord with one's inherent nature or character: *a natural fear of nuclear war; a grandparent's natural affection for a grandchild.* **Typical** stresses adherence to those qualities, traits, or characteristics that identify a kind, group, or category: *a typical American; a painting typical of the Impressionist school.*

noted *noted celebrated eminent famed famous illustrious notable preeminent renowned*
The central meaning shared by these adjectives is "widely known and esteemed": *a noted author; a celebrated musician; an eminent scholar; a famed scientist; a famous actor; an illustrious judge; a notable historian; a preeminent archaeologist; a renowned painter.*
   ✔ *Antonym:* **obscure**

nuance *nuance gradation shade*
The central meaning shared by these nouns is "a slight variation or differentiation between nearly identical entities": *sensitive to delicate nuances of style; gradations of feeling from infatuation to deep affection; subtle shades of meaning.*

nurture *nurture cultivate foster nurse*
The central meaning shared by these verbs is "to promote and sustain the growth and development of": *nurturing hopes; cultivating tolerance; foster friendly relations; nursed the fledgling business through an economic downturn.*

obligation *obligation responsibility duty*
These nouns refer to a course of action that is demanded of a

person, as by law or conscience. **Obligation** usually applies to a specific constraint arising from a particular cause: *"Then in the marriage union, the independence of the husband and wife will be equal, their dependence mutual, and their obligations reciprocal"* (Lucretia Mott). **Responsibility** stresses accountability for the fulfillment of an obligation: *"I believe that every right implies a responsibility; every opportunity, an obligation; every possession, a duty"* (John D. Rockefeller, Jr.) **Duty** applies especially to constraint deriving from moral or ethical considerations: *"I therefore believe it is my duty to my country to love it, to support its Constitution, to obey its laws, to respect its flag, and to defend it against all enemies"* (William Tyler Page).

oblige   *oblige accommodate favor*

The central meaning shared by these verbs is "to perform a service or a courteous act for": *obliged me by keeping the matter quiet; accommodating her by lending her money; favor an audience with an encore.*

✓ *Antonym:* **disoblige**

occurrence   *occurrence happening event incident episode circumstance*

These nouns all refer to something that takes place or comes to pass. **Occurrence** and **happening** are the most general: *an everyday occurrence; a happening of no great importance.* **Event** usually signifies a notable occurrence: *The events of the day are reported on the evening news.* *"Great events make me quiet and calm; it is only trifles that irritate my nerves"* (Queen Victoria). **Incident** may apply to a minor occurrence: *Errors are inescapable incidents in the course of scientific research.* The term may also refer to a distinct event of sharp identity and significance: *His debut at Carnegie Hall was the first of a succession of exciting incidents in his life.* An **episode** is an incident in the course of a progression or within a larger sequence: *"Happiness was but the occasional episode in a general drama of pain"* (Thomas Hardy). **Circumstance** in this comparison denotes a particular incident or occurrence: *"What schoolboy of fourteen is ignorant of this remarkable circumstance?"* (Thomas Macaulay).

offend   *offend insult affront outrage*

These verbs mean to cause resentment, humiliation, or hurt. To **offend** is to cause displeasure, wounded feelings, or repugnance in another: *"He often offended men who might have been useful friends"* (John Lothrop Motley). **Insult** implies gross insensitivity, insolence, or contemptuous rudeness resulting in shame or embarrassment: *". . . every chance he can get to insult and torment me, he takes"* (Harriet Beecher Stowe). To **affront** is to insult openly, usually intentionally: *Affronted at his impertinence, she stared at him coldly and wordlessly.* **Outrage** implies the flagrant violation of a person's integrity, pride, or sense of right and decency: *"Agnes . . . was outraged by what seemed to her Rose's callousness"* (Mrs. Humphry Ward).

offensive   *offensive disgusting loathsome nasty repellent repulsive revolting vile*

The central meaning shared by these adjectives is "extremely unpleasant to the senses or feelings": *an offensive remark; disgusting language; a loathsome disease; a nasty smell; a repellent demand; repulsive behavior; revolting food; vile thoughts.*

old   *old ancient archaic antediluvian obsolete antique antiquated*

These adjectives describe what belongs to or dates from an earlier time or period. **Old** is the most general term: *old lace; an old saying; old colleagues; an old Dutch painting.* **Ancient** pertains to the distant past: *"the hills, / Rock-ribbed, and ancient as the sun"*

(William Cullen Bryant). **Archaic** implies a very remote, often primitive period: *an archaic Greek bronze of the seventh century* B.C. *He was convicted under an archaic statute that had never been repealed.* **Antediluvian** applies to what is so old and outdated that it seems to belong to the period preceding the biblical Flood: *lived in a ramshackle, antediluvian tenement; "a branch of one of your antediluvian families"* (William Congreve). **Obsolete** indicates the fact of having fallen into disuse: *an obsolete custom; obsolete methods of research. "Either man is obsolete or war is"* (R. Buckminster Fuller). **Antique** is applied both to what is very old and to what is especially appreciated or valued because of its age: *"in hat of antique shape"* (Matthew Arnold). *She collects antique French furniture and porcelains.* **Antiquated** describes what is out of date, no longer fashionable, or discredited: *"No idea is so antiquated that it was not once modern. No idea is so modern that it will not someday be antiquated"* (Ellen Glasgow).

opportune   *opportune   seasonable   timely   well-timed*
The central meaning shared by these adjectives is "occurring, coming, or done at the right, fitting, or favorable time": *waited for the opportune moment; seasonable summer storms; a timely warning; a well-timed attack.*

✔ *Antonym:* **inopportune**

oppose   *oppose   fight   combat   resist   withstand   contest*
These verbs are compared as they mean to set someone or something in opposition to another, as in an effort to overcome or defeat. **Oppose** has the fewest connotations: *oppose a legislative bill; was opposed to nuclear reactors. "The idea is inconsistent with our constitutional theory and has been stubbornly opposed . . . since the early days of the Republic"* (E.B. White). **Fight** and **combat** suggest vigor and aggressiveness: *fight corruption; combating disease. "All my life I have fought against prejudice and*

intolerance" (Harry S. Truman). *"We are not afraid . . . to tolerate any error so long as reason is left free to combat it"* (Thomas Jefferson). To **resist** is to strive to fend off or offset the actions, effects, or force of: *"Pardon was freely extended to all who had resisted the invasion"* (John R. Green). *"My servants . . . resisted the adoption of this plan"* (A.W. Kinglake). **Withstand** often implies successful resistance: *"Neither the southern provinces, nor Sicily, could have withstood his power"* (Henry Hallam). To **contest** is to call something into question and take an active stand against it: *I don't contest your right to dispose of your property as you see fit, but I doubt the propriety of this bequest.*

orderly   *orderly methodical systematic*

These adjectives all mean proceeding in or observant of a prescribed pattern or arrangement. **Orderly** implies correct or customary procedure or proper or harmonious arrangement: *Firefighters supervised the orderly evacuation of the building. Workers set up chairs on the stage in orderly and symmetrical rows.* **Methodical** stresses adherence to a logically and carefully planned succession of steps: *The pattern supplies methodical instructions for cutting and assembling the parts of the garment. The methodical housekeeper performs tasks according to a schedule.* **Systematic** emphasizes observance of a coordinated and orderly set of procedures constituting part of a complex but unitary whole: *Scientists are conducting systematic research into antigens to combat immune disorders.*

origin   *origin inception source root*

These nouns signify the point at which something originates. **Origin** is the point at which something comes into existence: *The origins of some words are unknown.* *"Man with all his noble qualities . . . still bears in his bodily frame the indelible stamp of his lowly origin* (Charles Darwin). When *origin* refers to people, it means parentage or ancestry: *"He came . . . of mixed French and Scottish origin"* (Charlotte Brontë). **Inception** is the beginning, as of an action or process: *Between the inception of the litigation and its final disposition the plaintiff's first attorney retired.* **Source** can refer to the point of origin of a stream or a river: *"the Alpine sources of the Rhine"* (John Foster Kirk). In another sense the term signifies the point at which something springs into being or from which it derives or is obtained: *"one great original source of revenue . . . the wages of labor"* (Adam Smith). *"The mysterious . . . is the source of all true art and science"* (Albert Einstein). **Root** often denotes what is considered the fundamental cause of or basic reason for something: *"Lack of money is the root of all evil"* (George Bernard Shaw). *"Most of the problems a President has to face have their roots in the past"* (Harry S. Truman).

outline   *outline   contour   profile   silhouette*
The central meaning shared by these nouns is "a line defining the boundary and shape of an object, a mass, or a figure": *the outline of the mountains against the sunset; saw the contour of the island from the airplane; the profile of a king on a coin; saw the dark silhouette of the family waving farewell.*

overthrow   *overthrow   overturn   subvert   topple   upset*
The central meaning shared by these verbs is "to cause the downfall, destruction, abolition, or undoing of": *overthrow an empire; overturn existing institutions; subverting civil order; toppled the government; unable to upset the will.*

pacify   *pacify   mollify   conciliate   appease   placate*
These verbs all refer to allaying another's anger, belligerence, discontent, or agitation. To **pacify** is to restore calm to or establish peace in: *"The explanation . . . was merely an invention framed to pacify his guests"* (Charlotte Brontë). *An army was re-*

quired in order to pacify the islands. **Mollify** stresses the soothing of hostile feelings: *"In that case go ahead with the project," she said, mollified by his agreeable manner.* **Conciliate** usually implies winning over, often by reasoning and with mutual concessions: *"A wise government knows how to enforce with temper or to conciliate with dignity"* (George Grenville). **Appease** and **placate** suggest the satisfaction of claims or demands or the tempering of antagonism, often through the granting of concessions: *The child is adept at appeasing her parents' anger with a joke or compliment. Even a written apology failed to placate the indignant hostess.*

pain *pain ache pang smart stitch throe twinge*

The central meaning shared by these nouns is "a sensation of severe physical discomfort": *abdominal pain; aches and cramps in a leg; the pangs of childbirth; aspirin that alleviated the smart; a stitch in the side; the throes of dying; a twinge of arthritis.*

palliate *palliate extenuate gloss gloze whitewash*

The central meaning shared by these verbs is "to cause a fault or offense to seem less grave or less reprehensible": *palliate a crime; couldn't extenuate the malfeasance; glossing over an unethical transaction; glozing sins and iniquities; whitewashed official complicity in political extortion.*

pamper *pamper indulge humor spoil coddle mollycoddle baby*

These verbs all mean to cater excessively to someone or to his or her desires or feelings. To **pamper** is to gratify appetites, tastes, or desires, as for rich food or luxurious comforts: *Cosseted and pampered from earliest childhood, he believed the world had been invented for his entertainment. "He was pampering the poor girls's lust for singularity and self-glorification"* (Charles Kingsley). **Indulge** suggests a kindly or excessive lenience in yielding to wishes, inclinations, or impulses, especially those better left unfulfilled: *"The truth is, I do indulge myself a little the more in pleasure"* (Samuel Pepys). *"Pelham . . . felt that an ally so little used to control . . . might well be indulged in an occasional fit of waywardness"* (Thomas Macaulay). **Humor** implies compliance with or accommodation to another's mood or idiosyncrasies: *"Human life is . . . but like a froward child, that must be played with and humored a little to keep it quiet till it falls asleep"* (William Temple). **Spoil** implies oversolicitude or excessive indulgence that adversely affects the character, nature, or attitude: *"He seems to be in no danger of being spoilt by good fortune"* (George Gissing). **Coddle** and **mollycoddle** point to tender, overprotective care that often leads to weakening of character: *"I would not coddle the child"* (Samuel Johnson). *Stop mollycoddling me; I'm a grown person.* **Baby** suggests bestowing on someone the indulgence and attention one might give to an infant: *"I should like to be made much of, and tended — yes, babied"* (Adeline D.T. Whitney).

paragon   *paragon nonesuch nonpareil*
The central meaning shared by these nouns is "a person or thing so excellent as to have no equal": *Paris, the paragon of cities; a suspension bridge that is the nonesuch of beauty and utility; thought her grandchildren were nonpareils.*

partner   *partner colleague ally confederate*
These nouns all denote one who is united or associated with another, as in a venture or relationship. A **partner** participates in a relationship in which each member has equal status: *a partner in a law firm; husbands and wives who are ideal partners.* A **colleague** is an associate in an occupation, such as a profession: *a colleague and fellow professor.* An **ally** is one who associates with another, at least temporarily in a common cause: *The United States and the Soviet Union were allies in World War II.* A

confederate is a member of a confederacy, a league, or an alliance; sometimes the term signifies a collaborator in a suspicious venture: *The confederates, undefeated, pushed onward. The burglar was caught, but his confederate got away.*

patience   *patience long-suffering resignation forbearance*
These nouns all denote the capacity to endure hardship, difficulty, or inconvenience without complaint. **Patience** emphasizes calmness, self-control, and the willingness or ability to tolerate delay: *"Our patience will achieve more than our force"* (Edmund Burke). *"No fear can stand up to hunger, no patience can wear it out"* (Joseph Conrad). **Long-suffering** is long and patient endurance, as of wrong or provocation: *The general, a man by no means notable for docility and long-suffering, flew into a rage.* **Resignation** implies an unresisting acceptance of or submission to something trying, as out of despair or necessity: *Too timorous to protest the disrespect with which she was being treated, the young woman could only accept it with resignation.* **Forbearance** denotes restraint, as in retaliating, demanding what is due, or voicing disapproval or condemnation: *"It is the mutual duty of all to practice Christian forbearance, love, and charity towards each other"* (Patrick Henry). *The parents showed remarkable forbearance toward their defiant and unruly son.*

pause   *pause intermission recess respite suspension*
The central meaning shared by these nouns is "a temporary stop, as in activity": *a short pause in the conversation; a concert with the usual 15-minute intermission; the legislature's summer recess; toiling without respite; a suspension of work.*

pedantic   *pedantic academic bookish donnish scholastic*
The central meaning shared by these adjectives is "marked by a narrow, often tiresome focus on or display of learning and

especially its trivial aspects": *a pedantic style of writing; an academic insistence on precision; a bookish vocabulary; donnish refinement of speech; scholastic and excessively subtle reasoning.*

penitence   *penitence compunction contrition remorse repentance*

The central meaning shared by these nouns is "a feeling of regret for one's sins or misdeeds": *showed no penitence; ended the relationship without compunction; pangs of contrition; tears of remorse; sincere repentance.*

perceptible   *perceptible palpable appreciable noticeable discernible*

These adjectives apply to what is capable of being apprehended with the mind or through the senses as being real. **Perceptible** is the least specific: *After quite a perceptible pause, during which he consulted his notes, the lecturer continued.* **Palpable** applies both to what is perceptible by means of the sense of touch and to what is readily perceived by the mind: *"I felt as if my soul were grappling with a palpable enemy"* (Mary Wollstonecraft Shelley). *"The advantages Mr. Falkland possessed . . . are palpable"* (William Godwin). What is **appreciable** is capable of being estimated or measured: *Appreciable amounts of noxious waste are still being dumped into the harbor.* **Noticeable** means easily observed: *noticeable shadows under her eyes; a noticeable tremor in his voice.* **Discernible** means distinguishable, especially by the faculty of vision or the intellect: *The skyline is easily discernible even at a distance of several miles. The newspaper reports no discernible progress in the negotiations.*

perfect   *perfect consummate faultless flawless impeccable*

The central meaning shared by these adjectives is "being wholly without flaw": *a perfect diamond; a consummate per-*

former; faultless logic; a flawless instrumental technique; speaks impeccable French.

✔ Antonym: **imperfect**

perform   *perform execute accomplish achieve effect fulfill discharge*

These verbs signify to carry through to completion. To **perform** is to carry out an action, an undertaking, or a procedure; the word often connotes observance of due form or the exercise of skill or care: *The ship's captain performed the wedding ceremony. The orchestra and chorus performed an Easter oratorio. Sophisticated laser experiments are performed regularly in the laboratory.* **Execute** implies performing a task or putting something into effect in accordance with a plan or design: *"To execute laws is a royal office; to execute orders is not to be a king"* (Edmund Burke). *The violinist had the technical skill to execute the cadenza, with its double stops and harmonics, with brilliance.* **Accomplish** connotes the successful completion of something, often of something that requires tenacity or talent: *"Make one brave push and see what can be accomplished in a week"* (Robert Louis Stevenson). *He accomplished his purpose, the rapid acquisition of enormous profits, only by making risky investments.* To **achieve** is to accomplish something especially by dint of effort or despite difficulty; the term often implies a significant result: *"Some are born great . . . Some achieve greatness . . . And some have greatness thrust upon them"* (William Shakespeare). *Greater benefits can be achieved through diplomatic channels than by acts of aggression.* **Effect** suggests the power of an agent to bring about a desired result: *Even the antibiotics the doctor prescribed didn't effect a complete cure.* To **fulfill** is to live up to expectations or satisfy demands, wishes, or requirements: *It is unrealistic to hope that all one's desires can be fulfilled. She fulfilled her obligations to her parents.* To **discharge** an obligation or duty is to perform all the steps necessary for its fulfillment: *"I have* *found it impossible to carry the heavy burden of responsibility and to discharge my duties as King as I would wish to do"* (Edward VIII).

period *period epoch era age term*

These nouns refer to a portion or length of time. **Period** is the most general: *a short waiting period; one of the most difficult periods of her life; worked for a period of ten years; the Romantic period in music.* **Epoch** refers to a period regarded as being remarkable or memorable: *"We enter on an epoch of constitutional retrogression"* (John R. Green). An **era** is a period of time notable because of new or different aspects or events: *"How many a man has dated a new era in his life from the reading of a book"* (Henry David Thoreau). An **age** is usually a period marked by a particular distinctive characteristic: *the age of Newton; the Iron Age.* *"These principles form the bright constellation which has . . . guided our steps through an age of revolution and reformation"* (Thomas Jefferson). A **term** is a period of time to which limits have been set: *Senators are elected for a term of six years.*

periodic *periodic sporadic intermittent occasional fitful*

These adjectives all mean recurring or reappearing now and then. Something **periodic** occurs at regular or at least generally predictable intervals: *periodic feelings of anxiety.* **Sporadic** implies appearance or occurrence in scattered, irregular, unpredictable, or isolated instances: *a city subjected to sporadic bombing raids.* **Intermittent** describes something that stops and starts at intervals: *intermittent rain showers.* What is **occasional** happens at random and irregularly: *occasional outbursts of temper.* Something **fitful** occurs in spells and often abruptly: *fitful bursts of energy.*

permission *permission authorization consent leave license sanction*

The central meaning shared by these nouns is "approval for a course of action that is granted by one in authority": *was refused permission to smoke; seeking authorization to begin construction; gave their consent to the marriage; will ask leave to respond to the speaker; was given license to depart; gave sanction to the project.*

✔ Antonym: **prohibition**

physique *physique build constitution*
The central meaning shared by these nouns is "bodily structure or development": *a child of delicate physique; a stocky build; a robust constitution.*

pity *pity compassion commiseration sympathy condolence empathy*
These nouns signify sympathetic, kindly concern aroused by the misfortune, affliction, or suffering of another. **Pity** often implies a feeling of sorrow that inclines one to help or to show mercy: *"Pity is the feeling which arrests the mind in the presence of whatsoever is grave and constant in human sufferings and unites it with the human sufferer"* (James Joyce). **Compassion** denotes deep awareness of the suffering of another and the wish to relieve it: *"Compassion is not weakness, and concern for the unfortunate is not socialism"* (Hubert H. Humphrey). **Commiseration** signifies the expression of pity or sorrow: *"They not unfrequently wonder why, from being born blind, they should be held to be objects of commiseration"* (Benjamin C. Brodie). **Sympathy** as it is compared here denotes the act of or capacity for sharing in the sorrows or troubles of another: *"They had little sympathy to spare for their unfortunate enemies"* (William Hickling Prescott). **Condolence** is a formal, conventional expression of pity, usually to relatives upon a death: *We extended our condolences to the bereaved family.* **Empathy** is a vicarious identification with and understanding of another's situation, feelings, and mo-

tives: *Empathy for the criminal's childhood misery does not imply exoneration of the crimes he committed as an adult.*

plain   *plain modest simple unostentatious unpretentious*
The central meaning shared by these adjectives is "not ornate, ostentatious, or showy": *a plain hair style; a modest cottage; a simple dark suit; an unostentatious office; an unpretentious country church.*
   ✓ Antonym: **ornate**

plan   *plan blueprint design project scheme strategy*
The central meaning shared by these nouns is "a method or program in accordance with which something is to be done or accomplished": *has no vacation plans; a blueprint for the reorganization of the company; social conventions that are a product of human design; an urban-renewal project; a new scheme for power conservation; a strategy for capturing a major market share.*

plausible   *plausible believable colorable credible*
The central meaning shared by these adjectives is "appearing to merit belief or acceptance": *a plausible pretext; a believable excuse; a colorable explanation; a credible assertion.*
   ✓ Antonym: **implausible**

please   *please delight gladden gratify tickle*
The central meaning shared by these verbs is "to give pleasure to": *was pleased by their success; a gift that would delight any child; praise that gladdens the spirit; progress that gratified all concerned; compliments that tickle their vanity.*
   ✓ Antonym: **displease**

plentiful   *plentiful abundant ample copious plenteous*
The central meaning shared by these adjectives is "being fully as much as one needs or desires": *a plentiful supply of stationery;*

her abundant talent; ample space; copious provisions; a plenteous crop of wheat.

✓ *Antonym:* **scant**

poisonous   *poisonous mephitic pestilent pestilential toxic venomous virulent*

The central meaning shared by these adjectives is "having the destructive or fatal effect of a poison": *a poisonous snake; a mephitic vapor; a pestilent agitator; pestilential jungle mists; toxic fumes; venomous jealousy; a virulent form of cancer.*

poor   *poor indigent needy impecunious penniless impoverished poverty-stricken destitute*

These adjectives mean lacking the money or the means requisite to an adequate or comfortable life. **Poor** is the most general: *"Resolve not to be poor: whatever you have, spend less. Poverty is a great enemy to human happiness"* (Samuel Johnson). **Indigent** and **needy** refer to one in need or want: *The town government is responsible for assistance to indigent people. Local politicians used to distribute Thanksgiving turkeys to needy families.* **Impecunious** and **penniless** mean having little or no money: *"Certainly an impecunious Subaltern was not a catch"* (Rudyard Kipling). *If the breadwinner deserts the family, it will be left penniless.* One who is **impoverished** has been reduced to poverty: *The dictator, whose greed and excesses had produced an impoverished citizenry, fled the country.* **Poverty-stricken** means suffering from poverty and miserably poor: *"The poverty-stricken exiles contributed far more, in proportion . . . than the wealthy merchants"* (John Lothrop Motley). **Destitute** means lacking any means of subsistence: *Some nations have no middle class; one group is rich, while the other is destitute.*

postpone   *postpone defer shelve stay suspend*

The central meaning shared by these verbs is "to put off until a later time": *postponing our trip; deferred paying the bills; shelved the issue; stay an execution; suspending train service.*

posture   *posture attitude carriage pose stance*
The central meaning shared by these nouns is "a position of the body and limbs": *erect posture; an attitude of prayer; dignified carriage; a defiant pose; the alert stance of a batter in baseball.*

practice   *practice drill exercise rehearse*
The central meaning shared by these verbs is "to do or cause to do again and again in order to acquire proficiency": practice the shot put; drill pupils in the multiplication tables; exercising one's wits; an actor rehearsing a role.

praise   *praise acclaim commend extol laud*
These verbs mean to express approval or admiration. To **praise** is to voice approbation, commendation, or esteem: *"I come to bury Caesar, not to praise him"* (William Shakespeare). *"She was enthusiastically praising the beauties of Gothic architecture"* (Francis Marion Crawford). **Acclaim** usually implies hearty approbation warmly and publicly expressed: *The restoration of the frescoes is being widely but not universally acclaimed by art historians.* **Commend** suggests moderate or restrained approval, as that accorded by a superior: *The judge commended the jury for their patience and hard work.* To **extol** is to praise highly; the term suggests exaltation or glorification: *"that sign of old age, extolling the past at the expense of the present"* (Sydney Smith). **Laud** connotes respectful or lofty, often inordinate praise: *"aspirations which are lauded up to the skies"* (Charles Kingsley).

predict   *predict call forecast foretell prognosticate*
The central meaning shared by these verbs is "to tell about something in advance of its occurrence by means of special

knowledge or inference": *predict an eclipse; couldn't call the out-come of the game; forecasting the weather; foretold the collapse of the government; prognosticating a rebellion.*

predilection   *predilection bias leaning partiality penchant*
prejudice proclivity propensity
The central meaning shared by these nouns is "a predisposi-tion to favor a particular person, thing, point of view, or course of action": *a predilection for classical composers; a pro-American bias; conservative leanings; a partiality for liberal-minded friends; a penchant for exotic foods; a prejudice in favor of the underprivileged; a proclivity for self-assertiveness; a propensity for exaggeration.*

preliminary   *preliminary introductory*
prefatory preparatory
The central meaning shared by these adjectives is "going be-fore and preparing the way for something else": *a preliminary investigation; introductory remarks; an author's prefatory notes; preparatory steps.*

presume   *presume presuppose postulate posit assume*
These verbs signify to take something for granted or as being a fact. To *presume* is to suppose that something is reasonable, justifiable, sound, or possible in the absence of proof to the contrary: *"I presume you're tired after the long ride"* (Edith Whar-ton). *We cannot presume the existence of life on other planets.* **Pre-suppose** can mean merely to believe or suppose in advance; it can also mean to require as an antecedent condition: *It is unre-alistic to presuppose a sophisticated knowledge of harmony and counterpoint in a beginning music student. The evolution of species presupposes a process of natural selection.* **Postulate** and **posit** de-note the assertion of the existence, reality, necessity, or truth

of something, as something considered to be self-evident or axiomatic, as the basis for reasoning or argument: *"We can see individuals, but we can't see providence; we have to postulate it"* (Aldous Huxley). *Historical linguists posit a common ancestor from which both Romance and Germanic languages descend.* To **assume** is to accept something as existing or being true without proof or on inconclusive grounds: *Why do you assume that I'm angry? "We must never assume that which is incapable of proof"* (G.H. Lewes).

prevent   *prevent preclude avert obviate forestall*

These verbs mean to stop or hinder something from happening, especially by advance planning or action. **Prevent** implies anticipatory counteraction: *"The surest way to prevent war is not to fear it"* (John Randolph). To **preclude** is to exclude the possibility of the occurrence of an event or action: *"a tranquillity which . . . his wife's presence would have precluded"* (John Henry Newman). To **avert** is to ward off something about to happen: *Only quick thinking on the pilot's part averted a disastrous accident.* **Obviate** implies that something, such as a difficulty, has been anticipated and disposed of effectively: *"the objections . . . having . . . been obviated in the preceding chapter"* (Joseph Butler). **Forestall** usually suggests anticipatory measures taken to counteract, neutralize, or nullify the effects of something: *We installed an alarm system to forestall break-ins.*

produce   *produce bear yield*

The central meaning shared by these verbs is "to bring forth as a product": *a mine producing gold; a seed that finally bore fruit; a plant that yields a medicinal oil.*

proficient   *proficient adept skilled skillful expert*

These adjectives mean having or showing knowledge, ability,

or skill, as in a vocation, profession, or branch of learning. **Proficient** implies an advanced degree of competence acquired through training: *A proficient surgeon is the product of lengthy training and experience.* **Adept** suggests a natural aptitude improved by practice: *The dress designer was adept at draping and cutting the fabric without using a pattern.* **Skilled** implies sound, thorough competence and often mastery, as in an an art, a craft, or a trade: *Only the most skilled gymnasts are accepted for the Olympic team.* **Skillful** adds to *skilled* the idea of natural dexterity in performance or achievement: *The crafts teacher is skillful in knitting, crocheting, embroidery, and the use of the hand loom.* **Expert** applies to one with consummate skill and command: *A virtuoso is one who is expert in playing a musical instrument.*

profuse   *profuse exuberant lavish lush luxuriant prodigal riotous*
The central meaning shared by these adjectives is "given with, giving with, or marked by unrestrained abundance": *profuse apologies; an exuberant growth of moss; lavish praise; lush vegetation; luxuriant hair; a prodigal party giver; a riotous growth of ferns.*
   ✔ *Antonym:* **spare**

promise   *promise covenant engage pledge plight swear vow*
The central meaning shared by these verbs is "to declare solemnly that one will perform or refrain from a particular course of action": *promise to write soon; covenanting to exchange their prisoners of war; engaged to reorganize the department; pledged to uphold the law; plighted their loyalty to the king; swore to get revenge; vowed they would never surrender.*

proportion   *proportion harmony symmetry balance*
These nouns are compared as they mean aesthetic arrange-

ment, as in a design, marked by proper distribution of elements. **Proportion** is the agreeable or harmonious relation of parts within a whole: *The house, of Spanish colonial design, has rooms with graciousness of proportion and beautiful details.* **Harmony** is the pleasing interaction or appropriate combination of elements: *The harmony of her face is not diminished by her imperfect nose.* *Symmetry* and *balance* both imply an arrangement of parts and details on either side of a dividing line, but **symmetry** frequently emphasizes exact or mirror-image correspondence of parts, while **balance** often suggests dissimilar parts that offset each other to make a harmonious and satisfying whole: *Beds of iris were set out in perfect symmetry around a pool filled with water lilies. "In all perfectly beautiful objects, there is found the opposition of one part to another, and a reciprocal balance"* (John Ruskin).

propose   *propose pose propound submit*
The central meaning shared by these verbs is "to present something for consideration or discussion": *propose a solution to a problem; a situation posing many questions and problems; propound a theory; submitting a plan.*

proud   *proud arrogant haughty disdainful supercilious*
These adjectives mean filled with or marked by a high opinion of oneself and disdain for what one views as being unworthy. **Proud** can suggest dignity or justifiable self-respect or self-satisfaction, but it often implies conceit or vanity: *"There is such a thing as a man being too proud to fight"* (Woodrow Wilson). *"I pray God to keep me from being proud"* (Samuel Pepys). One who is **arrogant** is overbearingly proud and demands more power or consideration than is warranted: *"All sensibly gave him wide berth, for he was a dangerous-looking man, chewing a toothpick with the arrogant sullenness of one who is willing to commit vio-*

lence" (Stephen Hunter). **Haughty** suggests lofty, condescending pride, as by reason of high birth or station: *"An old and haughty nation proud in arms"* (John Milton). **Disdainful** emphasizes scorn or contempt: *"Nor [let] grandeur hear with a disdainful smile, / The short and simple annals of the poor"* (Thomas Gray). **Supercilious** implies haughty disdain: *"His mother eyed me in silence with a supercilious air"* (Tobias Smollett).

prudence   *prudence discretion foresight forethought circumspection*

These nouns are compared as they refer to the exercise of good judgment and common sense, especially in the conduct of practical matters. **Prudence,** the most comprehensive, implies not only caution but also the capacity for judging in advance the probable results of one's actions: *"She had been forced into prudence in her youth, she learned romance as she grew older"* (Jane Austen). **Discretion** suggests prudence coupled with wise self-restraint, as in resisting the impulse to take rash action: *"The better part of valor is discretion"* (William Shakespeare). **Foresight** implies the ability to foresee and make provision for what may happen: *She had the foresight to realize that once the ugly rumor had begun to circulate, only the truth could put it to rest.* **Forethought** suggests advance consideration of future eventualities: *An empty refrigerator illustrates a lack of forethought.* **Circumspection** implies discretion together with prudent heed for possible consequences, as out of concern for moral or social repercussions: *"The necessity of the times, more than ever, calls for our utmost circumspection, deliberation, fortitude and perseverance"* (Samuel Adams).

pull   *pull drag draw haul tow tug*

The central meaning shared by these verbs is "to cause something to move toward the source of an applied force": *pull a sled up a hill; drag furniture across the floor; draw up a chair; hauling wood from the forest; a car towing a trailer; tugging at the oars.*

✓ Antonym: **push**

punish   punish correct chastise discipline
castigate penalize

These verbs mean to subject a person to a penalty, such as loss, pain, or confinement, for an offense, a sin, or a fault. **Punish** is the least specific: *"The individual who refuses to defend his rights when called by his Government . . . must be punished as an enemy of his country and friend to her foe"* (Andrew Jackson). To **correct** is to punish so that the offender will mend his or her ways: *Regulations formerly permitted prison wardens to correct unruly inmates.* **Chastise** implies punishment, such as corporal punishment or a verbal rebuke, as a means of effecting improvement in behavior: *chastise a bully by giving him a thrashing; was roundly chastised for insolence.* **Discipline** stresses punishment inflicted by an authority in order to control an offender or to eliminate or reform unacceptable conduct: *The worker was disciplined for insubordination.* **Castigate** means to censure or criticize severely, often in public: *The judge castigated the attorney for badgering the witness.* **Penalize** usually implies a monetary penalty or the forfeiture of a privilege or gain because rules or regulations have been broken: *Those who file their income-tax returns after April 15 will be penalized.*

pure   pure absolute sheer simple unadulterated

The central meaning shared by these adjectives is "free of extraneous elements": *pure gold; absolute alcohol; sheer wine; a simple substance; unadulterated coffee.*

push   push propel shove thrust

The central meaning shared by these verbs is "to press against something in order to move it forward or aside": *push a baby carriage; wind propelling a sailboat; shove a tray across a table; thrust the package into her hand.*

✔ *Antonym:* **pull**

quibble   *quibble carp cavil niggle nitpick pettifog*
The central meaning shared by these verbs is "to raise petty or frivolous objections or complaints": *quibbling about minor points of grammar; an art critic who constantly carped; caviling about the price of a cup of coffee; an editor who niggled about commas; tried to get her to stop nitpicking all the time; pettifogging about a trivial clause in a contract.*

range   *range ambit compass orbit purview reach scope sweep*
The central meaning shared by these nouns is "an area within which something acts, operates, or has power or control": *the range of a supersonic jet; the ambit of municipal legislation; information not within the compass of this article; countries within the political orbit of a world power; hospital regulations under the purview of the department of health; outside the reach of the law; issues within the scope of an investigation; outside the sweep of federal authority.*

reach   *reach achieve attain gain compass*
All of these verbs mean to succeed in arriving at a goal or an objective. *Reach,* the least specific, like the other terms connotes the expenditure of effort: *reached shelter before the storm broke; reach an understanding; reach perfection.* **Achieve** suggests in addition the application of skill or initiative: *achieved international recognition.* **Attain** often implies the impelling force of ambition, principle, or ideals: *trying to attain self-confidence.* **Gain** connotes considerable effort in surmounting obstacles:

gained the confidence of the workers. **Compass** implies circumvention of impediments to success: *couldn't compass the assigned task.*

real   *real actual true existent*

These adjectives are compared as they mean not imaginary but having verifiable existence. **Real** implies that something is genuine or authentic or that what it seems or purports to be tallies with fact: *Don't lose the bracelet; it's made of real gold. My mother showed real sympathy for my predicament.* "*The general, in a well-feigned or real ecstasy, embraced him*" (William Hickling Prescott). **Actual** means existing and not merely potential or possible: "*rocks, trees . . . the actual world*" (Henry David Thoreau); "*what the actual things were which produced the emotion that you experienced*" (Ernest Hemingway). **True** implies that something is consistent with fact, reality, or the actual state of things: "*It is undesirable to believe a proposition when there is no ground whatever for supposing it true*" (Bertrand Russell). **Existent** applies to what has life or being: *Much of the beluga caviar existent in the world is found in the Soviet Union and Iran.*

reap   *reap garner gather glean harvest*

The central meaning shared by these verbs is "to collect": *reap grain; garner compliments; gathering mushrooms; glean information; harvested rich rewards.*

reason   *reason intuition understanding judgment*

These nouns refer to the intellectual faculty by means of which human beings seek or attain knowledge or truth. **Reason** is the power to think rationally and logically and to draw inferences: "*the rationalist whose reason is not sufficient to teach him those limitations of the powers of conscious reason*" (Friedrich

August von Hayek). *"Mere reason is insufficient to convince us of its* [the Christian religion's] *veracity"* (David Hume). **Intuition** is perception or comprehension, as of truths or facts, without the use of the rational process: *"Because of their age-long training in human relations — for that is what feminine intuition really is — women have a special contribution to make to any group enterprise"* (Margaret Mead). **Understanding** is the faculty by which one understands, often together with the comprehension resulting from its exercise: *"So long as the human heart is strong and the human reason weak, Royalty will be strong because it appeals to diffused feeling, and Republics weak because they appeal to the understanding"* (Walter Bagehot). *"The greatest dangers to liberty lurk in insidious encroachment by men of zeal, well-meaning but without understanding"* (Louis D. Brandeis). **Judgment** is the ability to assess situations or circumstances and draw sound conclusions: *"my salad days, / When I was green in judgment"* (William Shakespeare). *"At twenty years of age, the will reigns; at thirty, the wit; and at forty, the judgment"* (Benjamin Franklin).

rebellion   *rebellion revolution revolt mutiny insurrection uprising*

These nouns denote acts of violence intended to change or overthrow an existing order or authority. **Rebellion** is open, armed, organized resistance to constituted political authority that often fails of its purpose: *A rebellion in the officer corps led to chaos in the armed forces.* A **revolution** is the overthrow of one government and its replacement with another: *The 20th century has seen several major revolutions, which in turn have altered the balance of power among nations.* **Revolt** is rejection of and rebellion against a prevailing state of affairs or a controlling authority: *Fearing a taxpayers' revolt, the legislature passed a less confiscatory revenue bill.* **Mutiny** is revolt against constituted authority, especially by sailors: *The sailors, who had received low pay and poor rations, were finally in a state of mutiny.* **Insurrection** and **uprising** apply to popular revolts that are sometimes limited or are viewed as being the first indications of a more extensive rebellion: *The freedom fighters withdrew into the mountains, from which they mounted an insurrection against the junta. The 1956 uprising in Hungary was soon quelled by ruthless Soviet military action.*

recede   recede ebb retract retreat retrograde
The central meaning shared by these verbs is "to move backward": *a hairline that had receded; waters ebbing at low tide; a turtle retracting its head into its shell; a retreating army; academic standards that have retrograded.*

  ✔ Antonym: **advance**

reciprocate   reciprocate requite return
The central meaning shared by these verbs is "to give, take, or feel reciprocally": *doesn't reciprocate favors; consideration requited with callous disregard; return a compliment.*

recover   recover regain recoup retrieve
These verbs are compared as they mean to get back something lost or taken away. **Recover** is the least specific: *The police recovered the stolen car.* "*In a few days Mr. Barnstaple had recovered strength of body and mind*" (H.G. Wells). "*He . . . stood in the porch a minute to recover his composure*" (John Galsworthy). **Regain** suggests success in recovering something that has been taken from one: "*hopeful to regain / Thy Love*" (John Milton); "*regain'd my freedom with a sigh*" (Lord Byron). To **recoup** is to get back the equivalent of something lost: *The teacher, who had bought the book for the school library, felt entitled to recoup her expenses.* **Retrieve** pertains to the effortful recovery of something

(*retrieved the ball from the end zone*) or to the rectification of unfavorable consequences or the making good of something gone amiss or awry: "*a false step that he was never able to retrieve*" (John Morley). "*By a brilliant coup he has retrieved . . . a rather serious loss*" (Samuel Butler).

refer   *refer advert mention*
The central meaning shared by these verbs is "to call or direct attention to something": *referred to my indiscretion; adverting to childhood experiences; often mentions his old friend.*

refrain   *refrain abstain forbear*
The central meaning shared by these verbs is "to keep or prevent oneself from doing or saying something": *refrained from commenting; abstained from smoking; can't forbear criticizing their ineptitude.*

refuse   *refuse decline reject spurn rebuff*
These verbs all mean to be unwilling to accept, consider, or receive someone or something. **Refuse** usually implies determination and often brusqueness: "*The commander . . . refused to discuss questions of right*" (George Bancroft). "*I'll make him an offer he can't refuse*" (Mario Puzo). To **decline** is to refuse courteously: "*I declined election to the National Institute of Arts and Letters some years ago, and now I must decline the Pulitzer Prize*" (Sinclair Lewis). **Reject** suggests the discarding of someone or something as unsatisfactory, defective, or useless; it implies categoric refusal: "*He again offered himself for enlistment and was again rejected*" (Arthur S.M. Hutchinson). "*Emphasize your choice by utter ignoring of all that you reject*" (Ralph Waldo Emerson). To **spurn** is to reject scornfully or contemptuously: "*The more she spurns my love, / The more it grows*" (William Shakespeare). **Rebuff** pertains to blunt, often disdainful rejection:

"He had . . . forgotten himself, had gone too far in his advances, and had been rebuffed" (Robert Louis Stevenson).

regret   regret sorrow grief anguish woe heartache heartbreak

All of these nouns denote mental distress. **Regret** has the broadest range, from mere disappointment to a painful sense of loss, dissatisfaction, self-reproach, or longing, as over something lost, gone, done, or left undone: *He had hoped that our policy of not dealing with terrorists would be an example to other countries but soon realized, to his regret, that we didn't practice what we preached. She looked back with regret on the pain she had caused her family.* **Sorrow** connotes sadness caused by misfortune, affliction, or loss; it can also imply contrition: *"sorrow for his women, for his kinfolk, for his children, who needed his protection, and whom he could not protect"* (James Baldwin). **Grief** is deep, acute personal sorrow, as that arising from irreplaceable loss: *"Grief fills the room up of my absent child, / Lies in his bed, walks up and down with me"* (William Shakespeare). **Anguish** implies agonizing, excruciating mental pain: *"I pray that our heavenly Father may assuage the anguish of your bereavement"* (Abraham Lincoln). **Woe** is intense, often prolonged wretchedness or misery: *"the deep, unutterable woe / Which none save exiles feel"* (W.E. Aytoun). **Heartache** most often applies to sustained private sorrow: *The child's devastating problems are a source of untold heartache to the parents.* **Heartbreak** is overwhelming grief: *"Better a little chiding than a great deal of heartbreak"* (William Shakespeare).

relevant   relevant pertinent germane material apposite apropos

These adjectives all describe what relates to and has a direct bearing on the matter at hand. Something **relevant** is connected with a subject or issue: *The scientist corresponds with colleagues in order to learn about matters relevant to her own research.* **Pertinent** suggests a logical, precise relevance: *The professor has given the students a list of articles pertinent to the topic under discussion.* **Germane** implies close kinship and appropriateness: *"He's a serious student of the issues, always inquisitive about the facts, and aggressive in their pursuit. . . . he asks questions that are germane and central to the issue"* (Marlin Fitzwater). Something **material** is not only relevant but also crucial to a matter: *"Facts, the statement of which may reasonably be presumed likely to have such an influence on the judgment of the underwriter are called material facts"* (Joseph Arnould). **Apposite** implies a striking appropriateness and pertinence: *The successful copywriter is a master of apposite and evocative verbal images.* Something **apropos** is both to the point and opportune: *The thought may have been apropos, but I suppressed its expression out of consideration of their feelings.*

✔ Antonym: **irrelevant**

reliable   *reliable dependable responsible*
trustworthy trusty
The central meaning shared by these adjectives is "worthy of reliance or trust": *a reliable source of information; a dependable worker; a responsible used-car dealer; a trustworthy report; a trusty servant of the state.*

relieve   *relieve allay alleviate assuage lighten*
mitigate palliate
All of these verbs mean to make something less severe or more bearable. To **relieve** is to ease and make more endurable something causing discomfort or distress: *"that misery which he strives in vain to relieve"* (Henry David Thoreau). *"The counselor relieved her fears"* (Sir Walter Scott). **Allay** suggests relief at least for the time being from what is burdensome or painful: *"This*

music crept by me upon the waters, / Allaying both their fury and my passion / With its sweet air" (William Shakespeare). **Alleviate** connotes temporary lessening of distress without removal of its cause: "*No arguments shall be wanting on my part that can alleviate so severe a misfortune*" (Jane Austen). To **assuage** is to soothe or make milder: "*What shall assuage the unforgotten pain / And teach the unforgetful to forget?*" (Dante Gabriel Rossetti). **Lighten** in this comparison signifies to make less heavy or oppressive: *Congress endeavored to lighten the taxpayers' burden.* **Mitigate** and **palliate** connote moderating the severity, force, or intensity of something that causes suffering: "*I . . . prayed to the Lord to mitigate a calamity which seemed to me past the capacity of man to remedy*" (John Galt). "*His well-known financial ability made men turn to him in the hour of distress, as of all statesmen the most fitted to palliate it*" (William E.H. Lecky).

relinquish *relinquish yield resign abandon surrender cede waive renounce*

These verbs have in common the sense of letting something go or giving something up. **Relinquish,** the least specific, sometimes connotes unwillingness or regret: *can't bear to relinquish the idea.* **Yield** implies giving way, as to pressure or superior authority, often in the hope that such action will be temporary: *gradually had to yield ground.* **Resign** suggests unresisting submission or acquiescence, as that arising from hopelessness: *was forced by the scandal to resign the office to which he had been elected.* **Abandon** and **surrender** agree in implying no expectation of returning to or recovering what is given up, but the terms differ in that *surrender* implies the operation of compulsion, demand, or force: *abandoned all hope; refusing to surrender control.* **Cede** connotes formal transfer, as of rights or territory: *a province ceded by treaty.* **Waive** implies a voluntary decision to dispense with something, such as a claim or right: *waived all* *privileges.* To **renounce** is to relinquish something formally and usually as a matter of principle: *renounced his claim to the estate.*

rely   *rely trust depend reckon*

These verbs share the meaning "to place or have faith or confidence in someone or something." **Rely** implies complete confidence: *"You are the only woman I can rely on to be interested in her"* (John Galsworthy). **Trust** stresses confidence arising from belief that is often based on inconclusive evidence: *"It is better to suffer wrong than to do it, and happier to be sometimes cheated than not to trust"* (Samuel Johnson). *"I don't think I could trust myself to speak to him about it"* (Booth Tarkington). *Prepare yourself thoroughly for the performance; then trust in your talent to carry you through.* **Depend** implies confidence in the help or support of another: *Synthetic fuels should be developed; it is foolhardy to depend on Middle Eastern countries for our oil supplies.* **Reckon** implies a sense of confident expectancy: *"He reckons on finding a woman as big a fool as himself"* (George Meredith).

remember   *remember bethink recall recollect*

The central meaning shared by these verbs is "to bring an image or a thought back to the mind": *can't remember his name; bethought herself of her responsibilities; recalling her kindness; recollect how the accident happened.*

✔ Antonym: **forget**

replace   *replace supplant supersede*

These verbs are compared as they mean to turn someone or something out and place another in his, her, or its stead. To **replace** is to be or furnish an equivalent or a substitute in the place of another, especially another that has been lost, depleted, worn out, or discharged: *"A conspiracy was carefully engineered to replace the Directory by three Consuls"* (H.G. Wells). *"I* *succeed him* [Benjamin Franklin, as envoy to France]*; no one could replace him*" (Thomas Jefferson). **Supplant** often suggests the use of intrigue or underhanded tactics to take another's place: "*The rivaling poor Jones, and supplanting him in her affections, added another spur to his pursuit*" (Henry Fielding). The term does not, however, invariably have this connotation: "*The steam engine began to supplant the muscular power of men and animals*" (James Harvey Robinson). To **supersede** is to replace one person or thing by another held to be superior, more valuable or useful, or less antiquated: "*In our island the Latin appears never to have superseded the old Gaelic speech*" (Thomas Macaulay). "*Each of us carries his own life-form — an indeterminable form which cannot be superseded by any other*" (Carl Jung).

represent   *represent delineate depict limn picture portray*
The central meaning shared by these verbs is "to render or present a realistic image or likeness of": *a statue representing a king; cave paintings that delineate horses and hunters; a cartoon depicting a sea monster; the personality of a great leader limned in words; a country landscape pictured in soft colors; a book portraying life in the Middle Ages.*

resort   *resort apply go refer turn*
The central meaning shared by these verbs is "to repair to or fall back on someone or something in time of need": *never resorted to corporal punishment; apply to a bank for a loan; went to her parents for comfort; referred to his notes to refresh his memory; has no friends to turn to.*

responsible   *responsible answerable liable accountable amenable*
These adjectives share the meaning obliged to answer, as for one's actions, to an authority that may impose a penalty for

failure. *Responsible* often implies the satisfactory performance of duties, the adequate discharge of obligations, or the trustworthy care for or disposition of possessions: *"I am responsible for the ship's safety"* (Robert Louis Stevenson). *"The people had given him his command, and to the people alone he was responsible"* (J.A. Froude). *Answerable* suggests a moral or legal responsibility subject to review by a higher authority: *The court held the parents answerable for their minor child's acts of vandalism.* *Liable* may refer to a legal obligation, as to pay damages, or to a responsibility to do something, as to perform jury duty, if called on: *Wage earners are liable to income tax. During the war men between the ages of 18 and 35 were liable for military conscription.* *Accountable* especially emphasizes the requirement to give an account of one's discharge of a responsibility entrusted to one: *"The liberal philosophy holds that enduring governments must be accountable to someone beside themselves; that a government responsible only to its own conscience is not for long tolerable"* (Walter Lippmann). *Amenable* implies the condition of being subject to the control of an authority and therefore the absence of complete autonomy: *"She was not so amenable to the law as he"* (Jack London).

revere   *revere worship venerate adore idolize*

These verbs all mean to regard with the deepest respect, deference, and esteem. *Revere* suggests awe coupled with profound honor: *"At least one third of the population . . . reveres every sort of holy man"* (Rudyard Kipling). *Worship* implies reverent love and homage rendered to God or a god: *The ancient Egyptians, who were polytheists, worshiped a number of gods and sacred animals.* In a more general sense *worship* connotes an often uncritical but always very admiring regard: *"She had worshiped intellect"* (Charles Kingsley). *Venerate* connotes reverence accorded by virtue especially of dignity, character, or age: *"I ven-*

erate the memory of my grandfather" (Horace Walpole). To **adore** is to worship with deep, often rapturous love: *"O come, let us adore him, Christ the Lord!"* ("Adeste Fideles"). *A number of the students detested the subject but adored the teacher.* **Idolize** implies worship like that accorded an object of religious devotion: *He idolizes his wife and doesn't care who knows it.*

revive   revive restore resuscitate revivify

The central meaning shared by these verbs is "to give renewed well-being, vitality, or strength to": *rains that revive lawns and flowers; an invalid restored by quiet and fresh air; resuscitating old hopes and aspirations; a celebration that revivified our spirits.*

rich   rich affluent flush loaded moneyed wealthy

The central meaning shared by these adjectives is "having an abundant supply of money, property, or possessions of value": *a rich philanthropist; an affluent banker; a speculator flush with cash; not merely rich but loaded; moneyed aristocrats; wealthy corporations.*

   ✔ Antonym: **poor**

ridicule   ridicule mock taunt twit deride gibe

These verbs refer to making another the butt of amusement or mirth. **Ridicule** implies purposeful disparagement: *"My father discouraged me by ridiculing my performances"* (Benjamin Franklin). To **mock** is to poke fun at someone, often by mimicking and caricaturing his or her speech or actions: *"Seldom he smiles, and smiles in such a sort / As if he mock'd himself, and scorn'd his spirit"* (William Shakespeare). **Taunt** suggests mocking, insulting, or scornful reproach: *"taunting him with want of courage to leap into the great pit"* (Daniel Defoe). To **twit** is to taunt by calling attention to something embarrassing: *"The schoolmaster was twitted about the lady who threw him over"* (J.M. Barrie). **De-**

ride implies scorn and contempt: *Musical snobs often deride the harmonica as a serious instrument.* To *gibe* is to make taunting, heckling, or jeering remarks: *The child's classmates gibed at him for his timidity.*

right   right privilege prerogative perquisite birthright

These nouns apply to something, such as a power or possession, to which one has an established claim. *Right* refers to a legally, morally, or traditionally just claim: *"I'm a champion for the Rights of Woman"* (Maria Edgeworth). *"An unconditional right to say what one pleases about public affairs is what I consider to be the minimum guarantee of the First Amendment"* (Hugo L. Black). *"Our children are not individuals whose rights and tastes are casually respected from infancy, as they are in some primitive societies"* (Ruth Benedict). *Privilege* usually suggests a right not enjoyed by everyone: *"When the laws undertake to . . . grant . . . exclusive privileges, to make the rich richer and the potent more powerful, the humble members of society . . . have a right to complain of the injustice of their government"* (Andrew Jackson). *Prerogative* denotes an exclusive right or privilege, as one based on custom, law, office, or recognition of precedence: *It is my prerogative to change my mind.* A *perquisite* is a privilege or advantage accorded to one by virtue of one's position or the needs of one's employment: *"The wardrobe of her niece was the perquisite of her* [maid]*"* (Tobias Smollett). A *birthright* is a right to which one is entitled by birth: *Many view gainful employment as a birthright.*

rise   rise ascend climb soar tower mount surge

These verbs are compared as they mean to move upward from a lower to a higher position. *Rise* has the widest range of application: *We rose at dawn. The sun rises early in the summer. Fog was rising from the pond. Prices rise and fall.* *Ascend* frequently suggests a gradual step-by-step rise: *The plane took off and as-*

cended steadily until it was out of sight. "*Ascend above the restrictions and conventions of the world, but not so high as to lose sight of them*" (Richard Garnett). **Climb** connotes steady, often effortful progress, as against gravity: "*still climbing after knowledge infinite*" (Christopher Marlowe). "*You climb up through the little grades and then get to the top*" (John Updike). **Soar** implies effortless ascent to a great height: *A lone condor soared above the Andean peaks.* "*Well is it known that ambition can creep as well as soar*" (Edmund Burke). To **tower** is to attain a height or prominence exceeding that of anything in the surroundings: "*the tall Lombardy poplar . . . towering high above all other trees*" (W.H. Hudson). *Bach's gifts towered over those of his contemporaries.* **Mount** in this comparison connotes a progressive climb to a higher level: *Water mounted in the ship's hold. The blood mounted to her cheeks. Our expenses mounted fearfully.* **Surge** implies a tumultuous swelling or heaving force like that of waves: *The crowd of pedestrians surged ahead when the light turned green. I could feel indignation surging up in me.*

room   room elbowroom latitude leeway margin play scope

The central meaning shared by these nouns is "adequate space or opportunity for freedom of movement or action": *room for improvement; needed elbowroom to negotiate effectively; no latitude allowed in conduct or speech; allowed the chef leeway in choosing the menu; no margin for error; imagination given full play; permitting their talents free scope.*

rough   rough harsh jagged rugged scabrous uneven

These adjectives apply to what is not smooth but has a coarse, irregular surface. **Rough** describes something that to the sight or touch has inequalities, as projections or ridges: *rough bark; rough, chapped hands; a rough homespun fabric.* Something **harsh** is unpleasantly rough, discordant, or grating: *harsh burlap; the harsh cry of a crow.* **Jagged** refers to an edge or a surface with irregular projections and indentations: *a jagged piece of glass.* **Rugged,** which often refers to strength or endurance, especially in people, can also apply to land surfaces characterized by irregular, often steep rises and slopes: *a rugged, rocky trail; rugged countryside.* **Scabrous** means rough and scaly to the tactile sense: *a granular, scabrous spot on his cheek.* **Uneven** describes lines or surfaces of which some parts are not level with others: *uneven ground; uneven handwriting.*

rude   *rude crude primitive raw rough*

The central meaning shared by these adjectives is "marked by a lack of skill and finish": *a rude hut; a crude drawing; primitive kitchen facilities; a raw wooden canoe; a rough sketch.*

ruin   *ruin raze demolish destroy wreck*

These verbs mean to injure and deprive something — or, less often, someone — of usefulness, soundness, or value. **Ruin** usually implies irretrievable harm but not necessarily total destruction: *The fire ruined the books in the library. "You will ruin no more lives as you ruined mine"* (Arthur Conan Doyle). **Raze,** to level to the ground, **demolish,** to pull down or break to pieces, and the more general **destroy,** to tear down, can all imply reduction to ruins or even complete obliteration: *"raze what was left of the city from the surface of the earth"* (John Lothrop Motley). *The conquerors tried to raze the very name of the people's national hero from their memories. Both of the cars involved were demolished in the head-on accident. The prosecutor demolished the opposition's argument. "It became necessary to destroy the town in order to save it"* (Anonymous major in Vietnam). *"I saw the best minds of my generation destroyed by madness"* (Allen Ginsberg). To **wreck** is to ruin in or as if in a violent collision: *"The Boers* *had just wrecked a British military train"* (Arnold Bennett). When *wreck* is used in its extended sense, as in referring to the ruination of a person or his or her hopes or reputation, it implies irreparable shattering: *"Coleridge, poet and philosopher wrecked in a mist of opium"* (Matthew Arnold).

sad   *sad melancholy sorrowful doleful woebegone desolate*

These adjectives all mean affected with or marked by unhappiness, as that caused by affliction. **Sad** is the most general: *"Better by far you should forget and smile / Than that you should remember and be sad"* (Christina Rossetti). **Melancholy** can refer to a lingering or habitual state of mind marked by somberness or sadness: *The patient's face, though it was melancholy, brightened at the arrival of the guests.* **Sorrowful** applies to mental pain such as that resulting from irreparable loss: *"Even in laughter the heart is sorrowful"* (Proverbs 14:13). **Doleful** describes what is mournful, morose, or gloomy: *The chastised child looked at her father with a pathetic, doleful expression.* **Woebegone** suggests grief or wretchedness, especially as it is reflected in a person's appearance: *"His sorrow . . . made him look . . . haggard and . . . woebegone"* (George du Maurier). **Desolate** applies to one that is sorrowful to the point of being beyond consolation: *"No one is so accursed by fate, / No one so utterly desolate, / But some heart, though unknown, / Responds unto his own"* (Henry Wadsworth Longfellow).

same   *same identical selfsame very*

The central meaning shared by these adjectives is "not different in identity or nature from another or others": *wore the same dress twice; gave identical answers; saw the selfsame quotation in two newspapers; the very person who should have warned us.*

✓ Antonym: **different**

satisfy *satisfy answer fill fulfill meet*
The central meaning shared by these verbs is "to supply fully or completely": *satisfied all requirements; answered our needs; filling a purpose; fulfilled their aspirations; meeting her obligations.*

save *save rescue reclaim redeem deliver*
These verbs are compared in the sense of freeing a person or thing from danger, evil, confinement, or servitude. **Save,** the most general, applies to an act of keeping safe or preserving from danger, harm, or the consequences of evil: *The smallpox vaccine has saved many lives. A police officer saved the tourist from being cheated.* **Rescue** usually implies saving from immediate harm or danger by direct action: *rescue a rare manuscript from a fire; rescued sailors from a torpedoed ship.* **Reclaim,** applied to people, means to bring back, as from error to virtue or to right or proper conduct; it can also mean to return a thing to usefulness or productivity: *"To reclaim me from this course of life was the sole cause of his journey to London"* (Henry Fielding). *"The foundations of the capital were gradually reclaimed from the watery element"* (William Hickling Prescott). To **redeem** is to free someone from captivity or the consequences of sin or error or to save something from pawn or from deterioration or destruction; the term can imply the expenditure of money or effort: *The price exacted by the hijackers for redeeming the hostages was extortionate. He redeemed his ring from the pawnbroker.* **Deliver** in this comparison applies to liberating people from something such as misery, peril, error, or evil: *"consigned to a state of wretchedness from which no human efforts will deliver them"* (George Washington).

scatter *scatter disperse dissipate dispel*
These verbs are compared as they mean to cause a mass or an aggregate to separate and go in different directions. **Scatter**

usually refers to widespread, often haphazard distribution of components: "*the scattered driftwood, bleached and dry*" (Celia Laighton Thaxter). **Disperse** implies the complete breaking up of the mass or aggregate: "*only a few industrious Scots perhaps, who indeed are dispersed over the face of the whole earth*" (George Chapman). **Dissipate** usually suggests a reduction to nothing: "*Time dissipates to shining ether the solid angularity of facts*" (Ralph Waldo Emerson). **Dispel** suggests driving away or off by or as if by scattering: "*I thought, if I had caused the cloud, it was my duty to make an effort to dispel it*" (Emily Brontë).

secret   *secret stealthy covert clandestine furtive surreptitious underhand*
These adjectives mean deliberately hidden from view or knowledge. **Secret** is the most general: *a desk with a secret compartment; a secret marriage; secret negotiations.* **Stealthy** suggests quiet, cautious deceptiveness intended to escape notice: *heard stealthy footsteps on the stairs.* **Covert** describes something that is not overt but is concealed or disguised: *Students protested covert actions undertaken by the CIA.* **Clandestine** implies stealth and secrecy for the concealment of an often illegal or improper purpose: *a clandestine tryst; clandestine intelligence operations.* **Furtive** suggests the slyness, shiftiness, and evasiveness of a thief: *a menacing and furtive look to his eye.* Something **surreptitious** is stealthy, furtive, and often unseemly or unethical: *took a surreptitious glance at his watch; the surreptitious mobilization of troops in preparation for a sneak attack.* **Underhand** implies unfairness, deceit, fraud, or slyness as well as secrecy: *achieved success in business only by resorting to underhand methods.*

see   *see behold note notice espy descry observe contemplate survey view perceive discern remark*
These verbs refer to being or becoming visually or mentally

aware of something. *See,* the most general, can mean merely to use the faculty of sight but more often implies recognition, understanding, or appreciation: *"We must . . . give the image of what we actually see"* (Paul Cézanne). *"If I have seen further (than . . . Descartes) it is by standing upon the shoulders of Giants"* (Isaac Newton). **Behold** more strongly implies awareness of what is seen: *"My heart leaps up when I behold / A rainbow in the sky"* (William Wordsworth). **Note** and **notice** suggest close observation and a rather detailed visual or mental impression; *note* in particular implies careful, systematic recording in the mind: *Be careful to note where the road turns left. I have noted and overridden your protests. She didn't notice the run in her stocking until she had arrived at the office. I notice that you're out of sorts.* **Espy** and **descry** both stress acuteness of sight that permits the detection of something distant, partially hidden, or obscure: *"espied the misspelled Latin word in* [the] *letter"* (Los Angeles Times); *"the lighthouse, which can be descried from a distance"* (Michael Strauss). **Observe** emphasizes careful, closely directed attention: *"I saw the pots . . . red-hot . . . and observed that they did not crack at all"* (Daniel Defoe). **Contemplate** implies looking attentively and thoughtfully: *"It is interesting to contemplate an entangled bank, clothed with many plants of many kinds, with birds singing on the bushes"* (Charles Darwin). **Survey** stresses detailed, often comprehensive examination: *"Strickland looked away and idly surveyed the ceiling"* (W. Somerset Maugham). **View** usually suggests examination with a particular purpose in mind or in a special way: *The medical examiner viewed the victim's body. "He* [man] *viewed the crocodile as a thing sometimes to worship, but always to run away from"* (Thomas De Quincey). **Perceive** and **discern** both imply not only visual recognition but also mental comprehension; *perceive* is especially associated with insight, and *discern,* with the ability to distinguish, discriminate, and make judgments: *"We perceived a little girl* *coming towards us"* (Frederick Marryat). *"I plainly perceive [that] some objections remain"* (Edmund Burke). *Even with a magnifying glass I couldn't discern any imperfections in the porcelain. Many in the audience lack the background and taste to discern a good performance of the sonata from a bad one.* **Remark** suggests close attention and often an evaluation of what is noticed: *"Their assemblies afforded me daily opportunities of remarking characters and manners"* (Samuel Johnson).

seek   *seek hunt quest search*
The central meaning shared by these verbs is "to make an effort to find something": *seeking information; hunting through the telephone book for a number; questing after treasure; searched his face for his reaction.*

send   *send dispatch forward route ship transmit*
The central meaning shared by these verbs is "to cause to go or be taken to a destination": *sent the package by parcel post; dispatched a union representative to the factory; forwarding the mail to their new address; routed the soldiers through New York; shipping oil in tankers; transmitting money by cable.*

sentimental   *sentimental bathetic maudlin mawkish mushy romantic schmaltzy slushy soppy*
The central meaning shared by these adjectives is "excessively or insincerely emotional": *a sentimental soap opera; a bathetic novel; maudlin expressions of sympathy; mawkish sentiment; mushy effusiveness; a romantic adolescent; a schmaltzy song; slushy poetry; a soppy letter.*

separate   *separate divide part sever sunder divorce*
These verbs are compared as they mean to become or cause to become parted, disconnected, or disunited. **Separate** applies

both to putting apart and to keeping apart: *"In the darkness and confusion, the bands of these commanders became separated from each other"* (Washington Irving). *The Pyrenees separate France and Spain. The child's parents have separated.* **Divide** implies separation by or as if by cutting, splitting, or branching into parts, portions, or shares; the term is often used to refer to separation into opposing or hostile groups: *We divided the orange into segments.* *"[The rich] divide with the poor the produce of all their improvements"* (Adam Smith). *" 'A house divided against itself cannot stand.' I believe this government cannot endure permanently half slave and half free"* (Abraham Lincoln). **Part** refers most often to the separation of closely associated persons or things: *"None shall part us from each other"* (W.S. Gilbert). *"I remember the way we parted"* (Algernon Swinburne). **Sever** usually implies abruptness and force in the cutting off of a part from the whole or the breaking up of an association or a relationship: *"His head was nearly severed from his body"* (H.G. Wells). *The United States severed diplomatic relations with Cuba in 1961.* **Sunder** stresses violent tearing or wrenching apart: *The country was sundered by civil war into two embattled states.* **Divorce** implies the separation of the elements of a relationship or union: *"a priest and a soldier, two classes of men circumstantially divorced from the kind and homely ties of life"* (Robert Louis Stevenson).

serious   *serious sober grave solemn earnest sedate staid*
These adjectives are compared as they refer to the manner, appearance, disposition, or acts of persons and mean absorbed or marked by absorption in thought, pressing concerns, or significant work. **Serious** implies a concern with responsibility and work as opposed to play: *Serious students of music must familiarize themselves with the literature and idiom of all the important composers.* **Sober** emphasizes circumspection and self-restraint: *"a sober thoughtful man"* (Anthony Trollope). *"My sober mind*

was no longer intoxicated by the fumes of politics" (Edward Gibbon). **Grave** suggests the dignity and somberness associated with weighty matters: *"The soldier . . . of today is . . . a quiet, grave man, busied in charts, exact in sums, master of the art of tactics"* (Walter Bagehot). **Solemn** often adds to *grave* the suggestion of impressiveness: *The judge's tone was solemn as he pronounced sentence on the convicted murderer.* **Earnest** implies sincerity and intensity of purpose: *Both sides in the dispute showed an earnest desire to reach an equitable solution.* **Sedate** implies a composed, dignified manner: *"One of those calm, quiet, sedate natures, to whom the temptations of turbulent nerves or vehement passions are things utterly incomprehensible"* (Harriet Beecher Stowe). **Staid** emphasizes dignity and an often straitlaced observance of propriety: *"a grave and staid God-fearing man"* (Lord Tennyson).

severe   *severe stern austere ascetic strict*
These adjectives mean unsparing and exacting with respect to discipline or control. **Severe** implies adherence to rigorous standards or high principles; the term often suggests the imposition of harsh conditions: *"Praise or blame has but a momentary effect on the man whose love of beauty in the abstract makes him a severe critic on his own works"* (John Keats). **Stern** suggests unyielding disposition, uncompromising resolution, or forbidding appearance or nature: *"thought her husband a man fatally stern and implacable"* (George Meredith). **Austere** connotes sternness, qualities such as aloofness or lack of feeling or sympathy, and often rigid morality: *Austere officers demand meticulous conformity with military regulations.* **Ascetic** suggests self-discipline and self-denial and often renunciation of worldly pleasures for spiritual improvement: *"Be systematically ascetic . . . do . . . something for no other reason than that you would rather not do it"* (William James). **Strict** means requiring or

showing stringent observance of obligations, rules, or standards: *"He could not be severe nor even passably strict"* (W.H. Hudson).

shade   *shade penumbra shadow umbra umbrage*
The central meaning shared by these nouns is "an area of comparative darkness resulting from the blocking of light rays": *sitting in the shade; Earth's penumbra; in the shadow of the curtains; the umbra beyond the footlights; sheltered in the umbrage of a rain forest.*

shake   *shake tremble quake quiver shiver shudder*
These verbs mean to manifest involuntary vibratory movement. **Shake** is the most general: *The child's small body shook with weeping. The floor shook when she walked across the room.* **Tremble** implies quick, rather slight movement, as from excitement, weakness, or anger: *I could feel the youngster's hand tremble in mine. The apple blossoms trembled in the wind.* **Quake** refers to more violent movement, as that caused by shock or upheaval: *I was so terrified that my legs began to quake.* **Quiver** suggests a slight, rapid, tremulous movement: *"Her lip quivered like that of a child about to cry"* (Booth Tarkington). **Shiver** involves rapid, rather slight trembling, as of a person experiencing chill: *"as I in hoary winter night stood shivering in the snow"* (Robert Southwell). **Shudder** applies chiefly to convulsive shaking caused by fear, horror, or revulsion: *"She starts like one that spies an adder / . . . The fear whereof doth make him shake and shudder"* (William Shakespeare).

shapeless   *shapeless amorphous formless unformed unshaped*
The central meaning shared by these adjectives is "having no distinct shape": *a mass of shapeless slag; an amorphous cloud of*

insects; an aggregate of formless particles; an unformed personality; unshaped dough.

  ✔ *Antonym:* **shapely**

sharp   *sharp keen acute*

These adjectives all apply literally to fine edges, points, or tips: *a sharp knife; a keen blade; a leaf with an acute end.* Figuratively they indicate mental alertness and clarity of comprehension. **Sharp** suggests quickness and astuteness: *"a young man of sharp and active intellect"* (John Henry Newman). **Keen** implies clear-headedness and acuity: *Women with keen intelligent minds are making inroads in formerly male-dominated occupations.* **Acute** suggests penetrating perception or discernment: *an acute observer of politics and politicians.*

shelter   *shelter cover retreat refuge asylum sanctuary*

These nouns refer to places affording protection, as from danger, or to the state of being protected. **Shelter** usually implies a covered or enclosed area that protects temporarily, as from injury or attack: *A cold frame provides shelter for the seedlings. "And the dead tree gives no shelter"* (T.S. Eliot). **Cover** suggests something, as bushes, that conceals: *The army mounted the invasion under cover of darkness.* **Retreat** applies chiefly to a secluded place to which one retires for meditation, peace, or privacy: *Their cabin in the woods served as a retreat from the pressures of business.* **Refuge** suggests a place of escape from pursuit or from difficulties that beset one: *"vagrants and criminals, who make this wild country a refuge from justice"* (Sir Walter Scott). *"The great advantage of a hotel is that it's a refuge from home life"* (George Bernard Shaw). **Asylum** adds to *refuge* the idea of legal protection against a pursuer or of immunity from arrest: *"O! receive the fugitive and prepare in time an asylum for mankind"* (Thomas Paine). **Sanctuary** denotes a sacred or inviolable place of refuge: *Some of the political refugees found sanctuary in a monastery.*

shorten   *shorten abbreviate abridge curtail truncate*
The central meaning shared by these verbs is "to diminish the length, duration, or extent of by or as if by cutting": *smoking that will shorten her life; abbreviated the speech; abridging the rights of citizens; curtailed their visit; truncated the conversation.*
   ✔ *Antonym:* **lengthen**

shout   *shout bawl bellow holler howl roar whoop yell*
The central meaning shared by these verbs is "to say with or make a loud, strong cry": *fans shouting their approval; bawling out orders; bellowing with rage; hollered a warning; howling with pain; a crowd roaring its disapproval; children whooping at play; troops yelling as they attacked.*

show   *show display expose parade exhibit flaunt*
These verbs mean to present something to view. **Show** is the most general: *The jeweler showed the necklace to the customer. "She hated to show her feelings"* (John Galsworthy). **Display** often suggests an attempt to present something to best advantage: *The dealer spread the rug out to display the pattern. "Few 'letters home' of successful men or women display the graces of modesty and self-forgetfulness"* (H.G. Wells). **Expose** usually involves uncovering something or bringing it out from concealment: *The excavation exposed a staggering number of Bronze Age artifacts.* The term can often imply revelation of something better left concealed: *His comment exposed his insensitivity.* **Parade** usually suggests a pretentious or boastful presentation: *"He early discovered that, by parading his unhappiness before the multitude, he produced an immense sensation"* (Thomas Macaulay). **Exhibit** implies open presentation that invites inspection: *"The works*

of art, by being publicly exhibited and offered for sale, are becoming articles of trade" (Prince Albert). **Flaunt** implies an unabashed, prideful, often arrogant display: "*Every great hostelry flaunted the flag of some foreign potentate*" (John Dos Passos).

showy   *showy flamboyant ostentatious*
pretentious splashy
The central meaning shared by these adjectives is "marked by striking, often excessively conspicuous display": *a cheap, showy rhinestone bracelet; an entertainer's flamboyant personality; an ostentatious sable coat; a pretentious scholarly edition; a splashy advertising campaign.*

shrewd   *shrewd sagacious astute perspicacious*
These adjectives mean having or showing keen awareness, sound judgment, and often resourcefulness, especially in practical matters. **Shrewd** suggests a sharp intelligence, hardheadedness, and often an intuitive grasp of practical considerations: "*He was too shrewd to go along with them upon a road which could lead only to their overthrow*" (J.A. Froude). **Sagacious** connotes prudence, circumspection, discernment, and farsightedness: "*He was observant and thoughtful, and given to asking sagacious questions*" (John Galt). **Astute** suggests shrewdness, canniness, and an immunity to being misled: *An astute tenant always reads the small print in a lease.* **Perspicacious** implies penetration and clear-sightedness: *She is much too perspicacious to be taken in by such a spurious argument.*

shy   *shy bashful diffident modest coy demure*
These adjectives mean not forward but marked by a retiring nature, reticence, or a reserve of manner. One who is **shy** draws back from others, either because of a withdrawn nature or out of timidity: "*The poor man was shy and hated society*"

(George Bernard Shaw). **Bashful** suggests self-consciousness or awkwardness in the presence of others: *"I never laughed, being bashful. / Lowering my head, I looked at the wall"* (Ezra Pound). **Diffident** implies lack of self-confidence: *He was too diffident to express his opinion.* **Modest** is associated with an unassertive nature, absence of vanity, and freedom from pretension: *Despite her fame she remained the modest, unassuming person she had been as a student.* **Coy** usually implies feigned, often flirtatious shyness: *"yielded with coy submission"* (John Milton). **Demure** often denotes an affected shyness or modesty: *"I really don't know how to write a check," she said, with a demure sidelong glance.*

sign   sign badge mark token symptom note

These nouns are compared as they denote an outward indication of the existence or presence of something not immediately evident. **Sign** is the most general: *A high forehead is thought to be a sign of intelligence. "The exile of Gaveston was the sign of the barons' triumph"* (John R. Green). *"The V sign is the symbol of the unconquerable will of the occupied territories"* (Winston S. Churchill). **Badge** usually refers to something that is worn as an insignia of membership, is an emblem of achievement, or is a characteristic sign: *The sheriff's badge was shaped like a star. "Sweet mercy is nobility's true badge"* (William Shakespeare). **Mark** can refer to a visible trace or impression (*a laundry mark*) or to an indication of a distinctive trait or characteristic: *Intolerance is the mark of a bigot.* The term can also denote a lasting effect, as of an experience: *Poverty had left its mark.* **Token** usually refers to evidence or proof of something intangible: *sent flowers as a token of her affection.* **Symptom** suggests outward evidence of a process or condition, especially an adverse condition: *"dying of a hundred good symptoms"* (Alexander Pope); *"the gale having rather increased than shown any symp-*

toms of abating" (Frederick Marryat). **Note** applies to the sign of a particular quality or feature: *"the eternal note of sadness"* (Matthew Arnold).

silent   *silent reticent reserved taciturn secretive uncommunicative tightlipped*

These adjectives describe people who are sparing with speech. **Silent** often implies a habitual disinclination to speak or to speak out: *"the great silent majority"* (Richard M. Nixon). The term may also mean refraining from speech, as out of fear or confusion: *"He must be warned prior to any questioning that he has the right to remain silent"* (Earl Warren). **Reticent** suggests a tendency to keep one's thoughts, feelings, and personal affairs to oneself: *"She had been shy and reticent with me, and now . . . she was telling me aloud the secrets of her inmost heart"* (W.H. Hudson). **Reserved** suggests aloofness and reticence: *"a reserved man, whose inner life was intense and sufficient to him"* (Arnold Bennett). **Taciturn** implies unsociableness and a tendency to speak only when it is absolutely necessary: *"At the Council board he was taciturn; and in the House of Lords he never opened his lips"* (Thomas Macaulay). **Secretive** implies a lack of openness about or even concealment of matters that could in all conscience be discussed: *too secretive to disclose her vacation plans.* **Uncommunicative** suggests a disposition to withhold opinions, feelings, or knowledge from others: *Her uncle was a silent, uncommunicative Yankee farmer.* **Tightlipped** strongly implies a steadfast unwillingness to divulge information being sought: *The general remained tightlipped when reporters asked him about the rumored invasion.*

sleek   *sleek glossy satiny silken silky slick*

The central meaning shared by these adjectives is "having a smooth, gleaming surface": *sleek black fur; glossy auburn hair;*

satiny gardenia petals; silken butterfly wings; silky skin; slick seals and otters.

slide   *slide slip glide coast skid slither*

These verbs mean to move smoothly and continuously over or as if over a slippery surface. *Slide* usually implies rapid, easy movement without loss of contact with the surface: *coal sliding down a chute; "the drops sliding from a lifted oar"* (Theodore Roethke). *Slip* can refer to smooth, easy, and quiet passage: *"the jackals . . . slipping back to the hills"* (Lord Dunsany). More often, however, the term is applied to accidental sliding resulting in loss of balance or foothold: *slipped on a patch of ice and sprained his ankle. Glide* refers to smooth, free-flowing, seemingly effortless movement: *"four snakes gliding up and down a hollow"* (Ralph Waldo Emerson). *A submarine glided silently through the water. Coast* applies especially to downward movement resulting from the effects of gravity or momentum: *The driver turned off the engine and let the truck coast down the incline. Skid* implies an uncontrolled, often sideways sliding caused by a lack of traction: *The bus skidded on wet pavement. Slither* can mean to slip and slide, as on an uneven surface, often with friction and noise: *"The detached crystals slithered down the rock face for a moment and then made no further sound"* (H.G. Wells). The word can also suggest the sinuous, gliding motion of a reptile: *An iguana slithered across the path.*

sloppy   *sloppy slovenly unkempt slipshod*

These adjectives apply to people, their appearance, their way of thinking, or their work and mean marked by an absence of due or proper care or attention. *Sloppy* evokes the idea of careless spilling, spotting, or splashing; it suggests slackness, untidiness, or diffuseness: *a sloppy kitchen; sloppy dress. "I do not*

see how the sloppiest reasoner can evade that" (H.G. Wells).
Slovenly implies habitual negligence and a lack of system or
thoroughness: *a slovenly appearance; a slovenly writer; slovenly
inaccuracies.* **Unkempt** stresses dishevelment resulting from a
neglectful lack of proper maintenance: "*an unwashed brow, an
unkempt head of hair*" (Sir Walter Scott). *During the owners' absence the lawn became dreadfully unkempt.* **Slipshod** suggests a re-
laxed indulgence toward imperfection, a casual inattention to
detail, and a general absence of meticulousness: "*the new owners' camp . . . a slipshod and slovenly affair, tent half stretched,
dishes unwashed*" (Jack London); "*slipshod talk*" (George Eliot).

small   *small diminutive little miniature minuscule minute petite tiny wee*

The central meaning shared by these adjectives is "being notably below the average in size or magnitude": *a small house;
diminutive in stature; little hands; a miniature camera; a minuscule amount of rain; minute errors; a petite figure; tiny feet; a wee
bit better.*
  ✔ *Antonym:* **large**

smell   *smell aroma odor scent*

The central meaning shared by these nouns is "a quality that
can be perceived by the olfactory sense": *the smell of gas; the
aroma of frying onions; hospital odors; the scent of pine needles.*

social   *social companionable convivial gregarious sociable*

The central meaning shared by these adjectives is "inclined to,
marked by, or passed in friendly companionship with others":
*had a social cup of coffee; a companionable pet; a woman of con-
vivial nature; a gregarious person who avoids solitude; a sociable
conversation.*
  ✔ *Antonym:* **antisocial**

solve   *solve decipher resolve unravel*
The central meaning shared by these verbs is "to clear up or explain something puzzling or unintelligible": *solve a riddle; can't decipher his handwriting; resolve a problem; unravel a mystery.*

sour   *sour acid acidulous dry tart*
The central meaning shared by these adjectives is "having a taste like that produced by an acid": *sour cider; acid, unripe grapes; an acidulous tomato; dry white wine; tart cherries.*

spacious   *spacious ample capacious commodious roomy*
The central meaning shared by these adjectives is "having or affording a generous amount of space": *a spacious apartment; an ample kitchen; a capacious purse; a commodious harbor; roomy pockets.*

sparing   *sparing frugal thrifty economical*
These adjectives mean exercising or reflecting care in the use of resources, such as money. **Sparing** stresses restraint, as in expenditure: *sparing in bestowing gifts; neither profligate nor sparing of her time.* **Frugal** implies self-denial and abstention from luxury: *a frugal diet; a frugal farmer.* **Thrifty** suggests industry, care, and diligence in conserving means: *is excessively thrifty because he remembers the Depression.* **Economical** emphasizes prudence, skillful management, and the avoidance of waste: *an economical shopper; the most economical use of energy.*

speak   *speak talk converse discourse*
These verbs mean to express one's thoughts by uttering words. **Speak** and **talk,** often interchangeable, are the most general: *He ate his meal without once speaking to his dinner companion. "Why don't you speak for yourself, John?"* (Henry Wadsworth Longfellow). *"On an occasion of this kind it becomes more than a moral*

duty to speak one's mind. It becomes a pleasure" (Oscar Wilde). *I want to talk with you about vacation plans*. "*We must know . . . what we are talking about*" (Henry James). "*Let's talk sense to the American people*" (Adlai E. Stevenson). **Converse** stresses interchange of thoughts and ideas: "*With thee conversing I forget all time*" (John Milton). **Discourse** usually refers to formal, extended speech: "*striding through the city, stick in hand, discoursing spontaneously on the writings of Hazlitt*" (Manchester Guardian Weekly).

speed   speed hurry hasten quicken accelerate precipitate

These verbs mean to proceed or cause to proceed rapidly or more rapidly. **Speed** refers to swift motion or action: *The train sped through the countryside. Postal workers labored overtime to speed delivery of the Christmas mail.* **Hurry** implies a markedly faster rate than usual, often with concomitant confusion or commotion: *If you don't hurry, you'll miss the plane. Don't let anyone hurry you into making a decision you'll regret later.* **Hasten** suggests urgency and often eager or rash swiftness: *I hasten to respond to your invitation. Put the hot broth in the refrigerator for an hour to hasten cooling.* **Quicken** and especially **accelerate** refer to an increase in rate of activity, growth, or progress: *The dancer's breathing quickened as she approached the end of her solo. The runner quickened his pace as he drew near to the finish line. Despite efforts to eradicate it, corruption persists, though it doesn't accelerate. Heat greatly accelerates the deterioration of perishable foods.* **Precipitate** implies suddenness or impetuousness that often causes something to happen abruptly or prematurely: *The mere mention of the issue precipitated an outburst of indignation during the meeting.*

spend   spend disburse expend

The central meaning shared by these verbs is "to pay or give out money or an equivalent in return for something": *spent five dollars for a movie ticket; disbursing funds from the corporate account; expending energy on a project.*

✓ Antonym: **save**

spontaneous   *spontaneous impulsive instinctive involuntary automatic*

These adjectives mean acting, reacting, or happening without apparent forethought, prompting, or planning. **Spontaneous** applies to what arises naturally rather than resulting from external constraint or stimulus: *The two suddenly embraced in a spontaneous gesture of affection.* "*The highest and best form of efficiency is the spontaneous cooperation of a free people*" (Woodrow Wilson). **Impulsive** refers to the operation of a sudden urge or feeling not governed by reason: *Letting her friend borrow her car was an impulsive act that she later regretted.* **Instinctive** implies behavior prompted by instinct as a natural consequence of membership in a species: "*Nor is head-hunting, body-snatching, or killing for food instinctive or natural*" (Bronislaw Malinowski). The term also applies to what reflects or comes about as a result of a natural inclination or innate impulse: *Offering to help the accident victims seems as instinctive as breathing.* **Involuntary** refers to what is not subject to the control of the will: "*It [becoming a hero] was involuntary. They sank my boat*" (John F. Kennedy). **Automatic** suggests the unthinking, unfeeling functioning of a machine; it implies an unvarying mechanical response or reaction: *She accepted the subpoena with an automatic "thank you."*

stain   *stain blot brand stigma taint*

The central meaning shared by these nouns is "a mark of discredit or disgrace, as on one's good name": *a stain on his honor; the blot of treason; the brand of cowardice; the stigma of ignominious defeat; the taint of vice.*

stammer   stammer stutter

These verbs apply to hesitant, stumbling, or halting speech. To *stammer* is generally to speak with involuntary pauses or repetitions, as from nervousness or confusion: *The witness stammered and then fell silent. "He commanded himself sufficiently to stammer out his regrets"* (Frederick Marryat). *Stutter* usually refers to spasmodic repetition or prolongation of sounds, especially consonants, often as a result of a speech impediment: *Those who stutter often receive speech therapy. Caught shoplifting, the culprit stuttered a few transparent lies.*

standard   standard benchmark criterion gauge measure touchstone yardstick

The central meaning shared by these nouns is "a point of reference against which individuals are compared and evaluated": *a book that is a standard of literary excellence; a painting that is a benchmark of quality; educational criteria; behavior that is a gauge of self-control; government funding, a measure of the importance of the arts; success, a touchstone of opportunity, ambition, and ability; farm failures, a yardstick of federal banking policy.*

stay   stay remain wait abide tarry linger sojourn

These verbs mean to continue to be in a given place. *Stay* is the least specific, though it can also suggest that the person involved is a guest or visitor: *We stayed at home all evening. "Must you go? Can't you stay?"* (Charles J. Vaughan). *Remain* is sometimes synonymous with *stay* but more often implies continuing or being left after others have gone: *A few people came to boo but remained to applaud. Please remain for a minute at the end of the meeting; I want a word with you in private. Wait* suggests remaining in readiness, anticipation, or expectation: *"Your father is waiting for me to take a walk with him"* (Booth Tarkington). **Abide** implies continuing for a lengthy period: *"Abide with me"* (Henry Francis Lyte). **Tarry** and **linger** both imply a delayed departure, but *linger* more strongly suggests reluctance to leave: *"She was not anxious but puzzled that her husband tarried"* (Eden Phillpotts). *"I alone sit lingering here"* (Henry Vaughan). To **sojourn** is to reside temporarily in a place: *"He was sojourning at [a] hotel in Bond Street"* (Anthony Trollope).

steal   steal purloin filch snitch pilfer cop hook swipe lift pinch

These verbs mean to take another's property wrongfully, often surreptitiously. **Steal** is the most general: *stole a car; stealing a few moments for relaxation; research that was stolen by a colleague.* To **purloin** is to make off with something, often in a breach of trust: *purloined the key to his safe-deposit box.* **Filch** and **snitch** often suggest that what is stolen is of little value, while **pilfer** sometimes connotes theft of or in small quantities: *filched an ashtray from the restaurant; snitch a handkerchief; strawberries pilfered from the farmer.* **Cop, hook,** and **swipe** frequently connote quick, furtive snatching or seizing: *copped a necklace from the counter; planning to hook a fur coat; swiped a magazine from the doctor's waiting room.* To **lift** is to pick or take something up surreptitiously and keep it for oneself: *The pickpocket lifted my wallet.* **Pinch** suggests stealing something by or as if by squeezing it between the thumb and the fingers: *went into the study and pinched a dollar bill.*

steep   steep abrupt precipitous sheer

The central meaning shared by these adjectives is "so sharply inclined as to be almost perpendicular": *steep cliffs; an abrupt canyon; precipitous hills; a sheer descent of rock.*

stem *stem arise derive emanate flow issue originate proceed rise spring*

The central meaning shared by these verbs is "to come forth or come into being": *customs stemming from the past; misery arising from war; rights deriving from citizenship; disapproval emanating from the teacher; happiness that flows from their friendship; prejudice that issues from fear; a proposal originating in the Congress; a mistake that proceeded from carelessness; rebellion rising in the provinces; new industries springing up.*

stench *stench fetor malodor reek stink*

The central meaning shared by these nouns is "a penetrating, objectionable odor": *the stench of burning rubber; the fetor of polluted waters; the malodor of diesel fumes; the reek of stale sweat; a stink of decayed flesh.*

stiff *stiff rigid inflexible inelastic tense*

These adjectives are compared as they describe what is very firm and does not easily bend or give way. **Stiff,** the least specific, refers to what can be flexed only with difficulty (*a brush with stiff bristles; a stiff collar*); with reference to persons it often suggests a lack of ease, cold formality, or fixity, as of purpose: *"stiff in opinions"* (John Dryden). **Rigid** and **inflexible** apply to what cannot be bent without damage or deformation (*a table made of rigid plastic; an inflexible knife blade*); figuratively they describe what does not relent or yield: *"under the dictates of a rigid disciplinarian"* (Thomas B. Aldrich). *"In religion the law is written, and inflexible, never to do evil"* (Oliver Goldsmith). **Inelastic** refers largely to what lacks elasticity and so will not stretch and spring back without marked physical change: *an inelastic substance.* **Tense** means stretched tight; it is applied literally to body structures such as muscles and figuratively to what is marked by tautness or strain: *"that tense moment of expectation"* (Arnold Bennett).

stoop   *stoop condescend deign*
The central meaning shared by these verbs is "to descend to a level considered inappropriate to one's dignity": *stooping to contemptible methods to realize their ambitions; won't condescend to acknowledge his rival's greeting; didn't even deign to reply.*

stop   *stop cease desist discontinue halt quit*
The central meaning shared by these verbs is "to bring or come to a cessation": *stop arguing; ceased crying; desist from complaining; discontinued the treatment; halting the convoy; quit laughing.*
   ✔ Antonym: **start**

strange   *strange peculiar odd queer quaint outlandish singular eccentric curious*
These adjectives describe what deviates from the usual or customary. **Strange** refers especially to what is unfamiliar, unknown, or inexplicable: *"I do hate to be chucked in the dark aboard a strange ship. I wonder where they keep their fresh water"* (Joseph Conrad). **Peculiar** particularly describes what is distinct from all others: *The kitchen was redolent with the peculiar aromatic odor of cloves.* Something that is **odd** fails to accord with what is ordinary, usual, or expected, while something **queer** deviates markedly from the norm; both terms can suggest strangeness or peculiarity: *I find it odd that his name is never mentioned. "Now, my suspicion is that the universe is not only queerer than we suppose, but queerer than we can suppose"* (J.B.S. Haldane). **Quaint** refers to pleasing or old-fashioned peculiarity: *"the quaint streets of New Orleans, that most foreign of American cities"* (Winston Churchill). **Outlandish** suggests alien or bizarre strangeness: *"They were*

dressed in a quaint, outlandish fashion" (Washington Irving). **Singular** describes what is unique or unparalleled; the term often suggests an unusual or peculiar quality that arouses curiosity or wonder: *Such poise is singular in one so young.* **Eccentric** refers particularly to what departs strikingly from the recognized or conventional: *Many consider Berlioz's compositions to be innovative but eccentric.* **Curious** suggests strangeness or novelty that excites interest: *Americans living abroad often acquire a curious hybrid accent.*

streak   *streak strain vein*

The central meaning shared by these nouns is "an intermixture of an unexpected quality, as in a person's character": *a streak of humor; a strain of melancholy; a vein of stubbornness.*

strength   *strength power might energy force*

These nouns are compared as they denote the capacity to act or work effectively. **Strength** refers especially to physical, mental, or moral robustness or vigor: *"enough work to do, and strength enough to do the work"* (Rudyard Kipling). *"We are of course a nation of differences. Those differences don't make us weak. They're the source of our strength"* (Jimmy Carter). **Power** is the ability to do something and especially to produce an effect: *"I do not think the United States would come to an end if we lost our power to declare an Act of Congress void"* (Oliver Wendell Holmes, Jr.). **Might** often implies abundant or extraordinary power: *"With twenty-five squadrons of fighters he could defend the island against the whole might of the German Air Force"* (Winston S. Churchill). **Energy** in this comparison refers especially to a latent source of power: *"The same energy of character which renders a man a daring villain would have rendered him useful to society, had that society been well organized"* (Mary Wollstonecraft). **Force** is the application of power or strength: *"the overthrow of our institutions by force and violence"* (Charles Evans Hughes).

strut *strut swagger swank*

The central meaning shared by these verbs is "to walk or conduct oneself with exaggerated self-importance or affected superiority": *a pompous lecturer strutting back and forth across the
stage; a parvenu swaggering around at a party; a newly elected senator's wife swanking around town.*

subject *subject matter topic theme*

These nouns denote the principal idea or point of a speech, a
piece of writing, or an artistic work. **Subject** is the most general:
"Well, honor is the subject of my story" (William Shakespeare).
Matter refers to the material that is the object of thought or discourse: *"This distinction seems to me to go to the root of the matter"*
(William James). A **topic** is a subject of discussion, argument, or
conversation: *"They would talk of nothing but high life . . . with
other fashionable topics, such as pictures, taste, Shakespeare"*
(Oliver Goldsmith). **Theme** refers especially to a subject, an idea,
a point of view, or a perception that is developed and ex-
panded on in a work of art: *"To produce a mighty book, you must
choose a mighty theme"* (Herman Melville).

sufficient *sufficient adequate enough*

The central meaning shared by these adjectives is "being what
is needed without being in excess": *has sufficient income for a
comfortable retirement; bought an adequate supply of food; drew
enough water to fill the tub.*
  ✔ *Antonym:* **insufficient**

suggest *suggest imply hint intimate insinuate*

These verbs mean to convey thoughts or ideas by indirection.
Suggest refers to the calling of something to mind as the result
of an association of ideas or train of thought: *"his erect and careless attitude suggesting assurance and power"* (Joseph Conrad). To

imply is to suggest a thought or an idea that is unexpressed but that can be inferred from something else, such as a statement, that is more explicit: *The effusive praise the professor heaped on one of the students seemed to imply indifference toward or disapproval of the rest.* **Hint** refers to an oblique or covert suggestion that often contains clues: *He hinted that he would accept an invitation if it were extended. My imagination supplied the explanation you only hinted at.* **Intimate** applies to indirect, subtle expression that often reflects discretion, tact, or reserve: *She intimated that she and her husband were having marital problems.* To **insinuate** is to suggest something, usually something unpleasant, in a covert, sly, and underhanded manner: *The columnist insinuated — but never actually asserted — that the candidate had underworld ties.*

superfluous   *superfluous excess extra spare*
supernumerary surplus
The central meaning shared by these adjectives is "being more than is needed, desired, required, or appropriate": *delete superfluous words; trying to lose excess weight; found some extra change on the dresser; sleeping in the spare room; supernumerary ornamentation; surplus cheese distributed to the needy.*

supervise   *supervise boss overlook oversee superintend*
The central meaning shared by these verbs is "to have the direction and oversight of and performance of others": *supervised a team of investigators; bossed a construction crew; overlooking farm hands; overseeing plumbers and electricians; superintend a household staff.*

support   *support uphold back advocate champion*
These verbs are compared as they mean to give aid or encouragement to a person or cause. **Support** is the most general: *is being supported by friends in her effort to surmount the tragedy; "the*

policy of Cromwell, who supported the growing power of France against the declining power of Spain" (William E.H. Lecky). To **uphold** is to maintain or affirm in the face of a challenge or strong opposition: *"The Declaration of Right upheld the principle of hereditary monarchy"* (Edmund Burke). **Back** suggests material or moral support intended to contribute to or assure success: *"There is only one proved method of assisting the advancement of pure science — that of picking men of genius, backing them heavily, and leaving them to direct themselves"* (James B. Conant). **Advocate** implies verbal support, often in the form of pleading or arguing: *Scientists advocate a reduction in saturated fats in the human diet.* To **champion** is to fight for one that is under attack or lacks the strength or ability to act in its own behalf: *"championed the government and defended the system of taxation"* (Samuel Chew).

supposed   supposed conjectural hypothetical putative
reputed suppositious supposititious
The central meaning shared by these adjectives is "put forth or accepted as being true on inconclusive grounds": *the supposed cause of inflation; conjectural criticism; the site of a hypothetical colony; a foundling's putative father; the reputed author of the article; suppositious reconstructions of dead languages; supposititious hypotheses.*

  ✔ Antonym: **certain**

surprise   surprise astonish amaze astound
dumbfound flabbergast
These verbs mean to affect a person strongly as being unexpected or unusual. To **surprise** is to fill with often sudden wonder or disbelief as being unanticipated or out of the ordinary: *"Never tell people how to do things. Tell them what to do and they will surprise you with their ingenuity"* (George S. Patton). **Astonish** suggests overwhelming surprise: *The sight of such an enormous crowd astonished us.* **Amaze** implies astonishment and often be-

wilderment: *The violinist's virtuosity has amazed audiences all over the world.* **Astound** connotes shock, as from something unprecedented in one's experience: *We were astounded at the high cost of traveling in Japan.* **Dumbfound** adds to **astound** the suggestion of perplexity and often wordlessness: *His denial that he had witnessed the accident dumbfounded me.* **Flabbergast** is used as a more colorful equivalent of *astound, astonish,* or *amaze:* "*The aldermen . . . were . . . flabbergasted; they were speechless from bewilderment*" (Benjamin Disraeli).

surround   *surround circle compass encircle encompass environ gird girdle ring*
The central meaning shared by these verbs is "to lie around and bound on all sides": *a city surrounded by suburbs; a crown circling a king's head; a mountain peak compassed by fog; a belt encircling her waist; a lake that encompasses an island; oases environed by the desert; a castle girded by a moat; gardens girdling a bird bath; a dinner table ringed with guests.*

swerve   *swerve depart deviate digress diverge stray veer*
The central meaning shared by these verbs is "to turn away from a straight or prescribed course": *eyes that never once swerved from her face; won't depart from family traditions; deviated from their original plan; digressing from the principal topic; opinions that diverged; straying from the truth; veered the conversation away from politics.*

symbol   *symbol attribute emblem*
The central meaning shared by these nouns is "something associated with and standing for, representing, or identifying something else": *scales, the symbol of justice; the scepter, an attribute of royal power; the thistle, the emblem of Scotland.*

tardy   *tardy behindhand late overdue*

The central meaning shared by these adjectives is "not arriving, occurring, acting, or done at the scheduled, expected, or usual time": *tardy in making a dental appointment; behindhand with her car payments; late for the plane; an overdue bus.*

✔ Antonym: **prompt**

task   *task job chore stint assignment*

These nouns denote a piece of work that one must do. A *task* is a well-defined responsibility that is usually imposed by another and that may be burdensome: *"A man ought to read just as inclination leads him; for what he reads as a task will do him little good"* (Samuel Johnson). *Job* often suggests a specific short-term undertaking: *"did little jobs about the house with skill"* (W.H. Auden). *Chore* generally denotes a minor, routine, or odd job: *The farmer's morning chores included cleaning the stables and milking the cows.* *Stint* refers to a person's prescribed share of work: *Her stint as a lifeguard usually consumes three hours a day.* *Assignment* generally denotes a task allotted by a person in authority: *The reporter's assignment was to attend the trial and interview the principals at its conclusion.*

taste   *taste flavor relish savor smack tang*

The central meaning shared by these nouns is "a quality that can be perceived by the gustatory sense": *the salty taste of anchovies; the pungent flavor of garlic; the aromatic relish of freshly brewed coffee; the savor of rich chocolate; the spicy smack of curry sauce; the fresh tang of lemonade.*

teach   *teach instruct educate train school discipline drill*

These verbs mean to impart knowledge or skill. *Teach* is the most widely applicable: *teaching a child the alphabet; teaches po-*

litical science. "We shouldn't teach great books; we should teach a love of reading" (B.F. Skinner). **Instruct** usually suggests methodical teaching: *A graduate student instructed the freshmen in the rudiments of music theory.* **Educate** often implies formal instruction but especially stresses the development of innate capacities that leads to wide cultivation: *"All educated Americans, first or last, go to Europe"* (Ralph Waldo Emerson). **Train** suggests concentration on particular skills intended to fit a person for a desired role: *The young woman attends vocational school, where she is being trained as a computer technician.* **School** often implies an arduous learning process: *The violinist had been schooled to practice slowly to assure accurate intonation.* **Discipline** usually refers to the teaching of control, especially self-control: *The writer has disciplined himself to work between breakfast and lunch every day.* **Drill** implies rigorous instruction or training, often by repetition of a routine: *The French instructor drilled the students in irregular verbs.*

tear *tear rip rend split cleave*
These verbs mean to separate or pull apart by force. **Tear** involves pulling something apart or into pieces: *"She tore the letter in shreds"* (Edith Wharton). **Rip** implies rough or forcible tearing apart or away, often along a dividing line such as a seam or joint: *Carpenters ripped up the old floorboards.* **Rend** usually refers to violent tearing or wrenching apart: *"Come as the winds come, when / Forests are rended"* (Sir Walter Scott). To **split** is to cut or break something into parts or layers, especially along its entire length or along a natural line of division: *"They [wood stumps] warmed me twice — once while I was splitting them, and again when they were on the fire"* (Henry David Thoreau). **Cleave** most often refers to splitting with or as if with a sharp instrument: *"The apple's cleft right through the core"* (J.C.F. von Schiller).

teem *teem abound bristle crawl overflow swarm*

The central meaning shared by these verbs is "to be abundantly filled or richly supplied": *a street teeming with pedestrians; a garden abounding with flowers; roofs bristling with television antennas; a highway crawling with cars; a house overflowing with guests; a parade route swarming with spectators.*

temporary *temporary acting adinterim interim provisional*

The central meaning shared by these adjectives is "assuming the duties of another for the time being": *a temporary chairperson; the acting dean; an ad interim admissions committee; an interim administration; a provisional mayor.*

> ✓ Antonym: **permanent**

tend *tend attend mind minister watch*

The central meaning shared by these verbs is "to have the care or supervision of": *tended her plants; attending the sick; minded the furnace; ministering to flood victims; watched the house while the owners were away.*

tendency *tendency trend current drift tenor inclination*

These nouns are compared as they refer to the direction or course of an action or a thought. **Tendency** implies a predisposition to proceed in a particular way: *"The tendency of our own day is . . . towards firm, solid, verifiable knowledge"* (William H. Mallock). **Trend** often applies to a general or prevailing direction, especially within a particular sphere: *"the trend of religious thought in recent times"* (James Harvey Robinson). **Current** suggests a course or flow, as of opinion, especially one representative of a given time or place: *"[These] words . . . express the whole current of modern feeling"* (James Bryce). A **drift** is a tendency that depends for its direction or course on the impetus of something likened to a shifting current of air or water: *Polit-*

ical conservatives fear a drift toward communism in Latin America.
Tenor implies a continuous, unwavering course: *"His conduct was . . . uniform and unvarying in its tenor"* (Frederick Marryat).
Inclination usually refers to an individual's propensity for or disposition toward one thing rather than another: *"Man's capacity for justice makes democracy possible, but man's inclination to injustice makes democracy necessary"* (Reinhold Niebuhr).

theoretical   *theoretical abstract academic hypothetical speculative*

The central meaning shared by these adjectives is "concerned primarily with theories or hypotheses rather than practical considerations": *theoretical linguistics; abstract reasoning; a purely academic discussion; a hypothetical statement; speculative knowledge.*

think   *think cerebrate cogitate reason reflect speculate*

The central meaning shared by these verbs is "to use the powers of the mind, as in conceiving ideas or drawing inferences": *thought before answering; sat in front of the fire cerebrating; cogitating about business problems; reasons clearly; took time to reflect before deciding; speculating on what has happened.*

thoughtful   *thoughtful considerate attentive solicitous*

These adjectives mean having or showing concern for the well-being of others. Although *thoughtful* and *considerate* are often used interchangeably, **thoughtful** implies a tendency to anticipate needs or wishes, whereas **considerate** stresses sensitivity to another's feelings: *It was thoughtful of you to bring flowers. Apartment dwellers who have considerate neighbors are fortunate.* **Attentive** suggests devoted, assiduous attention: *The nurse was attentive to his patient, constantly checking to be sure she was comfortable.* **Solicitous** implies deep concern that often verges on anxiety or expresses itself in exaggerated and sometimes cloying attentiveness: *For heaven's sake, Mother, I am an adult! Stop being so solicitous.*

throw   *throw cast hurl fling pitch toss sling*
These verbs mean to propel something through the air with a motion of the hand or arm. **Throw** is the least specific: *throw a ball; threw the life preserver to the struggling swimmer; threw the book on the table.* **Cast** usually refers to throwing something light: *The angler cast her line into the stream.* **Hurl** and **fling** mean to throw with great force: *"Him the Almighty Power / Hurl'd headlong flaming from th' Ethereal Sky"* (John Milton). *The wedding guests were given confetti to fling at the bride and groom.* **Pitch** often means to throw with careful aim: *"a special basket in my study . . . into which I pitch letters, circulars, pamphlets and so forth"* (H.G. Wells). **Toss,** in contrast, usually means to throw lightly or casually: *"Campton tossed the card away"* (Edith Wharton). **Sling** stresses force of propulsion: *The cook's helper slung the peeled potatoes into a huge enamel pot.*

tight   *tight taut tense*
The central meaning shared by these adjectives is "not slack or loose on account of being pulled or drawn out fully": *a tight skirt; taut sails; tense piano strings.*

timid   *timid timorous*
The central meaning shared by these adjectives is "hesitating to take action or assert oneself out of fear, apprehensiveness, or lack of self-confidence": *too timid to protest; timorous of venturing an opinion.*

tire   *tire weary fatigue exhaust jade*
These verbs mean to cause or undergo depletion of strength,

energy, spirit, interest, or patience. *Tire* is the general, nonspecific term; it often suggests a state resulting from exertion, excess, dullness, or ennui: *Long hours of arduous hiking tired the scouts.* "*When a man is tired of London, he is tired of life*" (Samuel Johnson). *Weary,* like *tire,* is applicable to diminution of strength or endurance but often carries a stronger implication of dissatisfaction, as that resulting from what is irksome or boring: *found the journey wearying; soon wearied of their constant bickering.* *Fatigue* implies great weariness, as that caused by stress: *fatigued by the day's labors;* "*nothing so fatiguing as the eternal hanging on of an uncompleted task*" (William James). To *exhaust* is to wear out completely; the term connotes total draining of physical or emotional strength: "*Like all people who try to exhaust a subject, he exhausted his listeners*" (Oscar Wilde). *Jade* refers principally to dullness that most often results from overindulgence: *Even an exquisitely prepared dinner couldn't revive her jaded palate.*

tireless   *tireless indefatigable unflagging untiring unwearied weariless*

The central meaning shared by these adjectives is "having or showing a capacity for prolonged and laborious effort": *a tireless worker; an indefatigable advocate of equal rights; unflagging pursuit of excellence; untiring energy; an unwearied researcher; a weariless defender of freedom of the press.*

tool   *tool instrument implement utensil appliance*

These nouns refer to devices used in the performance of work. *Tool* applies broadly to a device that facilitates work; specifically it denotes a small manually operated device, such as a file, of the kind employed by carpenters and plumbers: *a box full of tools for repair jobs.* *Instrument* refers especially to one of the relatively small precision tools, such as a stethoscope or supersonic drill, used by trained professionals such as doctors and dentists: *had to sterilize all the instruments*. **Implement** is the preferred term for tools used in agriculture and certain building trades: *rakes, hoes, and other implements*. **Utensil** often refers to an implement, such as a pot or spoon, used in doing household work: *cooking utensils laid out on the table*. **Appliance** most frequently denotes a power-driven device, such as a toaster or refrigerator, that performs a specific function: *a store selling modern appliances*.

touch   *touch feel finger handle palpate paw*

The central meaning shared by these verbs is "to bring the hands or fingers into contact with so as to give or receive a physical sensation": *gently touched my hand; felt the runner's pulse; fingering his worry beads; handle a bolt of fabric; palpating the patient's abdomen; fans pawing a celebrity's arm*.

treat   *treat deal handle*

The central meaning shared by these verbs is "to act in a specified way with regard to someone or something": *treats his guests with courtesy; dealt rationally with the problem; handling a case with discretion*.

trial   *trial affliction crucible ordeal tribulation visitation*

The central meaning shared by these nouns is "distress or suffering that severely tests resiliency and character": *no consolation in their hour of trial; the affliction of a bereaved family; the crucible of revolution; the ordeal of being an innocent murder suspect; domestic tribulations; an epidemic considered to be a visitation*.

trouble   *trouble ail distress worry*

The central meaning shared by these verbs is "to cause anxious uneasiness in": *suffers memory lapses that trouble her chil-*

dren; asked him what's ailing him; a turn of events that has distressed us; has a high fever that worries the doctor.

truth   *truth veracity verity verisimilitude*

These nouns refer to the quality of being in accord with fact or reality. *Truth* is a comprehensive term that in all of its nuances implies accuracy and honesty: *"Every man is fully satisfied that there is such a thing as truth, or he would not ask any questions"* (Charles S. Peirce). *"We seek the truth, and will endure the consequences"* (Charles Seymour). *Veracity* is adherence to the truth: *"Veracity is the heart of morality"* (Thomas H. Huxley). *Verity* often applies to an enduring or repeatedly demonstrated truth: *"beliefs that were accepted as eternal verities"* (James Harvey Robinson). *Verisimilitude* is the quality of having the appearance of truth or reality: *"merely corroborative detail, intended to give artistic verisimilitude to an otherwise bald and unconvincing narrative"* (W.S. Gilbert).

turn   *turn rotate revolve gyrate spin whirl circle eddy swirl*

These verbs all mean to move or cause to move in a circle. *Turn,* the most general, means to move in a circular course: *a planet turning on its axis; turned and stared at me. Rotate* usually involves movement around an object's own axis or center: *The top rotated with decreasing speed as the spring wound down. Revolve* can have the same meaning as *rotate,* while in certain contexts it is distinguished from *rotate* as involving orbital movement: *The earth revolves around the sun. Gyrate* usually refers to revolving in or as if in a spiral course: *waltzers gyrating giddily.* To *spin* is to rotate rapidly, often within a narrow compass: *"He . . . spun round, flung up his arms, and fell on his back, shot through"* (John Galsworthy). *Whirl* applies to rapid or forceful revolution or rotation: *whirling snowflakes. Circle* refers to circular or ap-

proximately circular motion: *sea gulls circling above the ocean.*
Eddy usually denotes rapid circular movement like that of
a whirlpool: *Storm clouds eddied overhead.* **Swirl,** often interchangeable with *eddy,* sometimes connotes a graceful undula-
tion, spiral, or whorl: *The flood waters swirled wildly under the
bridge. The milliner swirled tulle lavishly above the brim of the hat.*

ugly ugly hideous ill-favored unsightly

The central meaning shared by these adjectives is "offensive to
the sense of sight": *ugly furniture; a hideous scar; an ill-favored
countenance; an unsightly billboard.*
  ✔ Antonym: **beautiful**

uncertainty uncertainty doubt dubiety skepticism suspicion mistrust

These nouns all refer to the condition of being unsure about
someone or something. **Uncertainty,** the least forceful, merely
denotes a lack of assurance or conviction: *I regarded my decision
with growing uncertainty.* **Doubt** and **dubiety** imply a questioning
state of mind that leads to hesitation in accepting a premise or
in making a decision: *"Doubt is part of all religion"* (Isaac Bashevis Singer). *On this point there can be no dubiety.* **Skepticism** generally suggests an instinctive or habitual tendency to question
and demand proof, as of truth or merit: *"A wise skepticism is
the first attribute of a good critic"* (James Russell Lowell). **Suspicion** is doubt as to the innocence, truth, integrity, honesty, or
soundness of someone or something; the word often suggests
an uneasy feeling that the person or thing is evil: *"I had rather
take my chance that some traitors will escape detection than spread
abroad a spirit of general suspicion and distrust"* (Learned Hand).
Mistrust denotes lack of trust or confidence, as in a person's
motives, arising from suspicion: *Corporate leaders viewed the
economist's recommendations with mistrust.*

unctuous   *unctuous fulsome oily oleaginous smarmy*
The central meaning shared by these adjectives is "insincerely, self-servingly, or smugly agreeable or earnest": *an ambitious and unctuous assistant; gave the dictator a fulsome introduction; oily praise; oleaginous hypocrisy; smarmy self-importance.*

unfortunate   *unfortunate hapless ill-fated ill-starred luckless unlucky*
The central meaning shared by these adjectives is "marked by, affected by, or promising bad fortune": *an unfortunate turn of events; a hapless victim; an ill-fated business venture; an ill-starred romance; a luckless prisoner of war; an unlucky accident.*
   ✔ Antonym: **fortunate**

unreasonable   *unreasonable irrational*
The central meaning shared by these adjectives is "not guided by or predicated on reason": *an unreasonable expectation; irrational fears.*
   ✔ Antonym: **reasonable**

unruly   *unruly ungovernable intractable refractory recalcitrant willful headstrong wayward*
These adjectives all mean resistant or marked by resistance to control. **Unruly** implies failure to submit to rule or discipline: *The little boy's parents think he is spirited, but his teacher finds him unruly.* One that is **ungovernable** is not capable of or amenable to being governed or restrained: *an ungovernable temper.* **Intractable** refers to what is obstinate and difficult to manage or control: *"Fox, as the less proud and intractable of the refractory pair, was preferred"* (Thomas Macaulay). **Refractory** implies stubborn resistance to control or authority: *as refractory as a mule.* One that is **recalcitrant** not only resists authority but rebels against it: *The university suspended the most recalcitrant demon-*

strators. **Willful** and **headstrong** describe one obstinately bent on having his or her own way: *Willful people cannot tolerate the slightest frustration of their wishes. His headstrong daughter is destined to learn from her own mistakes*. One who is **wayward** willfully and often perversely departs from what is desired, advised, expected, or required in order to gratify his or her own impulses or inclinations: *"a lively child, who had been spoilt and indulged, and therefore was sometimes wayward"* (Charlotte Brontë).

unspeakable   unspeakable indefinable indescribable ineffable inexpressible unutterable

The central meaning shared by these adjectives is "defying expression or description": *unspeakable misery; indefinable yearnings; indescribable beauty; ineffable ecstasy; inexpressible anguish; unutterable contempt*.

urgent   urgent pressing imperative exigent

These adjectives are compared as they mean compelling immediate attention. **Urgent** often implies that a matter takes precedence over others: *"My business is too urgent to waste time on apologies"* (John Buchan). **Pressing** suggests an urgency that demands that prompt measures be taken: *"The danger now became too pressing to admit of longer delay"* (James Fenimore Cooper). **Imperative** implies a need or demand whose fulfillment cannot be evaded or deferred: *As more nations acquire nuclear weapons the necessity for preventing war becomes imperative*. Something **exigent** requires swift action or remedy: *Her family's needs make exigent demands on her time and energy*.

use   use employ utilize

These verbs mean to avail oneself of someone or something in order to make him, her, or it useful, functional, or beneficial. To **use** is to put into service or apply for a purpose: *uses a hearing* *aid; used the press secretary as spokesperson for the administration; using a stick to stir the paint.* **Employ** is often interchangeable with *use: She employed her education to maximum advantage.* Unlike *use,* however, the term can denote engaging or maintaining the services of another or putting another to work: *"When men are employed, they are best contented"* (Benjamin Franklin). **Utilize** is especially appropriate in the narrower sense of making something profitable or of finding new and practical uses for it: *In the 19th century waterpower was widely utilized to generate electricity.*

usual   *usual habitual customary accustomed*

These adjectives apply to what is expected or familiar because it occurs frequently or recurs regularly. **Usual** describes what accords with normal, common, or ordinary practice or procedure: *"The parson said the usual things about the sea — its blueness . . . its beauty"* (George du Maurier). **Habitual** implies repetition and force of habit: *"He who permits himself to tell a lie once, finds it much easier to do it a second and third time, till at length it becomes habitual"* (Thomas Jefferson). **Customary** and **accustomed** refer to conformity with the prevailing customs or conventions of a group or with an individual's own established practice: *"It is the customary fate of new truths to begin as heresies and to end as superstitions"* (Thomas H. Huxley). *She resolved the difficulty with her accustomed resourcefulness and tact.*

vain   *vain empty hollow idle nugatory otiose*

The central meaning shared by these adjectives is "lacking value or substance": *vain regrets; empty pleasures; hollow threats; idle dreams; nugatory commentaries; an otiose belief in alchemy.*

valid   *valid sound cogent convincing telling*

These adjectives describe assertions, arguments, conclusions, reasons, or intellectual processes that are persuasive because they are well founded, as in fact, logic, or rationality. What is **valid** is based on or borne out by truth or fact or has legal force: *a valid excuse; a valid claim*. What is **sound** is free from logical flaws or is based on valid reasoning: *a sound theory; sound principles*. Something **cogent** is both sound and compelling: *cogent testimony; a cogent explanation*. **Convincing** implies the power to dispel doubt or overcome resistance or opposition: *convincing proof*. **Telling** means strikingly effective: *The attorney's summation was telling*.

vent   *vent express utter voice air*

These verbs mean to give outlet to thoughts or emotions. To **vent** is to unburden oneself of a strong pent-up emotion: *"She was jealous . . . and glad of any excuse to vent her pique"* (Edward G.E.L. Bulwer-Lytton). **Express,** a more comprehensive term, refers to communication both by verbal and by nonverbal means: *can't express the idea adequately in words; expressed her affection with a hug; "expressing emotion in the form of art"* (T.S. Eliot). **Utter** involves vocal expression; it may imply speech but can also refer to inarticulate sounds: *"The words were uttered in the hearing of Montezuma"* (William Hickling Prescott). *"The Canon uttered a resounding sigh"* (John Galsworthy). **Voice** denotes the expression in speech or writing of the outlook or viewpoint of a person or, often, of a group: *The judge voiced her satisfaction that the jury had reached a verdict. The majority leader rose to voice the party's opposition to the bill*. To **air** is to give vent to and often to show off one's feelings, beliefs, or ideas: *He wants a forum where he can air his favorite theory*.

versatile   *versatile all-around many-sided*
multifaceted multifarious

The central meaning shared by these adjectives is "having many aspects, uses, or abilities": *a versatile writer; an all-around athlete; a many-sided subject; a multifaceted undertaking; multifarious interests.*

vertical   *vertical upright perpendicular plumb*

These adjectives are compared as they mean being at or approximately at right angles to the horizon or to level ground. *Vertical* and especially *upright* are often used to signify contrast with what is horizontal; the terms do not always imply an exact right angle: *wallpaper with vertical stripes; an upright column.* *Perpendicular* and *plumb* are generally used to specify an angle of precisely 90 degrees: *a perpendicular escarpment; careful to make the doorjambs plumb.*

victory   *victory conquest triumph*

These nouns denote the fact of winning or the state of having won in a war, struggle, or competition. *Victory,* the most general term, refers especially to the final defeat of an enemy or opponent: *"Victory at all costs, victory in spite of all terror, victory however long and hard the road may be; for without victory there is no survival"* (Winston S. Churchill). *Conquest* connotes subduing, subjugating, or achieving mastery or control over someone or something: *"Conquest of illiteracy comes first"* (John Kenneth Galbraith). *Triumph* denotes a victory or success that is especially noteworthy because it is decisive, significant, or spectacular: *"If [a man] has a talent and learns somehow to use the whole of it, he has gloriously succeeded, and won a satisfaction and a triumph few men ever know"* (Thomas Wolfe).

vigor   *vigor dash punch verve vim vitality*

The central meaning shared by these nouns is "a quality of spirited force or energy": *intellectual vigor; played the piano with dash; an editorial with real punch; painted with verve; arguing with his usual vim; a decreased mental vitality.*

voluntary   *voluntary intentional deliberate willful willing*
These adjectives mean being or resulting from one's own free
will. **Voluntary** implies the operation of unforced choice: *"Igno-*
rance, when it is voluntary, is criminal" (Samuel Johnson). **Inten-**
tional applies to something undertaken to further a plan or realize an aim: *"In whatsoever houses I enter, I will enter to help the*
sick, and I will abstain from all intentional wrongdoing and harm"
(Hippocratic Oath). **Deliberate** stresses premeditation and full
awareness of the character and consequences of one's acts: *"In*
life courtesy and self-possession, and in the arts style, are the sensi-
ble impressions of the free mind, for both arise out of a deliberate
shaping of all things" (William Butler Yeats). **Willful** implies deliberate, headstrong persistence in a self-determined course of
action: *a willful waste of time.* **Willing** suggests ready or cheerful
acquiescence in the proposals or requirements of another:
"The first requisite of a good citizen . . . is that he shall be able and
willing to pull his weight" (Theodore Roosevelt).

voracious   *voracious gluttonous rapacious ravenous*
The central meaning shared by these adjectives is "having or
marked by boundless greed": *a voracious observer of the political*
scene; a gluttonous appetite; rapacious demands; ravenous for power.

wander   *wander ramble roam rove range meander*
stray gallivant gad
These verbs mean to move about at random or without destination or purpose. **Wander** and **ramble** stress the absence of a
fixed course or goal: *She wandered into the room. "An old man's*
wit may wander" (Lord Tennyson). *"They would go off together,*
rambling along the river" (John Galsworthy). *"Be not . . . ram-*
bling in thought" (Marcus Aurelius). **Roam** and **rove** emphasize
freedom of movement, often over a wide area: *"Herds of horses*
and cattle roamed at will over the plain" (George W. Cable). *"For*

ten long years I roved about, living first in one capital, then an-other" (Charlotte Brontë). **Range** suggests wandering in all directions: "*a large hunting party known to be ranging the prairie*" (Francis Parkman). "*The talk ranged over literary and publishing matters of mutual interest*" (Edward Bok). **Meander** suggests leisurely, sometimes aimless wandering over an irregular or winding course: "*He meandered to and fro . . . observing the manners and customs of Hillport society*" (Arnold Bennett). **Stray** refers to deviation from a proper course: "*He gave . . . strict directions . . . not to allow any of the men to stray*" (J.A. Froude). "*I ask pardon, I am straying from the question*" (Oliver Goldsmith). **Gallivant** refers to wandering about in search of pleasure: *The students gallivanted all over New York City during the class trip.* **Gad** suggests restless, pointless wandering: *My parents wanted me to stop gadding about unaccompanied in foreign cities.*

waste   *waste blow consume dissipate fritter squander*

The central meaning shared by these verbs is "to spend or expend without restraint and often to no avail": *wasted her inheritance; blew a fortune on a shopping spree; time and money consumed in litigation; dissipating their energies in pointless argument; frittering away her entire allowance; squandered his literary talent on writing commercials.*

   ✔ Antonym: **save**

way   *way route course passage pass artery*

These nouns refer to paths leading from one place or point to another. **Way** is the least specific: "*Many ways meet in one town*" (William Shakespeare). *We made our way on foot. Show me the way home.* **Route** refers to a planned, well-established, or regularly traveled way: "*They know the routes . . . of the trappers; where to waylay them*" (Washington Irving). "*Their one purpose of speed over the great ocean routes was achieved by perfect balance of spars* *and sails to the curving lines of the smooth black hull"* (Samuel Eliot Morison). *Course* suggests the path or channel taken by something, such as a river or a satellite, that moves: *"the stars in their courses"* (Judges 5:20); *"earth's diurnal course"* (William Wordsworth). *Passage* denotes a traversal over, across, or through something: *The yacht continued its passage with favorable winds. The passage between the buildings is dark and cramped.* *Pass* usually refers to a way affording passage around, over, or through a barrier: *"They had reached one of those very narrow passes between two tall stones"* (George Eliot). An *artery* is a main route for the circulation of traffic into which local routes flow: *The city council voted to close the central artery for extensive repairs.*

weak   *weak feeble frail fragile infirm*
decrepit debilitated

These adjectives mean lacking or showing a lack of strength. *Weak,* the most widely applicable, implies lack of physical, mental, or spiritual strength or deficiency of will or purpose: *"These poor wretches . . . were so weak they could hardly sit to their oars"* (Daniel Defoe). *"Like all weak men he laid an exaggerated stress on not changing one's mind"* (W. Somerset Maugham). *Feeble* suggests pathetic or grievous physical or mental weakness or hopeless inadequacy: *a feeble patient; a feeble intellect; a feeble effort.* *"We, who were the tall pine of the forest, have become a feeble plant and need your protection"* (Red Jacket). *Frail* implies delicacy, as of constitution, or lack of ability to endure or withstand: *"an aged thrush, frail, gaunt, and small, / In blast-beruffled plume"* (Thomas Hardy). *"Frail is our happiness, if this be so"* (John Milton). What is *fragile* is easily broken, damaged, or destroyed: *"a fragile dewdrop"* (John Keats). *"This city is for the King, whose body is fragile, a very unhealthy city"* (Lord Dunsany). *Infirm* implies enfeeblement: *"a poor, infirm, weak, and despis'd old man"* (William Shakespeare). *Decrepit* describes what is weakened, worn out, or broken down by hard use or the passage of time: *"childhood, manhood, and decrepit age"* (Francis Quarles). **Debilitated** suggests a gradual impairment of energy or strength: *Her already debilitated constitution is being further weakened by overwork and smoking.*

wet *wet damp moist dank humid*
These adjectives mean covered with or saturated with liquid. **Wet** describes not only what is covered or soaked (*a wet sidewalk; a wet sponge*) but also what is not yet dry (*wet paint*). **Damp** and **moist** both mean slightly wet, but *damp* often implies an unpleasant clamminess: *a cold, damp cellar; a moist breeze.* **Dank** emphasizes disagreeable, often unhealthful wetness: *a dank cave; dank tropical forests.* **Humid** refers to an unpleasantly high degree of moisture in the atmosphere: *hot, humid weather.*

whole *whole all entire gross total*
The central meaning shared by these adjectives is "including every constituent or individual": *a whole town devastated by an earthquake; all the class going on a field trip; entire freedom of choice; gross income; the total cost.*
  ✔ Antonym: **partial**

wonder *wonder marvel miracle phenomenon prodigy sensation*
The central meaning shared by these nouns is "one that evokes amazement or admiration": *saw the wonders of Paris; a marvel of modern technology; a miracle of culinary art; organ transplantation, a phenomenon of medical science; a musical prodigy; a performance that was the sensation of the season.*

wordy *wordy diffuse long-winded prolix verbose*
The central meaning shared by these adjectives is "given to

using or marked by the use of an excessive number of words":
*a wordy apology; a diffuse historical novel; a long-winded speaker;
a prolix, tedious lecturer; verbose correspondence.*

work   *work labor toil drudgery travail*

These nouns refer to physical or mental effort expended to produce or accomplish something. **Work** is the most widely applicable; it can refer both to the activity and the output of persons, machines, and the forces of nature: *"Which of us . . . is to
do the hard and dirty work for the rest — and for what pay?"* (John
Ruskin). *"A work that aspires . . . to the condition of art should
carry its justification in every line"* (Joseph Conrad). **Labor** usually
implies human work, especially of a hard physical or intellectual nature: *"a youth of labor with an age of ease"* (Oliver Goldsmith); *"where men must beg with bated breath for leave to . . . garner the fruits of their own labors"* (Roger Casement). **Toil** applies
principally to strenuous, fatiguing labor: *"I have nothing to offer
but blood, toil, tears and sweat"* (Winston S. Churchill). **Drudgery**
suggests dull, wearisome, or monotonous work: *"the drudgery
of penning definitions and marking quotations for transcription"*
(Thomas Macaulay). **Travail** connotes arduous work involving
pain or suffering: *"I have had my labor for my travail"* (William
Shakespeare).

writhe   *writhe agonize squirm*

The central meaning shared by these verbs is "to twist and
turn in discomfort or suffering": *writhing in pain; agonized over
the impending examination; squirming in embarrassment.*

yield   *yield relent bow defer submit capitulate succumb*

These verbs all mean to give in to what one can no longer oppose or resist. **Yield** has the widest application: *yield to an
enemy; wouldn't yield to reason; yielded to desire.* "The child . . .

soon yielded to the drowsiness" (Charles Dickens). To **relent** is to moderate the harshness or severity of an attitude or decision with respect to another over whom one has authority or influence: *"The captain at last relented, and told him that he might make himself at home"* (Herman Melville). **Bow** suggests giving way in defeat or through courtesy: *"Bow and accept the end / Of a love"* (Robert Frost). To **defer** is to yield out of respect or in recognition of another's authority, knowledge, or judgment: *"Philip . . . had the good sense to defer to the long experience and the wisdom of his father"* (William Hickling Prescott). **Submit** implies giving way out of necessity, as after futile or unsuccessful resistance. *"What must the King do now? Must he submit?"* (William Shakespeare). **Capitulate** implies surrender to pressure, force, compulsion, or inevitability: *"I will be conquered; I will not capitulate* [to illness]*"* (Samuel Johnson). **Succumb** strongly suggests submission to something overpowering or overwhelming: *"I didn't succumb without a struggle to my uncle's allurements"* (H.G. Wells).

young   young youthful adolescent immature juvenile puerile green

These adjectives are compared as they mean of, relating to, characteristic of, or being in an early period of growth or development. **Young** is the most general of the terms: *a young child.* **Youthful** suggests characteristics, such as enthusiasm, freshness, or energy, that are associated with youth: *youthful ardor.* **Adolescent** specifically implies the characteristics of those in the period between childhood and maturity: *adolescent insecurity.* **Immature** applies to what is not yet fully grown or developed; the term sometimes suggests that someone falls short of an expected level of maturity: *an emotionally immature adult.* **Juvenile** connotes immaturity, often childishness: *the juvenile* *pranks of the conventioneers.* **Puerile** is used derogatorily to suggest silliness, foolishness, or infantilism: *a puerile joke.* **Green** implies lack of training or experience and sometimes callowness: *The crew couldn't deal with the emergency. They were all green recruits.*

zest   *zest gusto relish*

The central meaning shared by these nouns is "keen, hearty pleasure or appreciation": *ate with zest; telling a joke with gusto; has no relish for repetitive work.*

SYNONYM INDEX

addle: confuse
adept: proficient
adequate: sufficient
ad interim: temporary
adjust: adapt
ad-lib: extemporaneous
admit: acknowledge
admixture: mixture
adolescent: young
adore: revere
adroit: dexterous
ADULTERATE
ADVANCE
ADVANTAGE
advantageous: beneficial
adventuresome: adventurous
ADVENTUROUS
advert: refer
advertise: announce
ADVICE
advice: news
ADVISE
advocate: support
AFFAIR
AFFECT
AFFECTATION
affection: love
affinity: likeness
AFFLICT
affliction: trial, burden[1]
affluent: rich
affray: conflict
affront: offend

afield: amiss
AFRAID
age: period, mature
AGELESS
aggravate: annoy
AGITATE
agonize: writhe, afflict
AGREE
agree: assent
aid: help
aide: assistant
ail: trouble
AIM
aim: intention
air: affectation, vent
AIRY
ALARM
alarm: fear, frighten
alert: aware, alarm
alien: foreign
alienate: estrange
all: whole
all-around: versatile
allay: relieve
alleviate: relieve
ALLOCATE
ally: partner
ALONE
alternative: choice
altitude: elevation
amalgam: mixture
amalgamate: mix
amass: gather

AMATEUR
amaze: surprise
AMBIGUOUS
ambit: range
ambrosial: delicious
ambuscade: ambush
AMBUSH
ameliorate: improve
amenable: responsible
amend: correct
AMENITY
AMISS
amorphous: shapeless
amour-propre: conceit
ample: spacious, plentiful
AMUSE
analogy: likeness
analytic: logical
ANALYZE
anatomize: analyze
ANCESTOR
anchor: fasten
ancient: old
ANGER
ANGRY
anguish: regret
animate: encourage
ANNOUNCE
ANNOY
ANSWER
answer: satisfy
answerable: responsible
ante: bet

antediluvian: old
anticipate: expect
antiquated: old
antique: old
antiseptic: clean
ANXIETY
ape: imitate
apologetic: apology
apologia: apology
APOLOGY
appall: dismay
apparatus: equipment
APPARENT
APPEAR
appease: pacify
APPLAUD
apple-polish: fawn
appliance: tool
apply: resort
APPOINT
appointment: engagement
apposite: relevant
appraise: estimate
appreciable: perceptible
APPRECIATE
APPREHEND
apprehensive: afraid
APPROPRIATE
appropriate: allocate
APPROVE
apropos: relevant
aptitude: ability
arbiter: judge

ARBITRARY
arbitrator: judge
arcane: mysterious
archaic: old
arctic: cold
ARGUE
argue: discuss,
    indicate
ARGUMENTATIVE
arise: stem
arm: branch
aroma: smell, fragrance
ARRANGE
array: display
arrogant: proud
arrogate: appropriate
ART
artery: way
ARTIFICIAL
artless: naive
ascend: rise
ascertain: discover
ascetic: severe
ASK
assay: estimate
assemble: gather
ASSENT
assess: estimate
assignation: engagement
assignment: task
assist: help
ASSISTANT
associate: join

assorted: miscellaneous
assuage: relieve
assume: presume
assurance: certainty
astonish: surprise
astound: surprise
astray: amiss
astute: shrewd
asylum: shelter
athletic: muscular
attain: reach
attend: tend
attentive: thoughtful
attest: indicate
attitude: posture
attribute: symbol
audacious: adventurous,
    brave
augment: increase
augur: foretell
august: grand
auspicious: favorable
austere: severe
AUTHENTIC
authorization: permission
AUTHORIZE
autochthonous: native
automatic: spontaneous
AVERAGE
avert: prevent
avow: acknowledge
await: expect
awake: aware

AWARE
awry: amiss
babel: noise
baby: pamper
back: support
BAD
badge: sign
badger: harass
bailiwick: field
bait: harass
BALANCE
balance: proportion
balloon: bulge
bamboozle: deceive
ban: forbid
BAND
BANISH
bank: heap
BANTER
barbarian: boor
bare: empty
BARGAIN
BARRAGE
barren: futile, empty
base: mean²
BASELESS
bashful: shy
baste: beat
bathetic: sentimental
BATTER
batter: beat
bawl: shout
BE

BEAR
bear: produce
beard: defy
BEAT
beat: defeat
BEAUTIFUL
befall: happen
befoul: contaminate
befuddle: confuse
beg: cadge
BEGIN
BEGINNING
begrudge: envy
beguile: deceive, charm
BEHAVIOR
behindhand: tardy
behold: see
being: existence
belabor: beat
beleaguer: besiege
BELIEF
believable: plausible
bellow: shout
belly: bulge
bemuse: daze
benchmark: standard
BEND
BENEFICIAL
BENEFIT
BENEVOLENT
benign: favorable
benumb: daze
BESIEGE

bespeak: indicate, book
BET
bethink: remember
betide: happen
betoken: indicate
betray: deceive
better: improve
bewitch: charm
BIAS
bias: predilection
bicker: argue
big: large
BINGE
birth: beginning
birthright: right
BITE
biting: incisive
BITTER
bizarre: fantastic
blab: gossip
BLACKBALL
blacklist: blackball
BLACKOUT
blamable: blameworthy
BLAME
blame: criticize
blameful: blameworthy
BLAMEWORTHY
blank: empty
BLAST
blend: mix, mixture
blight: blast
BLINK

BLOCK
blockade: besiege
BLOODY
BLOOM
blossom: bloom
blot: stain
blow: waste, botch
blubber: cry
blue: depressed
blueprint: plan
BLUNDER
BOAST
BODILY
BOIL
bold: brave
bombard: barrage
bona fide: authentic
BOOK
bookish: pedantic
BOOR
boost: lift
boot: dismiss
bootless: futile
bootlick: fawn
BORDER
BOREDOM
BORING
boss: supervise
BOTCH
bother: annoy
bounce: dismiss
boundless: infinite
BOUQUET

bouquet: fragrance
bow: yield
boycott: blackball
brag: boast
BRANCH
brand: stain, mark
brandish: flourish
BRAVE
brave: defy
BRAWL
brawny: muscular
BREACH
BREAK
break: demote
breakable: fragile
breathe: be
BREEZE
BRIGHT
bright: intelligent
brilliant: bright, intelligent
brim: border
brink: border
bristle: teem
brittle: fragile
BROACH
broad: broad-minded
broadcast: announce
BROAD-MINDED
broil: brawl
bromide: cliché
BROOD
BRUSH
buffet: beat

build: physique
BULGE
bum: cadge
bumble: blunder
bungle: botch
BURDEN[1]
BURDEN[2]
burly: muscular
BURN
burst: break
bury: hide
bushwhack: ambush
BUSINESS
business: affair
bust: demote
cache: hide
CADGE
cage: enclose
CALCULATE
CALL
call: predict
CALM
camouflage: disguise
CAMPAIGN
can: dismiss
cancel: erase
candid: frank
capacious: spacious
capacity: ability
capitalize: benefit
capitulate: yield
capricious: arbitrary
captious: critical

captivate: charm

CARE

care: anxiety

CAREFUL

CARESS

carp: quibble

carriage: posture

case: example

cashier: dismiss

cast: throw

castigate: punish

casual: chance

CATALYST

CATCH

categorical: explicit

cavil: quibble

cease: stop

ceaseless: continual

cede: relinquish

celebrated: noted

CELEBRITY

celerity: haste

censorious: critical

censurable: blameworthy

censure: criticize

CENTER

cerebrate: think

CERTAIN

CERTAINTY

certify: approve

certitude: certainty

CHAFE

chaff: banter

chagrin: embarrass

challenge: defy

champ: bite

champion: support

CHANCE

chance: happen

chaperon: accompany

char: burn

CHARGE

charge: care

charitable: benevolent

charity: mercy

CHARM

chastise: punish

cheer: encourage, applaud

cheerful: glad

cherish: appreciate

chic: fashionable

CHIEF

chilly: cold

CHOICE

choice: delicate

chore: task

CHRONIC

churl: boor

churn: agitate

cinch: breeze

cipher: calculate

circle: surround, turn

circuit: circumference

CIRCUMFERENCE

circumspection: prudence

circumstance: occurrence

circumstantial: detailed
CITIZEN
CLAIM
claim: demand
clamor: noise
clandestine: secret
CLEAN
cleanly: clean
CLEAR
clear: apparent
clear-cut: apparent, incisive
cleave: tear
clemency: mercy
CLEVER
CLICHÉ
climb: rise
cloak: clothe, disguise, hide
CLOSE
clot: coagulate
CLOTHE
coadjutant: assistant
coadjutor: assistant
COAGULATE
coalesce: mix
coast: slide
coddle: pamper
coerce: force
cogent: valid
cogitate: think
cognizant: aware
coincide: agree
COLD
colleague: partner

collect: gather
COLLISION
color: bias
colorable: plausible
colorless: dull
colossal: enormous
combat: oppose, conflict
combative: argumentative
combine: join
comely: beautiful
COMFORT
comfort: amenity
COMFORTABLE
commandeer: appropriate
commence: begin
commend: praise
COMMENT
commerce: business
commiseration: pity
commission: authorize
commodious: spacious
COMMON
common: general
commonplace: cliché
compact: bargain
companionable: social
company: band
compass: circumference,
    range, surround, reach
compassion: pity
compassionate: humane
compel: force
competence: ability

COMPLEX
complicated: complex, elaborate
component: element
composite: mixture
compound: mixture
comprehend: apprehend
compunction: penitence
compute: calculate
conceal: hide
concede: acknowledge
CONCEIT
concept: idea
conception: idea
concern: affair, anxiety
conciliate: pacify
conclude: decide
conclusion: decision
conclusive: decisive
concur: assent
concussion: collision
CONDEMN
condemn: criticize
condescend: stoop
conditional: dependent
condolence: pity
condone: forgive
conducive: favorable
conduct: accompany, behavior
confederate: partner
CONFER
confess: acknowledge

confirmed: chronic
confiscate: appropriate
CONFLICT
conform: agree, adapt
CONFUSE
congeal: coagulate
congregate: gather
conjectural: supposed
connect: join
conquer: defeat
conquest: victory
conscious: aware
consent: assent, permission
consequence: effect, importance
considerate: thoughtful
console: comfort
constant: continual, faithful
consternation: fear
constituent: element
constitution: physique
constrain: force
construe: explain
consult: confer
consume: eat, waste, monopolize
consummate: perfect
CONTAIN
CONTAMINATE
contemn: despise
contemplate: see
contend: discuss
contentious: argumentative

contest: conflict, oppose
contingent: dependent
CONTINUAL
continuous: continual
contour: outline
contract: bargain
contradict: deny
contravene: deny
contrition: penitence
convene: call
convenience: amenity
converse: speak
CONVERT
conviction: certainty
convincing: valid
convivial: social
convoke: call
convulse: agitate
cool: cold
coop: enclose
cop: steal
copious: plentiful
copy: imitate
cordial: gracious
core: burden²
corporal: bodily
corporeal: bodily
corps: band
CORRECT
correct: punish
correspond: agree
CORRUPT
counsel: advice, advise

COUNT
countenance: face
courageous: brave
course: way
covenant: bargain, promise
cover: shelter
covert: secret
covet: envy, desire
covetous: jealous
coy: shy
cozy: comfortable
crack: break
craft: art
crash: collision
crave: desire
crawl: teem
create: found
credence: belief
credible: plausible
credit: belief
CRISIS
crisp: incisive
criterion: standard
CRITICAL
CRITICIZE
crook: bend
cross: burden¹
crossroad: crisis
crow: boast
CROWD
crucial: decisive
crucible: trial
CRUDE

crude: rude
crusade: campaign
CRUSH
crush: crowd
CRY
cryptic: ambiguous
cuddle: caress
culpable: blameworthy
cultivate: nurture
cumbersome: heavy
curdle: coagulate
CURE
CURIOUS
curious: strange
current: flow, tendency
curtail: shorten
curve: bend
custody: care
custom: habit
customary: usual
cutting: incisive
dabbler: amateur
dainty: delicate
dally: flirt
damn: condemn
damp: wet
dank: wet
dare: defy
daredevil: adventurous
daring: adventurous
DARK
dash: blast, vigor
dashing: fashionable

date: engagement
daunt: dismay
dauntless: brave
dawn: beginning
DAZE
deal: distribute, treat, bargain
debase: adulterate, corrupt, degrade
debate: discuss
debauch: corrupt
debilitated: weak
DECEIVE
DECIDE
decipher: solve
DECISION
DECISIVE
declare: announce
decline: refuse
DECREASE
decree: dictate
decrepit: weak
DEEP
DEFEAT
DEFEND
defense: apology
defer: postpone, yield
definite: explicit
definitive: decisive
deft: dexterous
DEFY
DEGRADE
degrade: demote

dehydrate: dry

deign: stoop

dejected: depressed

delectable: delicious

delete: erase

deliberate: voluntary

DELICATE

delicate: fragile

DELICIOUS

delight: please

delineate: represent

deliver: save

delude: deceive

DEMAND

demean: degrade

demolish: ruin

DEMOTE

demure: shy

denote: mean[1]

denounce: criticize

DENY

depart: swerve

depend: rely

dependable: reliable

DEPENDENT

depict: represent

DEPLETE

deport: banish

deportment: behavior

deprave: corrupt

DEPRESSED

derelict: negligent

deride: ridicule

derive: stem

DESCRIBE

descry: see

deserve: earn

desiccate: dry

design: figure, plan

designate: allocate, appoint

DESIRE

desist: stop

desolate: sad

despairing: despondent

DESPISE

DESPONDENT

destiny: fate

destitute: poor

destroy: ruin

desultory: chance

detail: item

DETAILED

deter: dissuade

determination: decision

determinative: decisive

determine: discover, decide

detriment: disadvantage

develop: mature

DEVELOPMENT

deviate: swerve

DEVIATION

device: figure

devotion: love

devour: eat

DEXTEROUS

diaphanous: airy

DICTATE

DIFFER

DIFFERENCE

DIFFICULTY

diffident: shy

diffuse: wordy

digress: swerve

dilettante: amateur

dim: dark

diminish: decrease

diminutive: small

din: noise

DIP

direct: aim

DIRTY

DISADVANTAGE

disaffect: estrange

disaffirm: deny

disagree: differ

DISAPPEAR

disburse: spend

discern: see

discernible: perceptible

discharge: dismiss, perform

discipline: teach, punish

discombobulate: confuse

discomfit: embarrass

disconcert: embarrass

discontinue: stop

DISCOURAGE

discourage: dissuade

discourse: speak

DISCOVER

discrepancy: difference

discrete: distinct

discretion: prudence

DISCUSS

disdain: despise

disdainful: proud

disengage: extricate

disentangle: extricate

DISGUISE

DISGUST

disgusting: offensive

dishearten: discourage

DISMAY

dismay: fear

DISMISS

dispassionate: fair

dispatch: send, haste

dispel: scatter

dispense: distribute

disperse: scatter

dispirit: discourage

dispirited: depressed

DISPLAY

display: show

disputatious: argumentative

dispute: discuss

dissect: analyze

dissemble: disguise

dissimilarity: difference

dissimulate: disguise

dissipate: scatter, waste

DISSUADE

DISTINCT

distinct: apparent
distinction: difference
distress: trouble
DISTRIBUTE
diverge: swerve
divergence: deviation,
   difference
divert: amuse
divide: separate, distribute
divine: foretell
divorce: separate
dizzy: giddy
doctor: adulterate
DOCTRINE
dogma: doctrine
dole: distribute
doleful: sad
domain: field
donnish: pedantic
donnybrook: brawl
doom: condemn
double-cross: deceive
doubt: uncertainty
doughty: brave
douse: dip
downcast: depressed
downgrade: demote
downhearted: depressed
drab: dull
drag: pull
drain: deplete
DRAMATIC
drape: clothe

draw: pull
drawback: disadvantage
dread: fear
drift: tendency
drill: practice, teach
drive: campaign
drop: dismiss
drudgery: work
DRY
dry: sour
dubiety: uncertainty
duck: dip
ductile: malleable
DULL
DUMB
dumbfound: surprise
dunk: dip
dupe: deceive
dusky: dark
duty: obligation, function
dwell: brood
dwindle: decrease
dynamic: active
earmark: allocate
EARN
earnest: serious
earsplitting: loud
EASY
EAT
ebb: recede
eccentric: strange
ECCENTRICITY
ECHO

economical: sparing
eddy: turn
edge: border, advantage
educate: teach
educe: evoke
efface: erase
EFFECT
effect: perform
EFFECTIVE
effectual: effective
efficacious: effective
efficient: effective
efflorescence: bloom
effortless: easy
effulgent: bright
egoism: conceit
egotism: conceit
ELABORATE
elbowroom: room
election: choice
eleemosynary: benevolent
ELEGANCE
elegant: delicate
ELEMENT
elevate: lift
ELEVATION
elicit: evoke
ELIMINATE
eloquent: expressive
elucidate: explain
emanate: stem
EMBARRASS
emblem: symbol

embolden: encourage
emerge: appear
eminent: noted
empathy: pity
EMPHASIS
employ: use
empower: authorize
EMPTY
empty: vain
enchant: charm
encircle: surround
ENCLOSE
encompass: surround
ENCOURAGE
end: intention
ENDANGER
endemic: native
endorse: approve
endure: bear
ENEMY
energetic: active
energy: strength
enervate: deplete
ENFORCE
engage: book, promise
ENGAGEMENT
engross: monopolize
enigmatic: ambiguous
enjoin: forbid
enlarge: increase
enmesh: catch
ennui: boredom
ENORMOUS

enough: sufficient
ENRAPTURE
ensnare: catch
ensue: follow
entangle: catch
entertain: amuse
entire: whole
entrance: charm, enrapture
entrap: catch
envious: jealous
environ: surround
ENVY
episode: occurrence
epistle: letter
epoch: period
equilibrium: balance
EQUIPMENT
equipoise: balance
equitable: fair
equivocal: ambiguous
equivocate: lie
era: period
eradicate: eliminate
ERASE
ersatz: artificial
erudite: learned
erudition: knowledge
escort: accompany
esoteric: mysterious
esprit: morale
esprit de corps: morale
espy: see
essential: indispensable

establish: found
esteem: appreciate
ESTIMATE
ESTRANGE
eternal: infinite, ageless,
    continual
ethereal: airy
ethical: moral
evaluate: estimate
evanesce: disappear
evaporate: disappear
event: occurrence
eventual: last
evident: apparent
evil: bad
EVOKE
evolution: development
exact: demand
EXAGGERATE
examine: ask
EXAMPLE
excess: superfluous
EXCESSIVE
excoriate: chafe
excruciate: afflict
excuse: forgive
execute: perform
exercise: practice
exhaust: tire, deplete
exhibit: show
exigency: crisis
exigent: urgent
exile: banish

exist: be
EXISTENCE
existent: real
exorbitant: excessive
exotic: foreign, fantastic
expand: increase
expatriate: banish
EXPECT
expedient: makeshift
expedition: haste
expeditious: fast
expend: spend
EXPERIENCE
expert: proficient
expertise: art
EXPLAIN
explicate: explain
EXPLICIT
exploit: feat, manipulate
expose: show
expound: explain
express: vent, explicit
EXPRESSIVE
expunge: erase
exquisite: delicate
extend: increase
extenuate: palliate
extol: praise
extra: superfluous
extradite: banish
extraneous: irrelevant
extravagance: luxury
extravagant: excessive

extreme: excessive
EXTRICATE
exuberant: profuse
FACE
face: defy
facile: easy
facility: amenity
factor: element
faculty: ability
fade: disappear
fainéant: lazy
faint: blackout
FAIR
fair: average, beautiful
faith: belief
FAITHFUL
famed: noted
familiar: common
famous: noted
fanciful: fantastic
FANTASTIC
fascinate: charm
FASHION
FASHIONABLE
FAST
fast: faithful
FASTEN
FATE
fatigue: tire
fatuous: foolish
fault: blame
faultfinding: critical
faultless: perfect

favor: oblige
FAVORABLE
FAWN
faze: embarrass
FEAR
fearful: afraid
fearless: brave
FEAT
fecund: fertile
feeble: weak
feel: touch
fence: enclose
ferment: catalyst
FERTILE
fetor: stench
fetter: hamper
fib: lie
FIELD
fight: oppose, conflict
FIGURE
figure: calculate
filch: steal
fill: satisfy
filmy: airy
filthy: dirty
final: last
FINANCIAL
fine: delicate
finger: touch
fire: dismiss
FIRM
fiscal: financial
fit: adapt

fitful: periodic
fix: fasten
flabbergast: surprise
flabby: limp
flaccid: limp
flamboyant: showy
flash: moment
flashy: gaudy
flaunt: show
flavor: taste
flawless: perfect
fleet: fast
fleshly: bodily
flick: brush
flicker: flutter
fling: throw, binge
FLIRT
flit: flutter
flitter: flutter
flock: crowd
flood: flow
floppy: limp
florescence: bloom
flounder: blunder
FLOURISH
FLOW
flow: stem
flower: bloom
flush: bloom, rich
FLUTTER
flux: flow
focus: center
foe: enemy

FOLLOW
fondle: caress
fondness: love
FOOLISH
forbear: refrain
forbearance: patience
FORBID
FORCE
force: strength
forebear: ancestor
forecast: predict
forefather: ancestor
FOREIGN
foremost: chief
foresight: prudence
forestall: prevent
FORETELL
foretell: predict
forethought: prudence
FORGIVE
fork: branch
forlorn: despondent
formless: shapeless
FORTE
fortunate: happy
forward: send, advance
foster: nurture, advance
foul: dirty, contaminate
FOUND
fracas: brawl
fracture: break
FRAGILE
fragile: weak

FRAGRANCE
frail: weak
frangible: fragile
FRANK
fray: brawl
FREEDOM
free-for-all: brawl
freight: charge
fret: chafe, brood
fright: fear
FRIGHTEN
frigid: cold
frill: luxury
fritter: waste
front: defy
frosty: cold
FROWN
frugal: sparing
fruitful: fertile
fruitless: futile
fuddle: confuse
fulfill: perform, satisfy
fulsome: unctuous
fumble: botch
FUNCTION
furious: angry
further: advance
furtive: secret
fury: anger
fuse: mix
FUTILE
gad: wander
gain: reach

gainsay: deny
gall: chafe
gallivant: wander
gape: gaze
gargantuan: enormous
garish: gaudy
garner: reap
GATHER
gather: reap
GAUDY
gauge: standard
gaunt: lean²
gauzy: airy
GAZE
gear: equipment
gelid: cold
GENERAL
generic: general
genesis: beginning
genial: gracious
genuine: authentic
germane: relevant
gesticulation: gesture
GESTURE
gibe: ridicule
GIDDY
gigantic: enormous
gird: surround
girdle: surround
gist: burden²
glacial: cold
GLAD
gladden: please

glance: brush
glare: gaze
glean: reap
GLIB
glide: slide
gloss: palliate
glossy: sleek
glower: frown
gloze: palliate
gluttonous: voracious
gnaw: bite
go: resort
goal: intention
gory: bloody
gossamer: airy
GOSSIP
grace: elegance
GRACIOUS
gradation: nuance
GRAND
grandiose: grand
GRAPHIC
grasp: apprehend
gratify: please
grave: serious
graze: brush
great: large
green: young
gregarious: social
grief: regret
GRIEVE
grimy: dirty
gross: whole

grotesque: fantastic
groundless: baseless
guard: defend
GUIDE
guileless: naive
guilt: blame
guilty: blameworthy
gusto: zest
gyrate: turn
HABIT
habitual: chronic, usual
habitude: habit
halcyon: calm
hale: healthy
halt: stop
hammer: beat
HAMPER
handcuff: hamper
handicap: advantage,
    disadvantage
handle: touch, treat
handsome: beautiful
handy: dexterous
haphazard: chance
hapless: unfortunate
HAPPEN
happening: occurrence
HAPPY
happy: glad
HARASS
hard: firm
HARDEN
hardship: difficulty

hardy: healthy
harmonize: agree
harmony: proportion
harry: harass
harsh: rough
harvest: reap
HASTE
hasten: speed
hasty: fast
haughty: proud
haul: pull
hazard: endanger
head: crisis
headquarters: center
headstrong: unruly
heal: cure
HEALTHY
HEAP
heart: center
heartache: regret
heartbreak: regret
hearten: encourage
heave: lift
HEAVY
heedful: careful
hefty: heavy
height: elevation
HELP
help: improve
helper: assistant
hem: enclose
HERITAGE
hero: celebrity

heterogeneous: miscellaneous
HIDE
hide: block
hideous: ugly
hint: suggest
histrionic: dramatic
hobble: hamper
hog-tie: hamper
hoist: lift
hold: contain
holler: shout
hollow: vain
HONESTY
honor: honesty
hoodwink: deceive
hook: steal
hope: expect
hopeless: despondent
horde: crowd
horrify: dismay
horror: fear
hound: harass
hover: flutter
howl: shout
hub: center
hubbub: noise
huge: enormous
hullabaloo: noise
HUMANE
humanitarian: humane
humble: degrade
humdrum: boring, dull
humid: wet

humiliate: degrade
humor: mood, pamper
hunt: seek
hurl: throw
hurry: speed, haste
hypercritical: critical
hypothetical: theoretical,
 supposed
icy: cold
IDEA
identical: same
idiosyncrasy: eccentricity
idle: lazy, baseless, vain
idolize: revere
ignoble: mean[2]
ill-fated: unfortunate
ill-favored: ugly
illimitable: infinite
ill-starred: unfortunate
ill-treat: abuse
illustration: example
illustrious: noted
imbue: charge
IMITATE
immaculate: clean
IMMATERIAL
immaterial: irrelevant
immature: young
immediate: close
immense: enormous
immerse: dip
immoderate: excessive
IMPACT

impact: collision
impartial: fair
impeccable: perfect
impecunious: poor
imperative: urgent
imperil: endanger
impertinent: irrelevant
implement: tool, enforce
imply: suggest
import: mean[1], count, meaning, importance
IMPORTANCE
impose: dictate
imposing: grand
impoverish: deplete
impoverished: poor
impregnate: charge
impress: affect, impression
IMPRESSION
imprint: impression
IMPROVE
impulsive: spontaneous
in: fashionable
inarticulate: dumb
inaugurate: begin
incandescent: bright
inception: origin
incessant: continual
incident: occurrence
INCISIVE
inclination: tendency
incline: lean[1]
incorporeal: immaterial

INCREASE
indefatigable: tireless
indefinable: unspeakable
indescribable: unspeakable
INDICATE
indifferent: average
indigenous: native
indigent: poor
indignant: angry
indignation: anger
INDISPENSABLE
indolent: lazy
indulge: pamper
industry: business
ineffable: unspeakable
inelastic: stiff
inescapable: certain
inevitable: certain
inexpressible: unspeakable
infatuation: love
INFINITE
infirm: weak
inflate: exaggerate
inflexible: stiff
influence: affect
information: knowledge
infraction: breach
infringement: breach
ingenious: clever
ingenuous: naive
ingest: eat
ingredient: element
inheritance: heritage

initiate: begin
inordinate: excessive
inquest: inquiry
inquire: ask
INQUIRY
inquisition: inquiry
inquisitive: curious
inscrutable: mysterious
insinuate: suggest
inspirit: encourage
instance: example
instant: moment
instinctive: spontaneous
institute: found
instruct: teach
instrument: tool
insubstantial: immaterial
insulate: isolate
insult: offend
insurrection: rebellion
integrity: honesty
intellectual: intelligent
intelligence: news
INTELLIGENT
intent: intention
INTENTION
intentional: voluntary
interdict: forbid
INTERFERE
interim: temporary
interminable: continual
intermission: pause
intermittent: periodic

interpret: explain
interrogate: ask
intimate: suggest
intractable: unruly
intrepid: brave
intricate: elaborate, complex
introduce: broach
introductory: preliminary
intuition: reason
invest: besiege
investigation: inquiry
inveterate: chronic
invoke: enforce
involuntary: spontaneous
involved: complex
irate: angry
ire: anger
ireful: angry
irk: annoy
irksome: boring
irrational: unreasonable
IRRELEVANT
irritate: annoy
ISOLATE
issue: appear, stem
ITEM
jade: tire
jag: binge
jagged: rough
jar: collision
jaundice: bias
JEALOUS
jell: coagulate

jelly: coagulate
jeopardize: endanger
JERK
jiffy: moment
job: task
JOIN
jolt: collision
josh: banter
joyful: glad
joyous: glad
JUDGE
judgment: reason
juncture: crisis
just: fair
justification: apology
JUSTIFY
jut: bulge
juvenile: young
keen: cry, sharp
KEEP
keeping: care
kid: banter
kismet: fate
kisser: face
knack: art
knotty: complex
know-how: art
knowing: intelligent
KNOWLEDGE
kowtow: fawn
label: mark
labor: work
LACK

lackluster: dull
lambaste: beat
lambent: bright
lament: grieve
lank: lean²
lanky: lean²
LARGE
LAST
late: tardy
latitude: room
laud: praise
lavish: profuse
lax: negligent
LAZY
lead: guide
leading: chief
LEAN¹
LEAN²
leaning: predilection
learn: discover
LEARNED
learning: knowledge
leave: permission
leaven: catalyst
leavening: catalyst
leeway: room
legacy: heritage
leniency: mercy
lenity: mercy
lessen: decrease
LETTER
level: aim
liable: responsible

liberal: broad-minded
liberty: freedom
license: permission, freedom, authorize
LIE
lieutenant: assistant
lifelike: graphic
LIFT
lift: steal
light: easy
lighten: relieve
lighthearted: glad
LIKENESS
limn: represent
LIMP
limpid: clear
linger: stay
link: join
liquidate: eliminate
little: small
live: be
lively: active
load: adulterate
loaded: rich
loathsome: offensive
LOGICAL
lonely: alone
lonesome: alone
long-suffering: patience
long-winded: wordy
lookout: affair
loom: appear
lore: knowledge

lot: fate
LOUD
loud: gaudy
lout: boor
LOVE
lovely: beautiful
low: mean[2]
lower: frown
loyal: faithful
lucid: clear
luckless: unfortunate
lucky: happy
ludicrous: foolish
lumber: blunder
luminary: celebrity
luminous: bright
lurch: blunder
luscious: delicious
lush: profuse
lustrous: bright
luxuriant: profuse
LUXURY
mad: angry
magnificent: grand
magnify: exaggerate
maim: batter
main: chief
majestic: grand
MAKESHIFT
MALLEABLE
malodor: stench
maltreat: abuse
mammoth: enormous

manacle: hamper
maneuver: manipulate
mangle: batter
manifest: apparent
MANIPULATE
mannerism: affectation
mantle: clothe
many-sided: versatile
margin: border, room
marine: nautical
maritime: nautical
MARK
mark: sign
marshal: arrange
marvel: wonder
mash: crush
mask: disguise
massive: heavy
masterstroke: feat
material: relevant
materialize: appear
materiel: equipment
matter: subject, count
MATURE
maudlin: sentimental
maul: batter
mawkish: sentimental
MEAN[1]
MEAN[2]
meander: wander
MEANING
meaningful: expressive
measure: standard

meddle: interfere
mediocre: average
medium: average
meet: satisfy
melancholy: sad
melee: brawl
melodramatic: dramatic
MEMORY
mention: refer
mephitic: poisonous
merciful: humane
MERCY
meretricious: gaudy
merge: mix
merit: earn
metamorphose: convert
metaphysical: immaterial
methodical: orderly
métier: forte
mettlesome: brave
middling: average
might: strength
mimic: imitate
mind: tend
mindful: careful
mingle: mix
miniature: small
minister: tend
minuscule: small
minute: detailed, moment,
    small
miracle: wonder
MISCELLANEOUS

mislead: deceive
missive: letter
mistreat: abuse
mistrust: uncertainty
misuse: abuse
mitigate: relieve
MIX
mixed: miscellaneous
MIXTURE
mob: crowd
mock: ridicule
mode: fashion
MODERATE
modest: shy, plain
modish: fashionable
moist: wet
mollify: pacify
mollycoddle: pamper
MOMENT
moment: importance
monetary: financial
moneyed: rich
MONOPOLIZE
monotonous: boring
mooch: cadge
MOOD
moor: fasten
moot: broach
mope: brood
MORAL
MORALE
motif: figure
motley: miscellaneous

mound: heap
mount: rise
mourn: grieve
move: affect
muddle: confuse
muff: botch
mug: face
multifaceted: versatile
multifarious: versatile
multiply: increase
murky: dark
MUSCULAR
mushy: sentimental
muster: call
mute: dumb
mutilate: batter
mutiny: rebellion
MYSTERIOUS
NAIVE
name: appoint, celebrity
narcissism: conceit
narrate: describe
nascence: beginning
nasty: offensive, dirty
national: citizen
NATIVE
native: crude
natural: normal, naive
nauseate: disgust
NAUTICAL
naval: nautical
near: close
nearby: close

NEAT
necessary: indispensable
need: lack
needful: indispensable
needy: poor
negate: deny
negative: deny
neglectful: negligent
NEGLIGENT
NEWS
nictitate: blink
niggle: quibble
nigh: close
nimble: dexterous
nip: blast
nitpick: quibble
NOISE
nominate: appoint
nonesuch: paragon
nonpareil: paragon
NORMAL
nosegay: bouquet
nosy: curious
notable: noted, celebrity
note: letter, sign, see
NOTED
notice: see
noticeable: perceptible
notion: idea
NUANCE
nugatory: vain
nurse: nurture
NURTURE

object: intention
objective: fair, intention
obligate: force
OBLIGATION
OBLIGE
oblige: force
obscure: dark, ambiguous, block
observant: careful
observation: comment
observe: see
obsolete: old
obstruct: block
obviate: prevent
obvious: apparent
occasional: periodic
occult: mysterious
occur: happen
OCCURRENCE
odd: strange
odds: advantage
odor: smell
OFFEND
OFFENSIVE
office: function
offshoot: branch
ogle: gaze
oily: unctuous
OLD
oleaginous: unctuous
opaque: dark
open: frank
open-minded: broad-minded

opponent: enemy
OPPORTUNE
OPPOSE
option: choice
orbit: range
ordain: dictate
ordeal: trial
order: arrange
ORDERLY
ordinary: common
organize: arrange, found
orgy: binge
ORIGIN
originate: stem
ostentatious: showy
ostracize: blackball
otiose: vain
outcome: effect
outfit: equipment
outlandish: strange
OUTLINE
outrage: offend
outspoken: frank
overcome: defeat
overdue: tardy
overflow: teem
overhang: bulge
overlook: supervise
oversee: supervise
overstate: exaggerate
OVERTHROW
overturn: overthrow
own: acknowledge

PACIFY
PAIN
PALLIATE
palliate: relieve
palpable: perceptible
palpate: touch
palter: lie
PAMPER
pan: face
pandemonium: noise
pang: pain
panhandle: cadge
panic: fear, frighten
panoply: display
parade: display, show
PARAGON
paraphernalia: equipment
parch: burn, dry
pardon: forgive
parley: confer
parody: imitate
part: separate
partiality: predilection
particular: detailed, item
PARTNER
party: band
pass: way, crisis
passage: way
patent: apparent
PATIENCE
pattern: figure
PAUSE
paw: touch

peaceful: calm
peculiar: strange
pecuniary: financial
PEDANTIC
pedestrian: dull
peer: gaze
peeve: annoy
pellucid: clear
pen: enclose
penalize: punish
penchant: predilection
PENITENCE
penniless: poor
penumbra: shade
pepper: barrage
perceive: see
PERCEPTIBLE
perennial: continual
PERFECT
PERFORM
perfume: fragrance
perimeter: circumference
PERIOD
PERIODIC
periphery: circumference
permeate: charge
PERMISSION
perpendicular: vertical
perpetual: continual
perquisite: right
personage: celebrity
perspicacious: shrewd
pertinent: relevant

pervade: charge
pervert: corrupt
pester: harass
pestilent: poisonous
pestilential: poisonous
pet: caress
petite: small
pettifog: quibble
phenomenon: wonder
philanthropic: benevolent
physical: bodily
physiognomy: face
PHYSIQUE
picture: represent
pile: heap
pilfer: steal
pilot: guide
pinch: steal
pitch: throw
pith: burden²
PITY
placate: pacify
placid: calm
plague: harass
PLAIN
plain: apparent
PLAN
plastic: malleable
platitude: cliché
PLAUSIBLE
play: flirt, room
PLEASE
pledge: promise

plenteous: plentiful
PLENTIFUL
pliable: malleable
pliant: malleable
plight: promise
plucky: brave
plumb: vertical
point: aim
poise: balance
poison: contaminate
POISONOUS
polish: elegance
pollute: contaminate
pomp: display
ponderous: heavy
POOR
portion: fate
portray: represent
pose: propose, posture,
    affectation
posh: fashionable
posit: presume
POSTPONE
postulate: presume
POSTURE
posy: bouquet
pot: bet
pound: beat
poverty-stricken: poor
power: strength
PRACTICE
practice: habit
PRAISE

precipitate: speed
precipitous: steep
preclude: prevent
PREDICT
PREDILECTION
preeminent: noted
preempt: appropriate
prefatory: preliminary
preference: choice
prejudice: predilection, bias
PRELIMINARY
preoccupy: monopolize
preparatory: preliminary
preposterous: foolish
prerogative: right
prescribe: dictate
preserve: defend
press: crowd
pressing: urgent
PRESUME
presuppose: presume
pretense: claim
pretension: claim
pretentious: showy
pretty: beautiful
prevaricate: lie
PREVENT
primary: chief
prime: chief, bloom
primitive: rude
principal: chief
print: impression
privilege: right

prize: appreciate
probe: inquiry
probity: honesty
proceed: stem
proclaim: announce
proclivity: predilection
prodigal: profuse
prodigy: wonder
PRODUCE
productive: fertile
PROFICIENT
profile: outline
profit: benefit
profitable: beneficial
profound: deep
PROFUSE
progenitor: ancestor
prognosticate: predict
progress: development
prohibit: forbid
project: plan, bulge
prolific: fertile
prolix: wordy
PROMISE
promote: advance
promulgate: announce
propel: push
propensity: predilection
prophesy: foretell
propitious: favorable
PROPORTION
PROPOSE
propound: propose

proscribe: forbid
protect: defend
protrude: bulge
PROUD
providential: happy
province: field
provisional: temporary
proximate: close
PRUDENCE
publish: announce
puerile: young
PULL
pulp: crush
pummel: beat
punch: vigor
PUNISH
PURE
purge: eliminate
purloin: steal
purport: burden[2]
purpose: intention
purview: range
PUSH
push: campaign
pushover: breeze
puss: face
putative: supposed
quaint: strange
quake: shake
qualify: moderate
quarrel: argue
quarrelsome: argumentative
queer: strange

query: ask
quest: seek
question: ask
QUIBBLE
quick: fast
quicken: speed
quick-witted: intelligent
quirk: eccentricity
quit: stop
quiver: shake
quiz: ask
rack: afflict
racket: noise
radiant: bright
rag: banter
rage: anger
raise: lift, broach
ramble: wander
random: chance
RANGE
range: wander
rapacious: voracious
rapid: fast
rate: estimate, earn
ratify: approve
ratiocinative: logical
ration: distribute
rational: logical
rattle: embarrass
ravenous: voracious
ravish: enrapture
raw: crude, rude
rawboned: lean²

raze: ruin
razz: banter
REACH
reach: range
REAL
real: authentic
realistic: graphic
realm: field
REAP
rear: lift
REASON
reason: think
REBELLION
rebuff: refuse
recalcitrant: unruly
recall: remember
RECEDE
recess: pause
RECIPROCATE
recite: describe
reckon: calculate, rely
reclaim: save
recollect: remember
recollection: memory
recommend: advise
recommendation: advice
reconcile: adapt
recondite: ambiguous
recount: describe
recoup: recover
RECOVER
rectify: correct
rectitude: honesty

redeem: save
redolence: fragrance
redress: correct
reduce: decrease, demote
reecho: echo
reek: stench
REFER
refer: resort
referee: judge
reflect: echo, think
reform: correct
refractory: unruly
REFRAIN
refuge: shelter
REFUSE
regain: recover
regale: amuse
REGRET
regular: normal
rehearse: practice, describe
reject: refuse
relate: describe, join
relative: dependent
relent: yield
RELEVANT
RELIABLE
RELIEVE
RELINQUISH
relish: zest, taste
RELY
remain: stay
remark: see, comment
remedy: correct, cure

REMEMBER
remembrance: memory
reminiscence: memory
remiss: negligent
remorse: penitence
rend: tear
rendezvous: engagement
renounce: relinquish
renowned: noted
repel: disgust
repellent: offensive
repentance: penitence
repercussion: impact
REPLACE
reply: answer
report: describe
reprehend: criticize
reprehensible: blameworthy
REPRESENT
repulsive: offensive
reputed: supposed
require: demand
requisite: indispensable
requite: reciprocate
rescue: save
research: inquiry
resemblance: likeness
resentment: anger
reserve: book, keep
reserved: silent
resign: relinquish
resignation: patience
resist: oppose

resolve: decide, analyze, solve

RESORT

resort: makeshift

resound: echo

respite: pause

respond: answer

responsibility: obligation

RESPONSIBLE

responsible: reliable

restful: comfortable

restore: revive

result: follow, effect

resuscitate: revive

retain: keep

reticent: silent

retort: answer

retract: recede

retreat: shelter, recede

retrieve: recover

retrograde: recede

return: reciprocate

reverberate: echo

REVERE

revise: correct

REVIVE

revivify: revive

revolt: disgust, rebellion

revolting: offensive

revolution: rebellion

revolve: turn

rib: banter

RICH

RIDICULE

ridiculous: foolish

rig: equipment

RIGHT

righteous: moral

rigid: stiff

rigor: difficulty

rile: annoy

rim: border

ring: surround

riotous: profuse

rip: tear

ripen: mature

RISE

rise: beginning, stem

risk: endanger

roam: wander

roar: shout

robe: clothe

robust: healthy

rock: agitate

role: function

romantic: sentimental

ROOM

roomy: spacious

root: applaud, origin

rotate: turn

ROUGH

rough: rude

round: bend

rout: defeat

route: way, send

rove: wander

row: brawl

ruction: brawl
RUDE
rugged: rough
RUIN
rule: decide
rush: flow
sack: dismiss
SAD
safeguard: defend
sagacious: shrewd
SAME
sample: example
sanction: permission, approve
sanctuary: shelter
sanguinary: bloody
sanguineous: bloody
satiny: sleek
SATISFY
saturate: charge
SAVE
savor: taste
scabrous: rough
scare: frighten
SCATTER
scent: fragrance, smell
scheme: plan
schmaltzy: sentimental
scholarly: learned
scholarship: knowledge
scholastic: pedantic
school: teach
scope: room, range
scorch: burn

scorn: despise
scout: despise
scowl: frown
scrappy: argumentative
scrawny: lean^2
screen: block, hide
scrumptious: delicious
sear: burn
search: seek
season: harden
seasonable: opportune
seat: center
seclude: isolate
second: assistant, moment
SECRET
secrete: hide
secretive: silent
secure: fasten
sedate: serious
SEE
SEEK
seethe: boil
segregate: isolate
selection: choice
selfsame: same
sempiternal: infinite
SEND
sensation: wonder
sense: meaning
sensible: aware
sentence: condemn
SENTIMENTAL
SEPARATE

separate: distinct
sequel: effect
sequester: isolate
serene: calm
SERIOUS
set: coagulate
settle: decide
sever: separate
several: distinct
SEVERE
shackle: hamper
SHADE
shade: nuance
shadow: shade
shadowy: dark
shady: dark
SHAKE
shake: agitate, dismay
SHAPELESS
SHARP
sharp: fashionable
shatter: break
shave: brush
sheer: airy, pure, steep
SHELTER
shelve: postpone
shepherd: guide
shield: defend
ship: send
shipshape: neat
shiver: break, shake
shock: collision
SHORTEN

SHOUT
shove: push
SHOW
show: appear
shower: barrage
SHOWY
SHREWD
shrewd: clever
shroud: block
shudder: shake
SHY
sicken: disgust
siege: besiege
SIGN
sign: gesture
signal: gesture
significance: importance, meaning
significant: expressive
signification: meaning
signify: mean[1], count
SILENT
silhouette: outline
silken: sleek
silky: sleek
silly: foolish
similarity: likeness
similitude: likeness
simmer: boil
simple: pure, easy, plain, naive
simulate: imitate
simulated: artificial

sinewy: muscular

singe: burn

singular: strange

skepticism: uncertainty

skid: slide

skill: ability

skilled: proficient

skillful: proficient

skim: brush

skinny: lean[2]

slack: negligent

slant: lean[1]

slaver: fawn

SLEEK

slick: sleek, glib

SLIDE

sling: throw

slip: slide

slipshod: sloppy

slither: slide

slope: lean[1]

SLOPPY

slothful: lazy

slovenly: sloppy

slushy: sentimental

smack: taste

SMALL

smarmy: unctuous

smart: intelligent,
    fashionable, pain

smash: break, crush

SMELL

smooth: easy

smooth-tongued: glib

snap: jerk, breeze

snare: catch

snitch: steal

snoopy: curious

snug: comfortable

soar: rise

sob: cry

sober: serious

sociable: social, gracious

SOCIAL

sojourn: stay

solace: comfort

solemn: serious

solicitous: thoughtful

solicitude: anxiety

solid: firm

solitary: alone

SOLVE

somatic: bodily

sophisticate: adulterate

soppy: sentimental

sordid: mean[2]

sorrow: regret, grieve

sorrowful: sad

sort: arrange

sound: healthy, valid

SOUR

source: origin

souse: dip

SPACIOUS

spare: superfluous, lean[2]

SPARING

SPEAK
specialty: forte
specific: explicit
specimen: example
speculate: think
speculative: theoretical
speechless: dumb
SPEED
speed: haste
speedy: fast
SPEND
sphere: field
spick-and-span: neat
spin: turn
spiritual: immaterial
splashy: showy
splinter: break
split: tear, break
spoil: pamper
SPONTANEOUS
sporadic: periodic
spotless: clean
spree: binge
spring: stem
spruce: neat
spurn: refuse
squabble: argue
squalid: dirty
squander: waste
squash: crush
squirm: writhe
stack: heap
stagy: dramatic

staid: serious
STAIN
stake: bet
STAMMER
stamp: impression
stance: posture
stand: bear
STANDARD
stare: gaze
start: begin
startle: frighten
stately: grand
staunch: faithful
STAY
stay: postpone
steadfast: faithful
STEAL
stealthy: secret
STEEP
steer: guide
STEM
STENCH
stentorian: loud
stern: severe
stew: boil, brood
STIFF
stigma: stain
stink: stench
stint: task
stitch: pain
stodgy: dull
STOOP
STOP

stopgap: makeshift
straightforward: frank
strain: streak
STRANGE
strange: foreign
strategy: plan
stray: wander, swerve
STREAK
stream: flow
STRENGTH
stress: emphasis
strict: severe
strident: loud
strike: affect
STRUT
stumble: blunder
stun: daze
stupefy: daze
stupendous: enormous
stutter: stammer
style: fashion
stylish: fashionable
subdue: defeat
SUBJECT
subject: citizen, dependent
subjugate: defeat
submerge: dip
submit: propose, yield
subscribe: assent
subside: decrease
subsist: be
substance: burden[2]
subvert: overthrow

succeed: follow
succor: help
succumb: yield
suffer: bear, experience
SUFFICIENT
suffuse: charge
SUGGEST
summon: call
sunder: separate
supercilious: proud
SUPERFLUOUS
superintend: supervise
supernumerary: superfluous
supersede: replace
supervene: follow
SUPERVISE
supervision: care
supplant: replace
SUPPORT
SUPPOSED
suppositious: supposed
supposititious: supposed
sure: certain
surge: rise
surplus: superfluous
SURPRISE
surrender: relinquish
surreptitious: secret
SURROUND
survey: see
suspend: postpone
suspension: pause
suspicion: uncertainty

sustain: experience
swagger: strut
swank: fashionable, strut
swarm: teem
swear: promise
sweep: range
SWERVE
swift: fast
swipe: steal
swirl: turn
swoon: blackout
SYMBOL
symmetry: proportion
sympathy: pity
symptom: sign
syncope: blackout
synthetic: artificial
systematic: orderly
systematize: arrange
taciturn: silent
tackle: equipment
tag: mark
taint: contaminate, stain
talent: ability
talk: speak
tamper: interfere
tang: taste
tangle: catch
tangled: complex
tap: appoint
TARDY
tarry: stay
tart: sour

TASK
TASTE
taste: experience
tattle: gossip
taunt: ridicule
taut: tight
tawdry: gaudy
TEACH
TEAR
technique: art
tedious: boring
tedium: boredom
TEEM
telling: valid
temper: moderate, mood
TEMPORARY
TEND
TENDENCY
tenet: doctrine
tenor: tendency
tense: stiff, tight
term: period
terminal: last
terrify: frighten
territory: field
terror: fear
terrorize: frighten
testify: indicate
theatrical: dramatic
theme: subject
THEORETICAL
thing: forte
THINK

thought: idea
THOUGHTFUL
thrash: beat
thrifty: sparing
thrill: enrapture
throe: pain
throng: crowd
THROW
throw: confuse
thrust: push
ticket: mark
tickle: please
tide: flow
tiding: news
tidy: neat
TIGHT
tightlipped: silent
tilt: lean[1]
timeless: ageless
timely: opportune
TIMID
timorous: timid
tiny: small
tip: lean[1]
TIRE
TIRELESS
tiresome: boring
title: claim
toady: fawn
tocsin: alarm
toil: work
token: sign
tolerable: average

tolerant: broad-minded
tolerate: bear
TOOL
toothsome: delicious
topic: subject
topple: overthrow
torment: afflict
torture: afflict
toss: throw
total: whole
TOUCH
touch: affect
touchstone: standard
toughen: harden
tow: pull
tower: rise
toxic: poisonous
toy: flirt
trade: business
tradition: heritage
traffic: business
train: teach, aim
trammel: hamper
tranquil: calm
transfigure: convert
transform: convert
transgression: breach
transmit: send
transmogrify: convert
transmute: convert
transparent: clear, airy
transport: enrapture, banish
trap: catch

travail: work
traverse: deny
treasure: appreciate
TREAT
treat: confer
tremble: shake
tremendous: enormous
trenchant: incisive
trend: tendency
trendy: fashionable
trepidation: fear
trespass: breach
TRIAL
trial: burden[1]
tribulation: trial, burden[1]
trifle: flirt
trig: neat
trim: neat
triumph: victory
troop: band
TROUBLE
troupe: band
truckle: fawn
true: real, authentic, faithful
truism: cliché
truncate: shorten
trust: care, rely
trustworthy: reliable
trusty: reliable
TRUTH
tryst: engagement
tug: pull
TURN

turn: resort
twinge: pain
twinkle: blink
twit: ridicule
twitch: jerk
typical: normal
tyro: amateur
UGLY
ultimate: last
umbra: shade
umbrage: shade
umpire: judge
unadulterated: pure
unaffected: naive
unavailing: futile
unavoidable: certain
unbiased: fair
UNCERTAINTY
uncommunicative: silent
UNCTUOUS
undaunted: brave
undergo: experience
underhand: secret
understand: apprehend
understanding: reason
undoubted: authentic
uneven: rough
unflagging: tireless
unformed: shapeless
UNFORTUNATE
unfounded: baseless
ungovernable: unruly
uninspired: dull

unite: join
universal: general
unkempt: sloppy
unlikeness: difference
unlucky: unfortunate
unostentatious: plain
unprejudiced: fair
unpretentious: plain
unquestionable: authentic
unravel: solve
UNREASONABLE
unreasonable: excessive
UNRULY
unshaped: shapeless
unsightly: ugly
unsophisticated: naive
UNSPEAKABLE
untangle: extricate
untiring: tireless
unutterable: unspeakable
unwarranted: baseless
unwearied: tireless
uphold: support
upright: vertical
uprising: rebellion
uproar: noise
upset: overthrow
upshot: effect
urbanity: elegance
URGENT
usage: habit
USE
use: habit

useless: futile
usher: guide
USUAL
usurp: appropriate
utensil: tool
utilize: use
utter: vent
vacant: empty
vacuous: empty
vague: ambiguous
VAIN
vain: futile
valiant: brave
VALID
valorous: brave
value: appreciate
vanish: disappear
vanity: conceit
vanquish: defeat
vaporous: airy
variation: difference
varied: miscellaneous
vary: differ
vast: enormous
vaticinate: foretell
vaunt: boast
veer: swerve
vein: streak
venerate: revere
venomous: poisonous
VENT
venturesome: adventurous
veracity: truth

verbose: wordy
verge: border
verisimilitude: truth
verity: truth
VERSATILE
VERTICAL
vertiginous: giddy
verve: vigor
very: same
vex: annoy
vicissitude: difficulty
VICTORY
view: see
vigilant: aware
VIGOR
vigorous: healthy, active
vile: offensive
vim: vigor
violation: breach
virtuous: moral
virulent: poisonous
visage: face
visitation: trial
vitality: vigor
vitiate: corrupt
vivid: graphic
vogue: fashion
voice: vent
void: empty
VOLUNTARY
VORACIOUS
vow: promise
vulgar: common

vulgarian: boor
wager: bet
wail: cry
wait: stay
waive: relinquish
walkaway: breeze
walkover: breeze
wall: enclose
WANDER
wander: lack, desire
warning: alarm
warp: bias
warrant: justify
WASTE
watch: tend
watchful: aware, careful
wave: flourish
WAY
waylay: ambush
wayward: unruly
WEAK
wealthy: rich
weariless: tireless
weary: tire
wee: small
weep: cry
weigh: count
weight: importance
weighty: heavy
well: healthy
well-timed: opportune
WET
whimper: cry

whimsical: arbitrary
whirl: turn
whitewash: palliate
WHOLE
wholesome: healthy
whoop: shout
wicked: bad
willful: voluntary, unruly
willing: voluntary
win: earn
wink: blink
wish: desire
withhold: keep
withstand: oppose
witness: indicate
woe: regret
woebegone: sad
WONDER
wont: habit
word: news
WORDY
WORK

worry: brood, trouble, anxiety
worship: revere
wrangle: argue
wrath: anger
wrathful: angry
wreck: blast, ruin
wrench: jerk
WRITHE
wrong: amiss
yahoo: boor
yank: jerk
yardstick: standard
yeast: catalyst
yell: shout
YIELD
yield: produce, relinquish
YOUNG
youthful: young
yummy: delicious
ZEST

ANTONYM INDEX

admit: blackball
advance: recede
advantage: disadvantage
affirm: deny
agree: differ
ambiguous: explicit
amusement: boredom
antisocial: social
appear: disappear
aright: amiss
beautiful: ugly
blameless: blameworthy
careless: careful
certain: supposed
counterfeit: authentic
deliberation: haste
descendant: ancestor
different: same
dirty: clean
disadvantage: advantage
disagree: agree
disarrange: arrange
disbelief: belief
discourage: encourage
disoblige: oblige
dispensable: indispensable
displease: please
encourage: discourage

end: beginning
esteem: despise
far: close
finite: infinite
firm: limp
forget: remember
fortunate: unfortunate
hopeful: despondent
hot: cold
humility: conceit
illogical: logical
imperfect: perfect
implausible: plausible
indecisive: decisive
independent: dependent
ineffective: effective
inelegance: elegance
infertile: fertile
inhumane: humane
inopportune: opportune
insufficient: sufficient
intensify: moderate
irrelevant: relevant
large: small
lengthen: shorten
lively: dull
material: immaterial
minimize: exaggerate

moisten: dry

narrow-minded: broad-minded

necessity: luxury

nonexistence: existence

obscure: noted

opaque: clear

ornate: plain

partial : whole

particular: general

permanent: temporary

permit: forbid

persuade: dissuade

poor: rich

professional: amateur

prohibition: permission

promote: demote

prompt: tardy

pull: push

push: pull

reasonable: unreasonable

rejoice: grieve

relevant: irrelevant

repel: charm

retard: advance

save: spend, waste

scant: plentiful

shallow: deep

shapely: shapeless

simple: elaborate

small: large

soft: firm, loud

soften: harden

spare: profuse

start: stop

straighten: bend

unafraid: afraid

unclothe: clothe

uncritical: critical

unfashionable: fashionable

unfasten: fasten

unfit: adapt

ungracious: gracious

unhappy: happy

useful: futile